GAZZA AGONISTES

45

LITERATURE

 *at its Best*

FLYING IN TO LOVE
D M Thomas
'Ingenious, almost audacious, in his approach to history...
We witness Thomas at his most moving and complex'
The Sunday Times

A VENETIAN THEORY OF HEAVEN
William Rivière
'A hymn to beauty...the real hero is the city itself, with its dark,
thick waters and decaying beauties' *The Observer*

WE ALL LIVE IN A HOUSE CALLED INNOCENCE
Nigel Watts
'The most moving, tender and funny exposé of a sexist creep
I've ever read...a LUCKY JIM for the '90s' *Time Out*

THE ABSOLUTION GAME
Paul Sayer
'A distinctive and impressive piece of literature...He has
succeeded once more in generalising a particular situation
into an archetype' *The Independent*

CRYSTAL ROOMS
Melvyn Bragg
'A splendid Dickensian sweep of a book' *The Observer*

THE FOOD CHAIN
Geoff Nicholson
'An enjoyably black study of avarice and revenge...
compelling' *The Observer*

BET THEY'LL MISS US WHEN WE'RE GONE
Marianne Wiggins
'A writer of great originality, whose use of language is
dazzlingly inventive' *The Sunday Telegraph*

SACRED COUNTRY
Rose Tremain
'Hypnotic...curiously beautiful and strikingly original'
The Spectator

Hodder & Stoughton
A MEMBER OF THE HODDER HEADLINE GROUP

Editor: Bill Buford
Deputy Editor: Tim Adams
Managing Editor: Ursula Doyle
Editorial Assistant and Picture Researcher: Cressida Leyshon

Managing Director: Catherine Eccles
Financial Controller: Geoffrey Gordon
Marketing and Advertising: Sally Lewis
Circulation Manager: Lesley Palmer
Subscriptions Assistant: Nicki Reid
Office Assistant: Antony Stephenson

Picture Editor: Alice Rose George
Executive Editor: Pete de Bolla
US Publisher: Anne Kinard, Granta, 250 West 57th Street, Suite 1316, New York, NY 10107.

Editorial and Subscription Correspondence: Granta, 2–3 Hanover Yard, Noel Road, Islington, London N1 8BE. Telephone: (071) 704 9776. Fax: (071) 704 0474. Subscriptions: (071) 704 0470.
A one-year subscription (four issues) is £21.95 in Britain, £29.95 for the rest of Europe and £36.95 for the rest of the world.
All manuscripts are welcome but must be accompanied by a stamped, self-addressed envelope or they cannot be returned.

Granta is printed in the United States of America. The paper used in this publication meets the minimum requirements of American National Standard for Information Sciences—Permanence of Paper for Printed Library Materials, ANSI Z39.48-1984 ∞

Cover by Senate. Cover photograph: Syndication International.

Granta 45, Autumn 1993
ISBN 0140 140 646

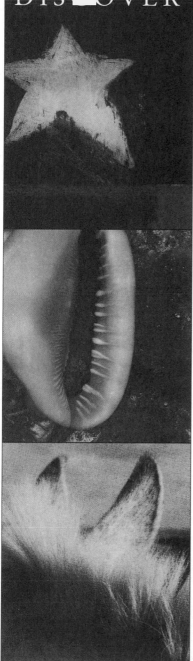

Dennis Stock © Magnum

IT'S THAT TIME AGAIN

Another Christmas: shopping, queueing, getting rained on, snowed
on, stepped on, ripped off, cheated, exploited and generally rendered miserable.

But if you give Christmas gift subscriptions to *Granta*, you will avoid all this.

The first issue will be despatched by us in time for Christmas, along
with a card announcing your gift. And next year, three more issues
of *Granta* will arrive, adding up to more than 1,000 pages of some
of the most lively, provocative, absorbing, entertaining,
distressing *and* comforting writing around.

To ensure that your gift arrives in time, please complete the order card bound into
this issue (you can't miss it—it's bright red) and return it Freepost to *Granta*.

CONTENTS

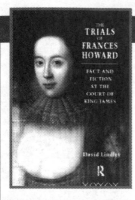

The Trials of Frances Howard

Fact and Fiction at the Court of King James
David Lindley

'A wife, a witch, a murderess and a whore' – Frances Howard was branded by the Jacobean court for the murder of Sir Thomas Overbury. But how many trials has she faced before and since then for the charge of 'deviant woman'? David Lindley challenges the verdict in a fascinating account of the cultural case against her.
October 1993: 256pp: illus. 16 b+w plates   Hb: £25.00

Crossing the Stage

Controversies on Cross-Dressing
Edited by Lesley Ferris

The sourcebook on theatrical cross-dressing – from Restoration 'breeches' to present day voguing. An indispensable buy for all those interested in performance in its different guises.
October 1993: 208pp: illus. 17 b+w plates   Hb: £35.00   Pb: £10.99

Outside in the Teaching Machine

Gayatri Chakravorty Spivak

In this exciting new work, Gayatri Spivak – teacher, feminist, literary theorist and cultural critic, addresses the issues of multiculturalism, international feminism and post-colonial criticism.
November 1993: 350pp   Hb: £35.00   Pb: £12.99

Shopping with Freud

Rachel Bowlby

Rachel Bowlby looks at some of the surprising ways in which the consumer subject appears in a wide range of writings, from 'Lolita and the poetry of advertising' to psychoanalysis and marketing psychology.
September 1993: 144pp   Hb: £35.00   Pb: £9.99

Available through booksellers.
For more information please contact:
Amelia La Fuente Sanchez, Routledge,
11 New Fetter Lane, London EC4P 4EE

ROUTLEDGE

Ian Hamilton
Gazza Agonistes

Newcastle

My first sighting of Paul Gascoigne was in 1987, when he was playing for Newcastle. I didn't exactly fall for him that day but I certainly looked twice. There was, as they say, 'something about him.' His giftedness was self-evident; he was a natural. You could tell that from his touch. However the ball came at him, fast, medium or slow, he welcomed it; he took it in his stride.

His appearance was unprepossessing. He was plump, twitchy and pink-faced, and on the small side. And he was cheeky in a puerile sort of way. He was always looking to nutmeg defenders when it would have been easier to pass them by. He wanted the ball *all the time*: for throw-ins, free kicks, corners—goal-kicks, if they had let him. He seemed fragile but he wasn't: there was a mean streak underneath the puppy fat. He was always glancing behind him, or from side to side, even when the ball was nowhere near. He talked a lot, played to the crowd, or tried to. At nineteen, Gascoigne came across as a trainee star, a star whose moment was—well, any second now.

I was intrigued by the way he related to his centre forward, a Brazilian called Mirandinha. Mirandinha had not long before scored for Brazil against England at Wembley, and when Newcastle signed him there had been a small fuss in the press. Wags said that the Newcastle board thought they were signing Maradona. For the most part, though, the appearance of a Brazilian in our English league was seen as a matter for great celebration. We would learn from Mirandinha. He would bring sunshine to our drizzly field of play.

What he actually brought was a repertoire of muttered curses and black looks, and in the game I watched most of them were directed at young Gascoigne—who was, in theory, his midfield supplier. The supply, it must be said, rarely arrived. When Mirandinha was unmarked, Gascoigne tended to ignore him, preferring instead to set off on an intricate, inventive and usually doomed run into the heart of the enemy's defence. When Mirandinha *was* marked, or merely unavailable, Gascoigne liked to zip classy first-time balls into spaces where the Brazilian should have been, but never was. For much of the game, Newcastle's

11

exotic foreigner was to be seen standing in the opposition's eighteen-yard box, hands on hips, eyes raised in exasperation to the heavens. Sunshine he was not.

Was the bumptious youth taking a rise out of his illustrious team-mate? Certainly Mirandinha seemed to think so. Midway through the second half, after yet another chance had failed to come his way, he strode over to Gascoigne and said something, something indignant, to judge from the arm-waving that went with it. And Gascoigne simply gaped back at him, as if to say: what *is* this? What have I done wrong? Why aren't you pleased with me?

And it was then, I think, that I began to wonder about this funny-looking kid, began to think he might be special. Gascoigne had not, I decided, been trying to make a monkey out of Mirandinha. On the contrary: he'd been trying to *impress* him, as one Brazilian, one artist, to another, young to old. And now, chastised for his selfishness, he was forlorn, perplexed. I don't think Gascoigne touched the ball again that afternoon. Mirandinha maybe got his goal, from someone else's pass; I can't recall. In any case, he never scored that many and was shortly on his way back to Brazil.

Was Gascoigne actually perplexed, or was he putting it all on? Or was he cast down because his virtuoso stuff had not come off? What if it *had* come off—as so often it so nearly did? Would he then have told the fuming Mirandinha where to go, told him he wasn't the only, perhaps not even the *real*, Brazilian in the team? He might well have done. For all his appearance of naughty-boy bewilderment, Gascoigne's cockiness probably ran just as deep, was just as fierce, as Mirandinha's pride. But then there was the sulk, the opting out. What did this signify? I noticed that, after his rebuke, Gascoigne started to make strange, spasmodic head movements and began muttering to himself. He kept licking his lips, flexing his jaw muscles, tucking his shirt in, pulling up his socks. And his face turned a more brilliant shade of pink. At the whistle, though, as the teams were walking from the field, he was immediately at Mirandinha's side, chattering and joking, linking arms, the best of friends. And the Brazilian's noble scowl seemed to be softening: perhaps this boy–man means no harm.

All this, I am aware, sounds fanciful and is perhaps

misremembered, written up. But if it is: well, that is the spectator's fate—we watch but in the end we have to guess. What I do know is that this was the day on which I became a Gascoigne fan-in-waiting, or in-hope. And it so happened that I rather badly needed a new soccer hero. Glenn Hoddle, my fixation for the past ten years, was on the wane. His admirers had grown weary of their long campaign to get his genius established in the England team. After his error against Russia in the European Nations Cup, we knew that the England manager at the time, Bobby Robson, would not pick him again. Jimmy Greaves was, of course, long gone. Steve Archibald had never quite shaped up. Richard Gough was a defender. All of these heroes used to play for Tottenham Hotspur. Was it possible for me to be smitten by a footballer who didn't play for Spurs? And was this Gascoigne true hero material? It seemed unlikely, but we'd see. So far, I told myself, we hadn't seen enough.

It helped, though, that Gascoigne was a Geordie. I had grown up in the North-East and I could just about recall the great days of Jackie Milburn and Bobby Mitchell, Cup winners three times in the 1950s. The black-and-white stripes had meant nothing much down south for thirty years, but for me they still had glamour. And I could remember the fervour, the near-desperation, of those Geordie fans. If Gascoigne did come good, became a Beardsley or a Waddle, the gratitude of Tyneside would be his.

Or would it? At that first game, the fans had seemed equivocal. A certain amount of dour North-Eastern grumbling could be heard: ponce, fairy and the like. But at Tottenham they said this kind of thing about Glenn Hoddle from time to time: it was an aspect of their adoration. Newcastle fans are different, though. They have been badly used; their adoration is *always* coloured with distrust. If Gascoigne did turn out to be as good as they wanted him to be, he would almost certainly be sold. What they really yearned for was a star who would be theirs for keeps and help them to win something big: a Jackie Milburn. Deep down they knew that there was not much chance of *that*.

Most soccer fans have a need to get hooked on the fortunes of a single player, to build a team around him, so to speak.

13

When England played well without Hoddle, I took a diminished pleasure in their triumph. What it chiefly signified to me, and to my co-worshippers, was that Glenn would not be in the team next time. On the other hand, if Glenn *had* played, had made the winning goal, our patriotic joy would have been boundless. Even at Tottenham, where my engagement really was supposed to encompass the whole team, victories were not complete unless Hoddle had had a significant hand in them. And it was much the same with Jimmy Greaves. How many Greaves fans, I wonder, wholeheartedly savoured that 1966 World Cup win? Greaves didn't. He left the stadium immediately after the presentations and skipped the banquet afterwards. How could we not skip it too?

I like to think that to be this kind of fan you have to be part yob, part connoisseur. To appreciate Hoddle's vision and finesse you need to have rare powers of discrimination. To fret for hours about whether or not he will do the business against Kuwait you need to be short of something else to think about. I also like to pretend that such a fan must be equipped with unusual qualities of loyalty, persistence and fortitude in the face of accumulating set-backs. With a pop star or an opera singer, when you turn up for a performance, you usually get more or less what you go to see, or hear. With soccer heroes, there is no such guarantee, or even likelihood: each performance is a new ordeal; the better the performer, the more determined the other side to stop him doing what he's good at. The odds against get higher all the time.

I remember once taking an American friend along to Tottenham's White Hart Lane to watch Jimmy Greaves. This player, I announced beforehand, is the best, simply the best: just wait and see. Greaves barely got a kick all afternoon. He was marked ferociously, man for man, or men for man. More than once he was hacked down just as he was about to set off on one of his legendary scampers towards the goal. After a few tumbles, he evidently decided that this was not to be his day. He slowed down, drifted here and there and altogether did the minimum—which, it has to be confessed, he was (also) quite good at. At one point, my companion was mystified to observe Greaves in the centre circle, idly chatting to the opposition's centre half, the most effective of his markers. Spurs, in the meantime, were under serious pressure at the other end.

It was at moments like this that the yob in me ('simply the best') hurriedly yielded to the connoisseur. I had already, so I said, perceived a dozen or more things to marvel at: not least, our hero's equable response to his tormentors. What a guy. And there had been one or two subtle flick-ons to be relished, the odd imaginative scurry into space, a couple of instant lay-offs under pressure. 'Did you see *that*?' I'd nudge my friend.

But he'd seen nothing much. And by the end, his smile was more patient than benign. 'Well sure,' he said, 'you can tell that he's got class.'

You couldn't, actually, unless you'd been at the Lane last week, when Greaves got four. 'The thing is,' I said, 'they wouldn't *let* him play.'

Would Paul Gascoigne ever inspire devotion of this order? During that 1986–87 season, I followed his progress as closely as I could from where I was. I watched Newcastle whenever they cropped up on television, which wasn't often, and I checked press reports of their games. Gascoigne, it transpired, was already a North-East celebrity. Born in Gateshead in 1967, he starred in local boys' teams and at fifteen had had a trial for Ipswich—where, ominously, he had been turned down by Bobby Robson. He signed apprentice forms for Newcastle a year later, after leaving school— where he had picked up two C.S.E.s (Grade 4) in English and Environmental Studies—and broke into the first team in August '85. Throughout that first season, he was in and out of the Newcastle side—dropped or injured—and it was not until 1986–87 that he began to make his mark. By the time I 'spotted' him, he had already had one or two run-outs with the England Under-21s and was in line for the Young Player of the Year award. Professional commentators, I learned, had been on to him from the beginning, and other clubs knew him to be Newcastle's danger-man. *Vide* that famous photograph of Vinnie Jones grabbing Gascoigne's 'personal bits and bobs' (as Gascoigne later described them). That was in February 1988. So much for my scouting expertise.

In fact, by 1988—within a year of my first sighting— Gascoigne was pencilled in as a candidate for England's 1990

15

World Cup squad. He was also giving the management some headaches—the sort of headaches England managers in particular seem prone to. Publicly Bobby Robson called him 'a little gem'. Privately, we now know, he was troubled by almost everything he heard about Gascoigne's 'character' and 'temperament'. In other words, it was looking like the usual story: the Hoddle story, the Greaves story—individual brilliance versus integrated team play, erratic flair versus dependable work-rate. Alf Ramsey, coach of England's World-Cup-winning team in '66, is said to have originated this managerial suspicion of flair players and bequeathed it to Don Revie, Ron Greenwood and then Bobby Robson. But it was there before Ramsey came along. Len Shackleton, also a Geordie and a joker, had been largely ignored by Walter Winterbottom in the 1950s. Shackleton's clownish ways were now regularly being compared to those of Gascoigne.

And with Gascoigne, it seemed, there would also be a dash of the George Best story, the Stan Bowles–Alan Hudson story—a precocious talent self-destroyed. Rumours from Newcastle spoke of drinking sprees and motoring offences, of mischief and subversion. Dave Sexton, the manager of the England Under-21 team, was renowned as one of soccer's 'deep thinkers'. In his spare time, he read Teilhard de Chardin and, when photographed, looked pensive and austere. Players were said to be in awe of him because they could never understand anything he said. Sexton picked Gascoigne for the Under-21s, then dropped him, then picked him again. The deep thinker could not make up his mind. He could see the talent but he hated the irreverence. At team talks, when Sexton unveiled his complex strategies, Gascoigne would be cracking jokes or pulling faces, or he would go off into a corner and ball-juggle. The boy could not sit still, could not keep quiet. When told off, he would be contrite, but the itch was plain to see: none of this talk really mattered. And when he took to the field, he played not for the team-plan but for himself, or so it seemed. Sometimes, according to Sexton, he was like a 'chicken with no head,' running in all directions, needlessly frantic and aggressive. He hogged the ball, held on to it too long and frequently lost possession in his own half of the field.

But then of course he might do something wonderful—like

beat three men, curl a free kick round the wall, split the defence with an outrageously angled pass. At such moments he was indeed a little gem. In spite of his lack of thoughtful preparation, Gascoigne scored twice against Yugoslavia's Under-21s and once against both Portugal and Russia. And he did plenty more besides. There were suggestions in the press that he was ready for promotion. In spite of Sexton's—and his own—misgivings, Bobby Robson 'knew, in my heart, that we could not possibly leave him out of the squad for the Word Cup finals in Italy. We would have to cater for him.' He may have known it in his heart, but he did not say it at the time. Gascoigne performed under a large question mark, and it is perhaps to his credit that he never seemed to notice it was there.

A recurrent managerial gripe was to do with Gascoigne's weight. As a child he was small for his age and noticeably fat. Scouts who came to view him usually gave him the thumbs-down at first sight. Robson's Ipswich rejection had more to do with the boy's shape than with his skill. And when Gascoigne joined Newcastle, the team trainer Colin Suggett almost gave up on him because of his compulsive eating. Suggett bullied and scolded and imposed every kind of punishing work schedule but he could not compete with the McDonalds and Mars Bars. Gascoigne lost weight in the morning and put it on again by nightfall.

On Jack Charlton's arrival as manager of Newcastle in 1984, Suggett was asked to provide an assessment of the club's playing resources. According to one chronicler, Suggett recommended to Charlton that Gascoigne—'a disruptive influence'—should be 'released'. Gascoigne was summoned to Charlton's office: to get the sack, it was assumed. After about half an hour, Charlton's door opened, and out came not Gascoigne but Big Jack, with tears running down his face, declaring, 'What a life that boy has had.' An early Gascoigne-watcher reckons that the soft-hearted Jack may have been conned: 'I don't know exactly what Gazza said, but he needed only to talk about his dad running off with someone else, and his mum being left on her own at home, and Jack would have been moved.' A diet was decreed, and the player was given two weeks 'to lose a stone—or leave.' He lost a stone—for the time being. And Charlton later mused: 'I've made some bad mistakes, but getting rid of Gazza would have been the worst.'

In most stories about Gascoigne's early years there are two kinds of authority-figure. There are the big-stick men like Colin Suggett, the drill sergeants. These bring out the delinquent in Gascoigne: nose-thumbing behind teacher's back, getting the lads to laugh at Sir's expense. And then there are the father-figures, shrewd, tolerant and humorous, ready to give talent room in which to breathe, to fool around, but stern and headmasterly when pushed too far. Gascoigne's own father had indeed left home and was something of an invalid: he had a brain haemorrhage in his mid-forties and since then had been unemployable—not quite the rock on which a son might lean. Despite his prankish instincts, Gascoigne did seem to need a senior, a guiding hand, and at Newcastle he was probably fortunate: Joe Harvey, Jack Charlton, Arthur Cox. Each appears to have acknowledged that the youngster needed to be 'catered for', that—perky as he was—he functioned on a worryingly short fuse.

Grinning and fidgeting, desperate for centre stage, this mischief-maker could easily be wounded, made to squirm. In Robin McGibbon's book, *Gazza*, there is an interesting account of the player's half-time response to Vinnie Jones's harassment of him during the 1988 Wimbledon encounter. Jones, in the celebrated photograph, is close-cropped, mean-mouthed, darkly gratified: he's not just grabbing, he's twisting. Gascoigne, cherubic, mop-haired, yelps in agony—who wouldn't? Jones, it transpired, had been detailed to nullify Newcastle's star, to 'give him a rude awakening.' 'Who does he think he is? He thought the whole day was about him and no one else. There were ninety minutes to be played and he was prancing about like he was man of the match already.' Thus Jones has recalled the pre-match warm-up. When the game started, he took to his task with relish. Throughout the first half, he followed Gascoigne everywhere, breathing down his neck, taunting him, threatening him, even spitting in his face. 'Stay where you are, Fat Boy, I'll be back,' he'd say when he had to go off to take a throw-in. And back he would come, slit-eyed and leering, the caricature tough.

And, sad to say, it worked. The Newcastle coach, John

Pickering, remembers that after forty-five minutes, Gascoigne was 'in total shock. His eyes were red from rubbing away the tears . . . Not one of us in the dressing-room had seen anyone treated so badly on a football pitch. Paul didn't say one word and he didn't even swear and shout about what had gone on—just sat in the dressing-room, staring into space.' Gascoigne himself has denied that the Jones experience seriously hurt him, but Pickering's account rings true. 'It moved him deeply,' he says. 'We lost him for a bit.' What, then, did this portend? Did Gascoigne's mischievous star turn require the good-humoured compliance of his victims—at least to the extent of playing by the rules? For the likes of Vinnie Jones, playing by the rules usually meant losing. And there were plenty more defenders where he came from.

It was not Jones's muscle that did the damage that day; it was the incessant nastiness, the sense he gave of despising the clown's party tricks. Gascoigne, still a football innocent, a lad who loved to play, to take the piss, had—so Pickering believed—been 'psyched' out of the game. When it came to a straight contest for the ball, Gascoigne was no softie. In the six months or so since I'd first seen him, he had somehow got leaner and bigger. His upper body was more muscular; he was beginning to get the burly, barrel-chested look of a Maradona or a Dave Mackay. Now *that* would be something for Vinnie Jones to ponder: a twinkletoes who packed a punch, a hard man who could dance.

Two weeks before the clash with Jones, Newcastle played Spurs at St James's Park. Spurs had to win, of course, but many of their fans also wanted Gascoigne to play well—or well enough for Spurs to want to buy him. Hoddle had gone by then, and there was a lot of press talk about Newcastle being ready to sell Gascoigne: to Manchester United, to Liverpool, even—unthinkably—to Wimbledon. Terry Venables, the Spurs manager, had not seen Gascoigne play. This, then, would be the crunch. Irving Scholar, the Spurs chairman, has described what happened:

> At one moment in the first half Gascoigne collected the ball just on the arc of the centre circle in his own half and strode forward. Fenwick went in very forcibly to try and dispossess him, but Gascoigne with just a shrug of

his hips shook him off, and Fenwick literally bounced off him . . . Terry and I looked round at each other. We didn't need to say anything, our eyes did the talking. Terry was astonished at the sheer power and strength of a player who was still only twenty, and I am convinced that at that moment Terry decided that Gascoigne was the signing that we both felt the club badly needed.

Paul Gascoigne was transferred to Tottenham in May 1988 for two million pounds—a British record. I didn't know it then and, in my delight at what seemed a correct, inevitable marriage, I doubt very much that I'd have cared, but Gascoigne dithered for some days before signing. It was not that he hated to leave Newcastle. He had been on the lookout for a transfer for some time: Newcastle, he believed, had exploited him from the beginning—at one stage paying him a miserly eighty-five pounds a week. And Newcastle did not want him to go. In February 1988, they offered him a new contract, worth 1,500 pounds a week, rather more than they could actually afford. He turned it down.

Gascoigne's then-agent, Alistair Garvie, got the impression, he said, that Gascoigne 'wanted away from the environment in which he was living.' In newspaper columns—he was already contracted to the *Sun*—the player spoke poignantly of his roots, his evenings with his real mates down at the Dunston Excelsior Working Men's Club, his rapport with the Geordie fans. In truth, though, the Geordie fans were another reason for him wanting to move on. He had never, he knew, entirely won them over. When he played less than brilliantly, they barracked him. When he played well, they reacted with suspicion: who was he trying to impress? He could never be sure of their esteem, and for Gascoigne this mattered quite a lot. It also puzzled him, and footballers are no good at being puzzled.

And he was always being told that he should leave—by other players, like Chris Waddle, a former Newcastle colleague who had gone to Spurs, and who now had for Gascoigne something of the status of an older brother; by the high-earners he ran into on his Under-21 trips; by the newspapers that traffic in fanciful transfer-talk; by the hangers-on who had spotted his market potential. By the time of the Spurs deal, Garvie—a one-time secretary of Newcastle United—had started to feel out of his depth. The Gazza-deals he had lined up in the North-East had brought him more trouble than profit—largely because Gazza, he reckoned, had become increasingly prickly and grasping. He called in a solicitor, Mel Stein, who was London-based but had Newcastle connections, and an accountant, Len Lazarus, to help with the fine print. By the time the transfer was completed, Stein and Lazarus had replaced him as Gascoigne's principal 'advisers'.

Why did Paul dither, then? Spurs fans more purist than I might well have been appalled to learn that Gascoigne's first choice was not Tottenham but Liverpool. Liverpool had shown an interest but wanted to hold off for a year. Gascoigne was not prepared to wait but, when approached by Spurs, he asked for a clause in his contract allowing him to leave 'if Liverpool come in at a later time.' Irving Scholar baulked at this: 'I didn't intend us to be a safe parking place for Liverpool.' Mel Stein persuaded Gascoigne to back down:

> Eventually they both returned to the room. Paul Gascoigne said: 'Mr Scholar, I have changed my mind about the conditions I was insisting upon the other day. I don't want any conditions in there concerning Liverpool. I'm a Tottenham Hotspur player and I promise you I will give you everything I have to repay your confidence in me.' He put out his hand and we shook.

This is the way everybody talks in soccer memoirs. In real life Gascoigne rarely uses the first person singular. He says 'us' when he means 'me'. And this Geordie trick of speech may have caused Scholar a few apprehensive moments during the contractual debate. When Gascoigne came down to London for the transfer talks, he insisted on bringing with him a small platoon of his best mates from Gateshead. The lads, he said, were to be housed with him in his posh Hadley Wood hotel. At around two a.m. on the morning after the contract had been signed, Scholar got a call from the hotel: could anything be done to restrain Mr Gascoigne and his colleagues? They were at that moment roaming the corridors, squirting each other with fire-extinguisher foam and engaging in loud Geordie banter. One of them, Five-Bellies Gardner, had been swimming in the hotel's miniature boating lake—a little noisily, they said. The following day, Scholar summoned the lads to his office for a dressing-down:

> But his friends completely disarmed me . . . They were lined up like naughty schoolboys waiting for the Headmaster to chastise them. Before I could say anything one of them, with a bowed head, looked up and said: 'Mr Scholar, I want to thank you for the best three days we've ever had in our lives.' With such an apology, how could anyone get annoyed with them?

Tottenham

Gascoigne's move to Tottenham had made him rich. Not rich like Irving Scholar or Terry Venables, perhaps, but rich enough—for him, for now and for the lads back home in Dunston. Gascoigne had grown up in poverty. Even in Gateshead terms, his family was perceived to be hard-up: four children, father out of work, mother having to do part-time menial jobs. 'Make me a millionaire,' Gascoigne told Garvie when the agent first approached him. The Tottenham deal had not quite done that but it had set him on the road. The signing-on fee was said to be 200,000 pounds, the salary around 125,000 a year. In addition there were perks: a house, a car and fat bonuses for good results. Manchester United had been ready to give Gascoigne 5,000 pounds each time he played for England, an offer Spurs no doubt had to top.

'Yeah, that's right, I'm going,' he said, in response to Newcastle fans who called him money-mad, accusations stoked by Newcastle's manager, Willie McFaul, who had offered Gascoigne the earth and been rebuffed, and by those of his former colleagues who could not resist the tabloid coin. 'I'm going to a better club, to make more money.' McFaul suggested that Fattie Gascoigne was riding for a southern fall, and the Newcastle chairman, Stan Seymour, called him 'George Best without the brains.' It was an acrimonious parting, and Gascoigne would later be hauled up before the Football Association for verbal retaliation: he ventured to call Seymour 'clueless' for having sold him to Spurs when his old contract still had a year to run. Gascoigne could scarcely be blamed for now and then losing his rag. When he said he 'belonged' in the North-East, he meant it. He found it hard to accept that the Geordie fans, who'd failed to love him, now saw him as a traitor. He too had been a Geordie fan. He had spent his boyhood dreaming about playing for the Magpies.

I couldn't believe the fixture list when I first saw it Spurs' first game of the 1988–89 season was against Newcastle at St James's Park. When Gascoigne ran on to the field, the crowd bombarded him with frozen Mars Bars: they were on sale outside the ground. Throughout the game they booed and chanted whenever he went near the ball: 'Fattie', 'Judas', 'Yuppie'. In those days it was commonplace for visiting London fans to mock the down-at-heel home crowd with lewd songs about unemployment. From the safety of the away-fans' enclosure they waved thick wads of cash and sent up rhythmic chants: 'Loadsamoney, Loadsamoney.' For the Tynesiders, to have Gascoigne owned by such as these was difficult to bear. What was wrong, they wondered, with the loadsamoney that Newcastle had offered him to stay? At St James's Park that day there seemed to be real hatred in the air. And, as with Vinnie Jones, Gascoigne caved in. He was taken off fifteen minutes before the end, booed all the way. Afterwards, he had to be smuggled out of the back door of his old club.

Throughout his first season at Tottenham, Gascoigne—by his own account—spent almost as much time on the motorway as he did in the deluxe quarters Spurs provided; a hotel first and then a house in Hertfordshire. 'The worst time,' he said, 'was whenever I picked up an injury. I would travel to the North-East after watching our game, but at five a.m. on the Sunday I would have to get up and rush down to White Hart Lane for treatment. As soon as that was finished I would climb into my car and head to the North-East again. On Monday it was a case of clambering out of bed at five a.m. and hurtling down to London. I know it was sheer lunacy, but just a few hours with my family and friends kept me from blowing my mind.'

When he went back to Dunston he had to be careful where he parked his black Mercedes and he kept his portable telephone well out of sight. On the other hand, he wanted to show these new toys to his friends. Surely the Mercedes alone—'190 2.6 complete with rear spoiler, low racing skirt and one-way reflective windows'—was proof enough that he'd been right to leave? He wanted the Excelsior to have a piece of his good fortune. Gascoigne may have been money-mad, but all reports of him agree that, when it came to his 'real mates', he was invariably ready with the readies—over-anxiously so, some reckoned. Certainly his Spurs paymasters might have wished that he could rid himself of one or two of his old ties.

Why should he, though? In the south, he was regarded with amusement as a Geordie hick. Irving Scholar, on first viewing him, observed that he 'was dressed in a slightly old-fashioned way, looking very much like a country boy on his first visit to the Smoke.' And then there were his country habits. At Newcastle, he used to chat up the middle-aged ladies who worked in the ticket office. They were, he said, his 'mums'. 'Do you fancy it?' he would ask Maureen, putting his hand up her skirt. And the mums would laugh it off. 'He'd drive you crackers but you couldn't help liking him—he was stupid, but not in a horrible way.'

At Spurs he tried a similar line with Scholar's assistant, a Ms Masterson, and she recoiled with distaste. 'He's going to be trouble,' she opined. His clothes, his dialect, his manners were all there to be mocked. But then he liked to raise a laugh. He was not easily embarrassed.

And there was the continuing problem of his weight. Later on Terry Venables would recall that when Gascoigne arrived at Spurs there was a section of the crowd that decided to target him—as Waddle, now a god, had once been targeted. 'They said he was miles overweight and too slow. It was a struggle for him at the start. But we couldn't force the weight off him for fear of weakening him.' Gascoigne's 'official weight' was eleven stone seven pounds, but, as he confessed, 'I can put on half a stone in a week. Then I've got to shift it in a week. I've learned to watch it though I admit I still let myself go on Sundays. Then I eat a lot because I know I'll be in next day to work it all off.' 'Eat a lot' we can take also to mean 'drink a lot'. For Gascoigne, the close season—June to August—amounted to three months of Sundays. When a new season kicked off he invariably looked out of shape.

As Britain's most expensive footballer, Gascoigne was also the target of the tabloids. For them the script was already written: simple Northern lad gets dazzled by bright lights. Before the new season with Tottenham had begun, at least three Gazza scandals were revealed. The 'night-club bust-up' story was followed swiftly by the 'high jinks on pre-season Swedish tour' story. Then came the 'former model tells all' tale: 'Gazza persuaded me to drive 180 miles to have sex with him.' Gascoigne was new to this game. His advisers wanted him to court publicity, to put his name to ghosted columns, to dress up for photo-shoots, to foster the lovable 'clown prince of soccer' image. He may even have believed that he had some good mates down Fleet Street way. Why then these lies, if lies they were? Why this intrusiveness, this dirt?

In his first year at Tottenham, Gascoigne did just enough to neutralize the terrace malcontents, without quite winning hearts and minds. At Tottenham, hearts and minds enjoy not being won, and it was lucky for him that his arrival coincided with the signing of Paul Stewart. Stewart was expensive too—over one million pounds from Manchester City—and he was good-looking in a beach-boy way, and vain. Also, he seemed to be no good; that is to say, *really* no good, not just a little slow to find his form. He was soon soaking up the derision that might have been Gascoigne's.

A cheeky goal against Arsenal in September earned Gascoigne a truce and, when he settled, he served up sufficient moments of high skill to compensate for his emerging tendency to disappear from games he could not dominate. Most of these moments came from dead-ball strikes—spectacular free kicks from thirty yards, Brazilian-style. Against Notts County, Derby, Q.P.R., he bent the ball so craftily into the top corner that the goalies could only stand and stare. Against Derby, the victim was Peter Shilton; against Rangers, David Seaman. To the fans, these details mattered. Shilton and Seaman put on airs. There were also several glorious near-misses, a fair supply of tricky solo runs and some incisive interplay with Waddle. Next year, it was believed, these two would click.

The season was crowned with a goal, against Luton, that sent the fans off happy for the summer break. Gascoigne got the ball deep inside his own half and moved forward, head high, chest out, arms spread, as if to say: 'Come on, then, take it off me if you can.' Then he accelerated and by the time Luton reacted he had reached the edge of their area, with only two men between him and the goal, one to his right, one to his left. The two hesitated as he ran towards them: should they close down the middle path or hold ground in case he swerved? He came at them dead straight, and gaining speed. They pounced, but they were half a second late. Instead of pincering the invader, they smacked into one another, face to face. He'd glided through the gap. The two sat there, marvelling, as Gascoigne stepped round the keeper and, with a delighted flourish, scored. For an English league game, this was an unusual goal. And yet it was also about as simple, as uninstructed, as a goal could be, a playtime joy.

Gascoigne's second year at Spurs, 1989–90, was the run-up to the World Cup finals in Italy, and every league game he played was treated as an argument for or against his inclusion in the England side. It was indeed the Hoddle saga all over again. In the months leading up to the 1982 Spain finals, the debate over Hoddle had been relentless and exasperating: one ineffectual game and he was written off. Could this brilliant but inconsistent player be fitted into a team plan? With Hoddle the fear was that he was too meek, too disinclined to put the boot in. With Gascoigne it was suspected that the boot might go in all too eagerly, that he would be the one to pick the fights.

In a game against Crystal Palace in November 1989, Gascoigne was booked for a foul and then argued with the referee. The *People* commented: 'If Gascoigne should produce this sort of over-the-top reaction in the steamy killing fields of the World Cup, God help him. And us!' And this was typical of his press coverage during the first weeks of the season. David Lacey of the *Guardian* complained that this novice lacked technique: 'Add to this an endless flow of backchat to officials and opponents and it is possible to believe that he still has some way to go before he reaches the stature as a player that he clearly is as a marketable media persona.' Gascoigne, said Lacey, was 'like the farmer's boy who discovered roast pork by burning down the pigsty. It is necessary to judge the end product against the amount of damage that may have been done along the way.' Patrick Barclay of the *Independent* sneered at Gascoigne's 'comic-book dribbling.'

And Gascoigne, impressively oblivious to such analyses, seemed intent on undermining his own cause. In 1989–90, he was booked ten times, often for 'dissent' but sometimes for taking a wild kick at an opponent. He broke his arm elbowing a Coventry defender in the face and was sidelined for a month. He threw a punch at Chelsea's John Bumstead, with Bobby Robson sitting in the stand.

'What can you do?' said Robson, after the Bumstead incident. And throughout the year he wavered publicly. He picked Gascoigne a few times as a substitute—ten minutes against Saudi Arabia, five against Denmark—but found it hard to take the ninety-minute plunge. He seemed to fear that by doing so he would be giving the wrong signals—to the player, to the press. At times he gave the impression that he merely wanted to be seen as a man who did not take decisions lightly. Certainly, on the subject of Gascoigne, he liked to think aloud. Against Albania, with England three up, Gascoigne was sent on for the final twenty minutes. He made one goal and scored another. Afterwards, Robson denounced him to the press for having disobeyed instructions. 'We needed two balls out there. One for Gascoigne, and one for the others.' His final verdict was: 'Daft as a brush.'

According to a team-mate, Gascoigne was 'hurt and angry'. Robson's crack had made him 'want to prove, more than ever, what he could really do.' But at England's next training session, he turned up with a brush shoved down his sock, and to Robson, the jest was further evidence that 'it was all just a bit of a laugh to him, really.' The boy was, well, just a boy. 'He's got to learn about the game, how to play it properly—he's still like a kid playing backstreet football. Lot of talent, lot of freshness, there's unbelievable things he'll do—but I'm talking about playing Argentina or Brazil, about being in the last eight in the world. You have to be utterly reliable.' Like Sexton, Robson could not take seriously a player who seemed not to take *him* seriously. At strategy talks, Gascoigne 'would listen to what I was saying and come back with "Oh, aye, all right. OK, I know,"' but Robson could see that his wisdom was going 'in one ear and out the other.'

If Gascoigne really was wounded by Robson's brush joke, he was not slow to turn the wound to profit. A joke-book called *Daft as a Brush* came out in November 1989, and there was talk of Gascoigne facing a charge from the Football Association of 'bringing the game into disrepute': the book carried a few swear-words and was rude about referees. Gascoigne swiftly 'disassociated himself' from the publication, and—according to Venables—was 'very upset' that he had been made to seem rough-tongued. The *Guardian* was not convinced: 'Reports that the player was in tears over the affair must be taken on trust, since the only previous recorded instance of Gascoigne's lachrymal ducts being tested was when the hand of one Vinnie Jones grabbed a tender part of his anatomy. Whatever the rights and wrongs of the present controversy, it is surely time for Gascoigne, and those who advise him, to decide if he is going to become an international footballer who is a bit of a character or a character who might have been an international footballer.'

This was snootily put—again by David Lacey—but there was truth in the suggestion that Gascoigne's handlers were butter-fingered, allowing the player to get into 'impish' promo-stunts when they should have been highlighting his 'maturity', his dedication to the cause. On the morning of a 'B' international against Italy, Gascoigne was pictured in one paper with his tongue out and a wild look on his face. The effect was to make him seem oafish and deranged, not at all the sort of man to whom you would entrust a nation's pride. And there were 'interviews' in which Gascoigne whinged about a 'conspiracy' to exclude him from the England team. To the *Sun* he confided that perhaps 'It would be better for everyone concerned if I was playing abroad . . . For a start I wouldn't be able to read the papers—even if I was getting stick.' When he was at Newcastle, he 'had no worries whatsoever. All I did there was think, eat and drink football . . . Everything was so uncomplicated . . . I love the game but I think I'm playing in the wrong era. You see games on telly and someone scores a great goal from 20 yards, but then you get the analysts saying someone was offside and criticising the defenders. It's all negative, when football was meant to entertain. That sort of thing does me in. It's like a cancer slowly killing a healthy body.'

Admittedly, it was not easy for Messrs Stein and Lazarus to package a fake Gascoigne when the real man was always likely to untie the parcel, but for those of us who were desperate to see Gascoigne perform in Italy, every day during the run-up to the World Cup was suspenseful. Would Gascoigne, or one of his allies, push Robson into a corner from which he might not be able to escape?

At the end of the 1989–90 season, Gascoigne put together a string of first-rate performances for Spurs. Against Nottingham Forest and Manchester United, he was at his try-and-stop-me best. He got booked against Forest for arguing with the referee and almost gave away a goal against United with one of his notorious forty-yard back-passes, but in both games he was the dominating figure. And Gary Lineker, playing alongside him, was looking good, not least because of Gascoigne's service. It was probably the United game that did the trick. In a two-one victory for Spurs, Gascoigne made United's Neil Webb and Bryan Robson seem cumbersome, not up to scratch. Neil Webb was ahead of Gascoigne in the England queue and Bryan Robson was, of course, the King. When Gascoigne scored, it was Robson he left standing. And the England manager was there to see it happen—and to see Gascoigne glowing with delight at his own mastery, every so often gesturing to Venables on the Spurs bench, as if to say: '*Now* he can't leave me out.'

A few days later, Gascoigne was in the England team against Czechoslovakia at Wembley. This, everyone agreed, would be the big one, the very last last chance. Before the game, according to Pete Davies in his book *All Played Out*, Gazza was more than usually 'coiled up'. 'In the tunnel beforehand, he nearly decapitated me, bouncing a ball off the wall bare inches from my head, with a really manic aggression.' And team-mate Tony Dorigo has recalled that, 'He was nervous and tense, and sweating up through the stress of it all. I noticed his face getting redder than usual, and his twitches were more evident that day too. I don't know any player

29

who had so much expected of him as Gazza had on that night.'

And in the opening moments of the game, we feared the worst. Gascoigne was diving into tackles, he looked frenzied; he would surely break something or get booked. The referee seemed to be telling him to watch it, but it was not at all clear that he was listening. And then he found relief: a stunningly accurate long pass that sent Steve Bull in for England's first goal. Gascoigne seemed to know then that he'd done it, that now he could relax and simply play. And play he did, as if the field belonged to him, but with subtlety and calm. He even managed to make Bull look deadly. Scored one, made three was Gazza's final tally, and the goal he scored was a beauty, a last-minute solo flourish.

It was by far the best game he had played for England, and this time there could be no talk of errant individualism, of not playing for the team. It was he who had made the team look like a team. There had been a few of his old tricks, but on the whole it was his imaginative distribution that had most impressed. Afterwards, Jozef Venglos, the Czech manager, seemed baffled: 'Gascoigne does not look like an English footballer,' he said.

'Maybe it's the old French blood in me coming out,' was Gazza's explanation. 'It's when I start eating the snails and garlic that I'll get worried.' He said this a year later. On the night he was less affable. As the hero left the field, a television crew approached him for a quote. He brushed them off: 'I hate the press.' And yet that same morning he had appeared in a circus clown's rig-out on the back page of the *Daily Mirror*. 'The cameramen,' says Davies, 'tapped their heads and turned away.' And Bobby Robson? At the press conference he was invited to admit that Gascoigne had finally arrived. He said: 'All right, tonight he's passed the test. He's slimmer, fitter, he's matured, far better discipline. But you're still not a player after one match.' To Don Howe, his assistant, he said much the same—or says he said: 'Right, we'll have to see if he can do it again. We won't leave him out—we'll pick him again against different opposition and see if he can do it again.'

So, we could breathe again. We could even start looking forward to the summer. And it probably did wonders for Gascoigne's relationship with Robson that on the morning when the England squad assembled for the flight to the World Cup, the pair of them were in the news. ROBSON FINALLY ADMITS: I'M QUITTING, was one headline. Beneath it, in much larger, blacker type was GASCOIGNE WINE BAR PUNCH UP. Robson would be leaving his job after the World Cup—he would become manager of PSV Eindhoven in the Netherlands—and although the Football Association were denying that he had been sacked, they were not trying to make him change his mind.

The Gascoigne story was one that we seemed to have read before: Gazza, outside wine bar with girlfriend (twenty-one-year-old Dunston lass Gail Pringle) is approached by thirty-one-year-old out-of-work non-drinker Anthony Marshall. Marshall says something and Gazza proceeds to black his eye, break his nose and chip several of his front teeth—all by himself. 'I was also dragged along the pavement,' said Marshall, 'badly scourging my left shoulder.' Gascoigne had been questioned by police and then let go. Marshall's mother thought the player should have been locked up.

Arriving at Luton airport, Gascoigne was surrounded by reporters. 'Give it a rest,' he said. 'Why don't you sling it?' Later, according to one of these reporters, 'he had a twenty-minute heart to heart with Robson at a side-table in their hotel restaurant.' Robson, we learned, had greeted Gazza with: 'I hear you've had a day of it as well.' At last the two had bonded: manager and player, wise father–dodgy son, co-victims of the scribblers. Robson made no mention of the wine bar story; nor, at the time, did Gascoigne. Later on, though, when a team-mate suggested he should sue, he said: 'Nah, I whacked the cunt, didn't I?'

World Cup Hero

The antitheses had been there all along but in July 1990, after Gascoigne's World Cup triumph, they were given a new formulation. His immaturity was now being hymned as 'childlike'; his aggression was 'fire', 'guts', 'determination'; his yob prankishness sprang from a simple need to 'entertain'. If Gascoigne had listened to any of the sermons he'd been given by the press over the years, he would have had good reason now to jeer. What if, as advised, he *had* matured? Would Bobby Robson now be calling him 'a lovely boy, really a lovely boy'?

It was the tears in Turin that pitched Gascoigne from soccer bad-boy to the status of national celebrity. England's semi-final tie against West Germany was seen on television by millions who barely knew the rules of football. They knew enough, though, to grasp that our best player had been made to cry. It did not matter that Gascoigne's grief was first of all for himself: the tears came when he was shown the yellow card, which would have meant being suspended for the final if England reached it. The point was: England lost and they had gone down stirringly, unluckily, with grit. The warrior's tears were felt as patriotic tears, our tears. At the very end of the game, the unchildlike Stuart Pearce was crying too, but no one noticed. By then we were *all* crying, and it was Gazza who had shown the way, who'd been the first to sense how badly this defeat was going to hurt.

I know of at least one Gascoigne fan who was glad that England lost the penalty shoot-out. A World Cup Final without Gazza, he said, would have been unbearable, a joyless second best. As it was, the player's Turin tears achieved symbolic resonance, the stuff of posters, T-shirts, scarves and mugs. Shrouds, maybe. If England had triumphed, had gone on to win the Cup, they would have been just tears. They may even have been read as further evidence of Gascoigne's instability. Who could forget Gary Lineker's gesture to the England bench just after Gazza's booking? He had a finger to his head as if to indicate that Gascoigne had gone mental, that he'd cracked.

In fact he didn't crack—in that game or in any other. For a minute or so after the booking he was out of action: gulping for air, doing his strange neck-jerk thing, but looking blank, as if he had forgotten where he was. And then he conquered it, he rallied and began looking for the ball. It is not often that a soccer match affords such close-ups. And it was perhaps this flash of inner drama, this visible raising of his game, that the *Independent* had in mind when it declared: 'If you believe football is a noble pursuit, Gascoigne, in that moment, was noble.'

Opposite: Paul Gascoigne in the game against Cameroon in the 1990 World Cup quarter-finals.

Photo: Colorsport

'Noble' is not a word that the back pages often have much use for, but on this day it did not seem out of place. And we too had been ennobled. From the split-second against Holland when an explosive pirouette took him through two startled Dutch defenders, Gascoigne had altered our expectations; he had even put a strain on our vocabulary. In that instant we, as fans, moved up a league. At last and maybe just for once we had a player of world class—or rather a player who was not afraid to *be* world class, who could treat the Gullitts and Van Bastens, the Baggios and Viallis, as if they were just another mob of big lads in some Gateshead school yard. It was rumoured that during the Dutch game Gazza had made fun of Gullitt's dreadlocks and asked Rijkaard how much he was getting from A.C. Milan. We loved to hear about this kind of thing. We were so used to treating the opposition with respect and to being more than happy when they almost did the same for us. This Gazza was sublimely disrespectful.

We had not reached the World Cup semi-finals since 1966, and, but for Gascoigne, we would not, in 1990, have got beyond the last sixteen. Against the Cameroons it was his heroic surge that won us the penalty that mattered; against both Egypt and Belgium it was one of his pin-point free kicks that saved the day. And altogether he seemed able to raise the team's morale, it's 'self-belief'. Clench-fisted, pop-eyed, snarling, he often looked just like a fan. He looked fanatical. On the terraces each week you can see that kind of angry, life-or-death commitment, and it's not a pretty sight. With Gazza, it was translated to the pitch, a grudge come true. The 1990 World Cup has been described as one of the most boring of all time. But not for us. We will remember it as the best since 1970. With '70, apart from Banks's save and that photo of Bobby Moore and Pele swapping shirts, it is names like Astle and Bonetti that stick in the mind—two losers. This 1990 loss, we felt certain, would always be recalled as Gascoigne's victory.

H ow then to repay him?
     When the England team returned from Italy, a grateful nation was more than ready with the spoils. One hundred and twenty thousand fans were at Luton airport for the great home-coming and most of them, it seemed, had turned out to welcome

Photo: Bob Thomas Sports Photography

Gascoigne with England manager Bobby Robson after the Cameroon game.

Gascoigne. And although they may not have expected to find their hero laurelled and aloof, eyes modestly downcast, chin resolute, even the most resilient of his admirers were nonplussed by Gazza's coronation garb: a pair of gigantic tie-on plastic boobs plus pendulous beer belly. There he was, atop a roofless bus, the apotheosis of yuk, and grinning wickedly as if he had pulled off some stylish comic coup.

For those soccer aesthetes who had begun to portray him in the subtlest of heroic hues, this was a cruel coming down to earth. We had seen Gazza before dressed as a clown, as a cowboy, even as a sugar-plum fairy, and we had heard more than enough about his over-the-top japes: how he filled Chris Waddle's tea-kettle with shampoo, spiked Bobby Robson's pre-match orange juice, booked sunbed sessions for black team-mates, and so on. We knew about these things and we had learned to live with them, or so we said. Even during the World Cup he had pulled a few clod-hopping stunts. These too we were able to forgive. When, before one match, he stuck his tongue out during the national anthem, this meant he was relaxed, puckishly unfazed. When he threw his drink at Paul Parker because Parker was caught talking to the press, this meant that he was suitably fired-up. All this we could handle. After all, the lads seemed to get a lift from Gazza's pranks. They thought he was nutty, but he made them laugh. And they seemed to like it when he told reporters to fuck off. Well, fair enough. These plastic boobs, though, coming when they did, and on television, just as we were musing most sagaciously upon his merits, his complexities, somehow had the impact of a personal rebuff. One thing was clear: our hero didn't need to be worshipped by the likes of us.

Seen in this way, the boobs rig-out could perhaps be filed under 'personal integrity', read as a sturdy declaration of intent. Gazza would remain unspoiled, or remain spoiled, as some might think. 'I want to be mesel,' he'd often said. We would soon be learning more about that self, more maybe than we wished to know.

At Luton, when the fans dispersed, Gazza was able to slip away into his father's Dormobile and make for Gateshead. He was accompanied by the *Mail on Sunday*, which had paid a fortune for his first exclusive interview since the World Cup. The *Mail on Sunday* was there when Gazza arrived at the door of the Excelsior and said: 'I'm gaggin' for a pint.'

> It was very, very emotional, what happened in the club that night. This was England, that special part of it, saying: He is one of ours.
>
> You have seen our Gazza, and now you know what it means to be a Geordie. Now you know about the skill and the wit and the passion and the humour, and, above

Opposite: Gascoigne and team-captain Terry Butcher after England's 5-4 defeat to Germany in the World Cup semi-final.

all, the utter determination—no matter how tough the going gets—not to let anyone roll over them.

Hardy wrote about another England in another time and called it The Return of the Native. This was The Return of the Hero—young Paul, born 22 years ago not far from the club in a terraced council house in Pitt Street . . .

Paul has been coming here since he was eight. The bairn in the corner with the Coke and the packet of crisps, while his Dad . . . bought his pints. Ever since then Paul has been part of the heart of the place. He says: 'It's the only place I come in, shut the doors, chalk my name up on the snooker board, and just be me. Just the same as everybody else.'

This was July 1990, and for the next three months Gascoigne was rarely off the front pages of the *Sun*, *Star*, *Mirror* and *Today*. The *Sun* had him under contract for a 120,000 pounds, and this meant that its three rivals had to appoint full-time Gazza-watchers to follow him from Wogan to Madame Tussauds to Downing Street, where he scored a PR bull's-eye by giving Thatcher a big hug: 'She's cuddly, like me.' For the Downing Street visit he sported a mustard-yellow suit with floral beach-shirt—an ensemble that helped to earn him the Menswear Association's award of Britain's Best Dressed Man.

The papers were now full of Gazza's 'estimated earnings'. There were lists of his endorsement contracts: football boots, sportswear, aftershave (his Brut sponsors had to smile when he said, 'It's for pooftahs, isn't it?'). There were catalogues of his memorabilia—from duvet covers to real-tears crying dolls—and breakdowns of his personal appearance fees: two grand for opening a pizza parlour, three grand for a supermarket, a hundred grand for a television commercial. Stein and Lazarus, we learned, were 'fielding' fifty calls a day. They no longer projected Gazza, they protected him. If even half the offers were accepted, the player would have no time in which to play. Lazarus announced: 'We are only proceeding with those deals where we are satisfied with the companies plus the quality and image of the product, to

Photo: Rex Features

protect Gazza's good character.'

Luckily, Gascoigne's family rallied round; they were prepared to share the load. For 3,000 pounds you could get to photograph his mother; for 1,000 pounds she would give you an interview—about herself. For speaking of her son she charged extra. His sister Anne-Marie was more expensive. Two thousand pounds to talk about her acting career; 2,000 for a photograph. For Paul-talk much, much more. Gascoigne's own price was 10,000 pounds per interview.

Now and again Gazza was prepared to talk for free. In October, he released a pop record, a version of Lindisfarne's 'Fog on the Tyne' (on the B-side you got 'Geordie Boy', with lyrics by Lazarus and Stein). For the record launch, Gascoigne agreed to 'meet the press'. An inspired interviewer from *Time Out* turned up

39

bearing gifts—a battery-operated seal that did football tricks and an inflatable guitar—and as a result got something of a scoop: a Gazza interview that was not entirely grudging and defensive. The presents went down well; they broke the ice. 'Cheers mate. Brilliant. Thanks very much.' In gratitude, Gazza tried hard to say something about his musical tastes: 'Phil Collins, I think every one of his is fantastic. Billy Ocean. I dunno. I just like a good song. I'm not really a big music man.' The 'Fog on the Tyne' recording was, he said, an attempt to emulate Glenn Hoddle and Chris Waddle, who in the eighties had had a hit with 'Diamond Lights'. 'They done it so I thought it would be good to follow them. Theirs did well—didn't it?—got to number eleven.' He then started strumming his rubber guitar. 'I'll keep this, use it on me next video. I bet you I do. I wish I'd had it beforehand, it would have been great on the video.'

So far, so good. When *Time Out* switched to soccer, Gascoigne 'visibly relaxed'. But then he was asked about the press:

> The English press treat football like a joke. All they do is look for bad bits; every week, bad bits. You never see the good side of it. They've been writing great about me but people should realise that I had nearly two years of shit off them, you know. Nearly two years of absolute crap, slaughtered by them.
>
> With myself they've been really good. But the news people, the news guys, have been right bastards. I'd love to see some of them come into the local pub I go to in Newcastle and see how brave they are then. They're all soft; all they can do is write the front page of the newspaper and give somebody stick. They're cowards.
>
> Girls I wasn't seeing but they put them in the paper, a girl I was supposed to be having an affair with, which was untrue. Some girls go in the paper and say, I've been with Paul Gascoigne. I mean, it's all right for me, she could be a good-looking girl so the lads are like 'cor!' even though I don't like it. What does this girl feel like? She must feel like a right tart.
>
> They camp out at the end of the drive in cars, like little

Photo: Rex Features

kids. I mean those people have got to go back to their families. Imagine one of them going home and his wife saying, 'How did your day go?' 'Great. I sat outside Gascoigne's house all day and all night waiting for him to come out.' His wife must say, 'What do you want to do that for, you prick?'

This at least sounded like something Gascoigne might actually have said. And the sense of grievance was well-founded. The press attitude to Gazzamania was not so much ambivalent as straightforwardly two-faced. He was canonized at the back of the paper and terrorized at the front. In August, at the height of his celebrity, the news guys decided to take over his 'love life', which hitherto had not been much discussed. Since his move to Spurs, Gascoigne had lived in Hertfordshire with Gail Pringle, his girlfriend from Dunston. During the World Cup, Gail went out to join him for the last days of the tournament and was eagerly sized up by the hacks. 'It was all so predictable,' said one, 'the first time any of us saw her, we knew her days were numbered. How long would it be, asked the cynics, before this lovely, unspoiled girl would be replaced by a Stringfellows bimbo? The truth is, alas, these days that for any girl who finds the frog turned into a handsome prince, life is unlikely to end happily ever after.'

And so it came to pass. A month after the World Cup, one Heidi Shepherd appeared on the *Sun* front page in suspender-belt, G-string and 'provocatively opened black leather jacket.' Heidi, the *Sun* said, was Gazza's new delight. A few days later, the *Mail on Sunday* signed up Gail Pringle's lachrymose account of 'How I Lost Gazza to the World'. Things used to be so wonderful, she said. 'When we were together we just rented a video and picked up a bottle of Asti Spumante with a Chinese takeaway. We liked curling up on the couch together.' After the World Cup, everything had changed. 'When he came back from Italy, he was always looking over his shoulder. We were living in a goldfish bowl.' And then came Heidi Shepherd—or rather, then came the *Sun*'s photograph of Heidi Shepherd. 'When the papers had a story about Paul and another woman he would always deny it and tell me not to believe what I read. But now I don't know what to believe.'

The truth seems to have been that Gascoigne had indeed wanted to move on, that Heidi Shepherd—a Dunston neighbour— was largely a *Sun* fantasy, and that it was Gail who made the break, telling the supportive *Mail on Sunday*: 'The truth is that if he had been a postman or something we would have been happy forever.' But for Gazza there would soon be other Heidis. In October, blonde dental assistant Natalie Barnes admitted to the *Star* that she was 'the new lady in his life.' The *Star* sent one of its girl-sleuths to confront the 'Romeo soccer star' with these new allegations. 'We thought the fun-loving superstar would be delighted to chat about his sexy new pal . . . but fiery Gazza seemed to think we were stirring things up. When I walked up the path of his luxury home, he rushed out with a huge pan of minestrone soup and tipped it all over me.' Meanwhile, Natalie was already lamenting the end of the affair. On her birthday, she said, Gazza had done her wrong, choosing to go off 'for a riotous West End night out while she sobbed broken-hearted over his absence.'

These Gazza romances were identically structured: simple, home-loving, marriage-seeking lovely gives all to beer-swilling sexual opportunist. What Gascoigne liked above all, the papers said, was bevvying with his coarse-grained Gateshead cronies, but with the occasional element of 'Cor!' The bet was that *Star* and *Sun* readers, male and female, would instantly recognize the type—as, no doubt, they did. And so presumably did Gascoigne, but the coverage still seemed to get him down. He appeared at times to be genuinely baffled by the motivation: was he loved, or wasn't he? Why the destructiveness, the wish to wound? After Tottenham's first game of the new season, he declared: 'I'm fed up with all this girl-talk. I have split up with Gail but I don't want to have another girlfriend. It took me twenty-five minutes to get going playing football because of all this hype about a new girlfriend. It seems the only place I am safe these days is out there on the football pitch.'

'He's a very sensitive boy,' Tottenham coach Terry Venables had said, even before the Turin tears, and during the first months of the new season he had to repeat it more than once. Gascoigne started well, as if relieved to be back where he was 'safe', where he knew what to do and who to be. And he was welcomed. Every ground he played at was packed out, and he knew that the extra fans were there because of him. Post-Italy euphoria was evident, and although cries of 'fat boy' and 'big-head' were heard from some opposition fans, there was an odd suspension of the usual enmities. When Spurs played away, with Gascoigne and Lineker on show, supporters were able to relive those great moments of the summer.

Throughout September, Gascoigne was ablaze: a hat-trick against Derby, four against Hartlepool in the Rumbelows Cup, a stunner against Manchester City, and, in between, some breath-taking moments of high skill. For five weeks, he was unstoppable. Perhaps the will to stop him was not there. After all, players are fans too and would also have been glued to the World Cup. By October, though, things had begun to tighten up, and Gazza found himself back in the old routine: the shirt-tugging, the sneaky elbows, the wind-up repartee. Against Aston Villa on 1 October, he was tracked everywhere by Paul Birch, got into a spitting-fight with him and later took a swing at Paul McGrath. 'He was pulled back nearly every time he went past someone,' said Venables, 'and that is frustrating for supporters. They want to see what happens when he has gone past them.'

43

Well, some do. Against Q.P.R. a week later there was another flare-up, and Gascoigne was booked for yelling at the referee. Venables again sprang to his defence. Was the manager suggesting that Gascoigne deserved special protection? This notion was swiftly worked up into a 'talking point', and several papers began dusting down their sermons from the year before. David Miller in *The Times* intoned: 'Gascoigne needs protection from himself.' His 'immaturity' was still a problem. He thinks he's funny, Miller said, but his play-acting was in truth 'about as funny as a puncture.' Stuart Jones, also in *The Times*, seemed to agree: 'Gascoigne is going to cause some explosions unless he learns to lengthen his fuse.' There could be no excuse for his excessive 'petulance'. Mostly the fouls on him were occasioned by his 'running style': 'With his arms flailing, his elbows flapping and his hands grasping he resembles a late commuter attempting in desperation to board a train which is leaving the platform. Anyone in his way risks having the contours of their upper body instantly and painfully rearranged.' True enough, perhaps, but wasn't this the same 'determined' style that we'd been drooling over just eight weeks before?

There was an unpleasant hint of backlash, too, in the way the papers resurrected the old Vinnie Jones dispute. After Spurs played Sheffield United—where Vinnie was now lodged—Jones called Gascoigne 'flash', 'a bottler' and (rather oddly) 'not the same lad I knew eighteen months ago.' He predicted that Gascoigne would 'get hurt one day with all that standing on the ball and taking the piss. Whenever I play against him, he disappears. He never came out for the game. He didn't fancy it. I said, "Come on, take me on," but he bottled it.' Gascoigne had indeed been substituted in the second half, after a largely anonymous performance. He had spent most of his time on the pitch making rude gestures to Dave Bassett, the United manager, who—pre-match—had called Gascoigne 'a buffoon'. 'Gascoigne,' said Bassett, 'goes around ruffling hair and making gestures and gets away with it. But if my kids behaved like him they would be given a good smack and sent to their room.'

All this was given headline treatment, but the whole thing somehow seemed contrived. So too did Gascoigne's run-in with George Best. In the papers and on television, Best was being

George Best with friend (23 April 1993).

prodded for his verdict on Gascoigne and, when it came, it was brutally dismissive. He was tired, he said, of seeing his own name crop up in pieces about Gazza. Was Gazza as good as Best had been? Would Gazza go the same way—i.e., downhill, and self-propelled? Best's view was that Gascoigne wouldn't last: 'He's not good enough. He's a false idol. He's hailed as a superstar because there aren't any, there's a void. There's more to the making of a superstar than a couple of fair games in an abysmal World Cup. I survived because I was the best. Twenty years ago he would have been an average midfield player.' If Gascoigne had anything, he said, it was a sort of childish ebullience, but this would quickly fade. He gave Gazza two or three seasons at the most. It was sad to hear Best talk this way, with seeming bitterness, but it was sad also to hear Gascoigne, invited to respond, describe his precursor as a 'scum bastard' and a 'drunken fat man'.

In October, England played its first game since the World Cup—a European Nations Cup qualifier against Poland, at Wembley. When the England team ran out, Gascoigne lingered in the dressing-room and then trotted out alone, to a tumultuous welcome. But after the match, England's new manager, Graham Taylor, said that England had been playing with ten men—and it was pretty clear that the missing one, in his view, had been Gascoigne, who had made small impact in a two-nil victory for England. Taylor's comments induced a familiar chill in the hearts of all Gazza-fanciers: were we going to go through all *that* again?

Indeed we were. England's next big game was against the Republic of Ireland—the team we cannot beat, the team that knows how to stamp out midfield artistry. Three days before the match, a piece in *The Times* by Stuart Jones gave us the warning light: 'What should Graham Taylor do with Paul Gascoigne?'—a question that would have been unthinkable three months before.

After Italy, and so soon after Italy, it was infuriating to hear the old worries trundled out: 'Gascoigne runs this way, he runs that. And the ball never comes for Lineker. Gascoigne is off on some private excursion, rousing the terraces but too often not allowing his colleagues to join him on the trip.' This was unfair. If Jones had been at White Hart Lane throughout September, he would have seen Lineker miss at least three chances made for him by Gascoigne. He would also have noticed that three of Gazza's goals came from Lineker 'assists'. The two could play together very well.

But Graham Taylor did drop Gascoigne for the Ireland game. It was not, he said, a Gazza sort of match. The pitch was heavy, and so too were the Irish. To replace him, he brought in Gordon Cowans, a player who had worked under him at Aston Villa: a skilful player but wraith-like, past his best and not in the least suited to the Republic's mud and muscle. Cowans did nothing against Ireland but then nor did anybody else: it was a dreary, watchful draw, one-one. Taylor was neither shamed nor vindicated. Afterwards he said: 'I'm not saying that Gordon Cowans is a better player than Paul Gascoigne. What I am saying is that in this

Opposite: Graham Taylor at the press conference following the Ireland–England game.

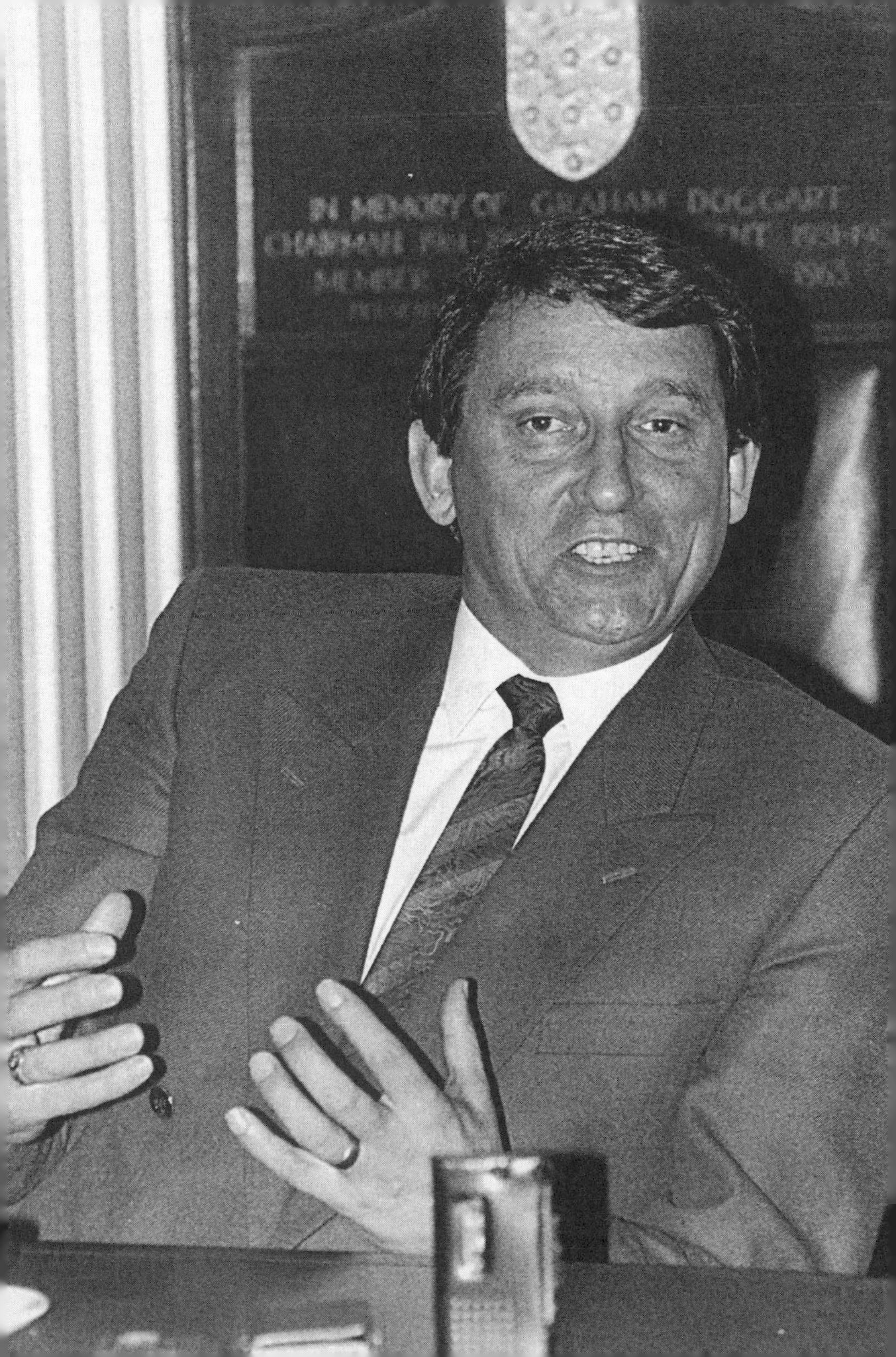
IN MEMORY OF GRAHAM DOGGART

particular game I picked the right side to meet what I knew would happen. It mattered that we kept a clear mind when the onslaught was on.'

A clear mind? Was this a hint? Taylor prides himself on his communication skills, but he also likes to suggest that he knows more than he is saying. He went on:

> I would find it very hard to believe that the things that are written about Paul don't affect a boy of twenty-three. Because he is such a gifted footballer, it has to be of concern to me as England manager but it is something I cannot control. It was not a question against the Republic of playing Cowans instead of Gascoigne, it was a question of the team. You can talk about the flaws you may believe are in his character, but I won't. Whatever I think has to be left to me and the player to discuss privately. Throughout my career, when I have had something of a private nature to discuss, it has remained between the player and me.

What did this mean? What was it, of a private nature, that he and Gascoigne needed to discuss? Gazza himself was silent, humbly accepting his demotion, so it seemed. A couple of years later, Taylor would tell us more about this Irish incident. In the meantime, though, we Gazzamanes were left with the feeling that a tide had turned, that something might go wrong, or had gone wrong.

Don't Cry for Gazza

'Who is Gazza?' asked Mr Justice Harman in the High Court in September 1990. The judge was hearing an application from Paul Gascoigne Ltd for an injunction against Penguin Books' impending *Gazza*, an 'unauthorized biography' by Robin McGibbon. The argument for the plaintiff was that the name 'Gazza' had been trademarked and that McGibbon was in breach of copyright.

'Paul Gascoigne is a very well-known footballer,' explained Michael Silverleaf, Gazza's counsel.

'Rugby or Association football?' asked the judge.

And at this Silverleaf seemed to wilt: 'Association football. He plays for Tottenham Hotspur Football Club and played in the World Cup this summer. As a result of his performance he has come to be very greatly recognized by the public in this country.'

The judge still didn't get it. 'Isn't there an operetta called *La Gazza Ladra?*' he inquired. Silverleaf could not say. The judge went on: 'Do you think Mr Gascoigne is more famous than the Duke of Wellington was in 1815?'

'I have to say I think it's possible,' said Silverleaf. For Mr Justice Harman, this revelation was enough to swing the case in Penguin's favour. The Iron Duke, he seemed to recall, had had no 'right of action' against upstart biographers, although he disapproved of them. Silverleaf's plea that 'times have changed' was met with a final, withering riposte: 'But the law fortunately hasn't . . . I cannot see that Mr Gascoigne has at this time any reputation in this class of goods which could be appropriated by the defendants by publication of this work.'

A defeat, then, for Gazza—or rather for Mel Stein and his legal team. Stein's concern in bringing the suit, or so it seemed, was that McGibbon's book would come out before his own ghost-work-in-progress, *Gazza: My Life in Pictures.* Stein's literary plans for Gazza were ambitious. After *My Life in Pictures* there would be *Gazza's Football Year.* Each of these publications would be billed as 'by Paul Gascoigne with Mel Stein' and each would be heavily pictorial—about fifty words a page. Even so, they would maintain an affable control of Gascoigne's image. He would come across in them as a shrewd, modest, quick-witted, easy-going sort of guy, with a workmanlike command of tabloid prose. If there were rough edges, Paul would be seen as fortunate to have a sophisticate like Stein to watch over him. Len Lazarus would also receive a grateful mention in both works.

McGibbon's book, although reverential and somewhat stodgily composed, was in a different bracket, and not at all aimed at the juvenile-fan readership that Stein seemed to be soliciting. In commercial terms, there was no rivalry, and the trademark argument had scant hope of success since Gascoigne had been known publicly as 'Gazza' long before Mel Stein took over his affairs. Was there something else, then, in the book, that brought the case to court? Gascoigne later complained—'with Mel Stein'—that the book was full of inaccuracies but he offered no examples. He might plausibly have argued that it was too thorough. McGibbon, a former *Sun* journalist, had done some serious leg-work in the North-East. He had amassed several tape-hours of interviews with Gascoigne's early circle: school-friends, team-mates, teachers, coaches. In consequence, his book was rich in data, some of it merely homely or sentimental, some of it intriguing.

Only one disclosure could be thought of as provocative, and was indeed seized on as a scoop. 'Gazza's Tragic Secret' was on the *News of the World* front page shortly before McGibbon's book appeared. The secret was to do with the player's much-discussed 'mentality', his nerves. McGibbon had discovered that when Gazza was twelve he had seen one of his friends knocked over by a car and killed. The shock had left him with a string of nervous ailments. There were nightmares, bouts of insomnia, crying jags and so on—but there had also been a perceptible change in his day-to-day behaviour. Gascoigne developed severe facial twitches, he stammered, he blinked all the time. There was 'a nervous swallow, a clearing of the throat, which came out as a high-pitched squeak . . . some muscular reaction forced the noise out, particularly when he was under pressure.' Later the squeak turned into a bark. According to one of the Newcastle scouts, Gazza 'would get rid of one affliction, then another would start. When the barking stopped I'd say, "You've got rid of the dog, then, Paul." By then, he had developed another nervous habit—a dry cough or something. I don't think he knew he was doing it. Other lads used to take the mickey and mimic him.'

For Gascoigne's more ruminant admirers, this information seemed to invest their hero with new glamour. For the first time, his off-the-field personality had something more to offer than obscenities and ale, something that rendered him susceptible to abstract speculation. We had seen his spasmodic head movements start up at high-pressure moments during the World Cup. We'd seen him twitch and blink, pull faces, gulp. If we'd been close enough, we might have heard him bark. Now we could connect these symptoms to his child psychology, to a trauma that was itself to be admired: after all, it was not little Gazza who had been knocked over by a car; it was his mate.

There was speculation too that Gascoigne might be suffering from a form of Tourette's Syndrome. Victims of this ailment display 'an excess of nervous energy, and a great production of strange motions and notions: tics, jerks, mannerisms, grimaces, noises, curses, involuntary imitations and compulsions of all sorts, with an odd elfin humour, and a tendency to antic and outlandish kinds of play.' They also show 'a capacity for inspired improvisation.' This did sound like our man. It could also be made to sound like an over-eager version of Lear's Fool. An all-licensed Gascoigne might not be too amusing, but there was much literary appeal in the idea that his yob-nonsense and his soccer artistry might be clinically conjoined.

In *The Man Who Mistook his Wife for a Hat,* Oliver Sacks tells the story of Ray, a Tourette's sufferer who had been fired from a dozen jobs because of his condition. His marriage was in trouble, and his friends, although they liked him, could not help but laugh. It was not just the facial tics that had antagonized employers: there were also the problems of his impatience, his pugnacity and his coarse 'chutzpah'. Ray was given to 'involuntary cries of "Fuck!" or "Shit!"' when he became excited. At games, though, he excelled,

> partly in consequence of his abnormal quickness of reflex and reaction, but especially, again, because of 'improvisations', 'very sudden, nervous, *frivolous* shots' (in his own words), which were so unexpected and startling as to be virtually unanswerable.

Sacks cured Ray with drug treatment so that he now enjoys a new 'spaciousness and freedom' in his life. His wife loves him again, and his friends 'value him as a person—and not simply as an accomplished Tourettic clown.' On the other hand, Ray no longer plays sport very often, and if he does he finds that he has lost his special gift:

> he no longer feels 'that urgent killer instinct, the instinct to win, to beat the other man'; he is less competitive, then, and also less playful; and he has lost the impulse, or the

knack, of sudden 'frivolous' moves which take everyone by surprise. He has lost his obscenities, his coarse chutzpah, his spunk. He has come to feel, increasingly, that something is missing.

We did not want something of Gascoigne to go missing. And yet, in the light of McGibbon's revelations and Taylor's gnomic remarks after the Ireland game, we were now more than ever inclined to think of his talent as unstable, under threat. The feeling was well captured by Karl Miller, who saw the World Cup warrior as 'a highly charged spectacle on the field of play: fierce and comic, formidable and vulnerable, urchin-like and waif-like, a strong head and torso with comparatively frail-looking breakable legs, strange-eyed, pink-faced, tense and upright, a priapic monolith in the Mediterranean sun.'

And another don, John Casey, called Gazza 'the weeping, doomed, inarticulate idol of the working classes.' But if doomed, doomed to what? George Best thought that Gascoigne's gift would simply peter out, he would outgrow it; others believed it would be coached out of him by functional team managers like Taylor; some feared that Gascoigne would do the job himself, that he so little understood the nature of his own genius that he would be unable to protect it from the excesses to which his personality was irreversibly inclined. Or should he go to see Professor Sacks? On New Year's Day 1991, in a televised game against Manchester United, Gascoigne was sent off for swearing at the referee. Afterwards he raised press guffaws by pleading that, yes, he may well have sworn, but he was not swearing *at* the referee—an explanation which Sacks might not have been surprised by.

The Manchester United game we can now see as the final act of Gazzamania's benign phase. He had been worshipped and he had been warned, and there he was, still at it, was the general cry. But for his sending off, Tottenham might have beaten United that day and thus kept up their perky start to the season. As it was, all hope of winning the Championship must now be written off. For Spurs, it might be said, what's new? But 1990–91 was different from other seasons; this year it mattered that Spurs *seemed* to have a chance of doing well. English clubs had only just been re-admitted to European competitions, after having been banned following the deaths at Heysel stadium, and Tottenham badly needed to persuade the Midland Bank that they would be in on the proceeds.

For several months, the club had been keeping the lid on a worsening financial crisis. During the eighties, Tottenham Hotspur plc, under the chairmanship of Irving Scholar, had been leaking money into various low-grade, money-grabbing schemes that had gone wrong. To make a Spurs fan squirm you had only to mention the executive box mania, the flotation, the diversification into 'leisure-industry' pursuits, the Saatchi and Saatchi ad campaign, the computerized ticketing, the 0898 Hotline, the Hummel shirt fiasco. When Spurs sold Chris Waddle to Marseille for four and a half million pounds, supporters large and small whinged in the streets, or on the East Stand scaffolding, and they whinged some more when it was revealed that the Waddle loot was needed to offset the losses of a Spurs-owned ladies fashion-wear concern. What it all added up to by 1991 was a debt of around fifteen million pounds with interest running at three million pounds a year.

In this year of all years, then, Spurs needed to win something. They also needed to sell something—or somebody. To get into Europe they now had to capture either the Rumbelows Cup (from which they would shortly be eliminated) or, better by far, the F.A. Cup. To do this, they looked to Lineker and Gascoigne, their most saleable assets. The thirty-year-old Lineker would not fetch much more than the one million pounds they had paid for him (by IOU). Gascoigne, however, was—in age terms—not yet at his peak and might be worth, well, anything: press estimates since the World Cup had ranged from five to fifteen million.

In the end, Spurs went for a best-of-both-worlds solution to the problem: Gazza, according to their master-plan, would win the Cup for them and *then* be sold.

Throughout the second half of the season, Gascoigne was kept out of the rough-and-tumble of the League. He had developed a troublesome groin injury which would eventually need surgery. It was decided that this injury would be nursed from Cup-tie to Cup-tie, and an operation was timed for 11 March. On 10 March, Spurs beat Notts County in the sixth round. This meant they would play Arsenal in the semi-final on 14 April. Gazza thus had a month in which to recover from the operation and to get match-fit.

And how Spurs needed him. In each of the earlier rounds, it was his contribution that had got them through. Against Blackpool in round three, his free kick had set up the winning goal, and against Oxford (round four) he ran the game, scoring twice and sending Venables into raptures: 'Over the years you can always compare a current player with somebody from the past, a player always reminds you of somebody. But in the case of Paul Gascoigne, I don't know anyone who has played like him.' Venables ended up by describing a cross between Dave Mackay and Tommy Harmer, with a dash of Maradona for good measure. The Oxford manager did not demur: 'Gascoigne was so sharp it was unbelievable. You can't stop him. We needed twelve men out there . . . [but] he would still have done the things he did.'

And so it went on. Against Portsmouth (round five) Gascoigne scored two goals, one with his head, and against Notts County (round six), he won the game in the last minute. No one could remember a Cup-run in which so much had turned on the performance of an individual player, round by round, over the full distance. Well, nearly the whole distance. The big one, against Arsenal, was viewed with dread by experienced Spurs fans. The hype was intensive, the match was at Wembley and Arsenal were top of the league: it was the sort of game Spurs *always* lose. And yet they won—thanks largely to a spectacular Gascoigne free kick in the fifth minute. Some sense of what this masterpiece of a goal meant to the Spurs faithful, the triumph, the astonishment, can be gleaned from the writings of one Stuart Mutler, editor of the *Spur*:

> When that big bastud of a free-kick left the right peg of Paul Gascoigne on 14 April, 1991, you could have peeled me off the roof of Wembley Stadium. It was a moment that encapsulated all that was . . . that was . . . BOLLOCKS! Words fail me (as usual).
>
> Is Gascoigne going to crap on the Arse? He is y'know. GET *IN* THERE, YOU F---ER. Boring I know but that's the way it was.

I can't remember what *I* said when Gazza's shot went in but I don't suppose it was much prettier. Even now, among Spurs fans, a mention of 'the free kick against Arsenal' induces a moment of silent, beaming homage. And for decades this is likely to be so. It was for us what Michael Thomas's last-minute, end-of-the-season, championship-winning goal against Liverpool was for Arsenal, except that *they* were on the receiving end of *ours*.

Spurs went on to beat Arsenal three-one, and the calculators were out in the directors' box. Negotiations had already begun for Gascoigne's transfer, and this goal may have added another million to the fee. Since February Spurs had been checking the Italian market. The big clubs, Juventus and Milan, had shown a tentative interest but had not come through with solid offers. The one really enthusiastic response was from Lazio of Rome. Just before the Notts County game they tabled a bid of five million pounds: a three-year contract, a house, a gang of bodyguards and a hefty signing-on fee, probably one million. For both club and player, the offer was seductive. Even so, Spurs stalled: Gazza, they announced publicly, was not for sale. By March the transfer fee had climbed to eight million: there were handshakes but no signatures. Venables and Scholar, in their separate ways, were trying to raise money elsewhere: each of them had staked his job on the promise that Gascoigne would not be sold.

Lazio meanwhile were telling *their* fans that Gazza—this 'poet and peasant of the free kick'—would very soon belong to them. As a result, the club's VIP membership scheme (5,000 pounds a head) was doing well. On 25 April, a Spurs contingent plus Mel Stein flew out to Rome, and by the twenty-sixth the deal was done—three weeks before the Cup Final against Nottingham Forest. Gascoigne himself had not yet agreed his 'personal terms', and Venables was still pleading with him not to go, saying that signing for Lazio would be like signing for Norwich. On Cup Final day, though, we knew that this would be Gascoigne's last game for Spurs. Gazza indeed had said as much: 'If I said no, Spurs would go to the wall. I could never have that on my conscience.' For the fans, it was all a bit bewildering. They had been told that winning the Cup would mend the club's finances, but now it seemed that

Gazza's Cup heroics had been a farewell gift.

Spurs hadn't actually won the Cup yet, but everyone believed they would, and that Gazza would produce some crowning marvel, the icing on a cake which to some of us already looked a little stale. Gascoigne knew what was required of him, and before the game Terry Venables was edgy: 'I do fear for Gazza with all the pressure he's under. The world is watching him. It's too much. He's only human.' Later on, Irving Scholar would accuse Venables of 'turning the key' on his already wound-up star. In the tunnel, as the teams waited to make their entrances, Gascoigne was sweating and twitching; he was breathing like a bull, somebody said.

None of this was evident during the pre-match presentations. Gascoigne kissed the hand of Princess Di instead of shaking it: cocky but not too cocky. As soon as the game started, though, it became clear that he was on the rampage. After five minutes he launched a chest-high kick at Gary Parker, a foul which in some games might have got him a red card. Would that it had. A few minutes later, Gary Charles carried the ball to the edge of the Spurs penalty area and was about to be closed down by van den Hauwe. And then, into our picture, out of nowhere, came Gazza at high speed. He caught Charles with a swiping tackle and the pair of them went down, with Charles on top and Gascoigne's right leg twisting as he fell. A free kick for Forest which Stuart Pearce hoofed into the Spurs net.

Nil-one. Gascoigne was OK, it seemed. He shuffled back to the halfway line, looking shamefaced. At the restart, though, he ran half a dozen paces and then fell. This time he stayed down, and somehow we knew that it was bad: the physio was leaning over him for far too long, too many of his team-mates gathered round. Then came the stretcher. The cameras closed in, but Gascoigne had an arm across his face. Nayim came on as a substitute and a bit later we saw an ambulance parked at the players' entrance. The word was that Gascoigne had broken his right leg.

Famously it was much worse than that. The player had ruptured an anterior cruciate ligament, the ligament that controlled the movement of his knee joint. This was an injury we'd heard about—much feared, it had ruined a number of promising careers; Brian Clough's, for one. Even if Gazza's knee was saved, it would

Photo: Malcolm Croft (Press Association)

be months before he could play again. Lazio's general manager was at the Wembley game. Would he want Gascoigne now? Would anyone? Mel Stein has recalled: 'It was a nightmare. It was the Jewish sabbath, so I couldn't ride. I walked thirteen miles home from Wembley on the North Circular without knowing what was happening. "Paul's been four times on the phone already, crying," my wife told me when I got in. "Do you think Lazio will still take me?" he kept asking when I got through to him, and I told him, "Of course they will."'

On Sunday, everyone assessed the damage. There was a certain amount of sorrowing for Gazza, but not much: even the Stuart Mutlers could not get round the fact that Gascoigne had 'brought it on himself.' It was, said Mutler, 'Haywire City. Yeah, *'course* I knew he was capable of such acts of stupidity. But it was freaking me out to the point of total insanity. I still wanted to love him! But for the Gaz to plummet from such a towering high . . . ? No. I could no longer defend the man. I had to expel him from my soul. Paul Gascoigne. You are a Bastard. Get Out of my Life.'

And the *Mail on Sunday* more or less agreed: 'There can be not a scrap of pity for Paul Gascoigne, who entered the game with the mindless fury of a demented child and left, damaged and discredited, upon a stretcher.'

In England the fear that a great talent may have been destroyed was less pressing than the need to pontificate, to gloat. Luckily for Gascoigne, and for the Tottenham finances, the Italians were more generous. 'We consider him still in the family,' said the Lazio president Gianmarco Calleri. 'We've suffered a mortal blow. Gascoigne is a player of whom we have become very fond, a person we like very much, and I, at this point, say that we won't leave Gascoigne on his own.' In Italy, the tackle on Charles was seen as mistimed, badly executed, but not crazy. They saw worse each week in the Italian league—as we did in ours, they might have added. Before leaving London, the Lazio officials visited Gazza in hospital, gave him a 5,000-pound gold watch and told him to get better soon.

Lazio were somewhat less soft-hearted when it came to dealing with the Spurs money-men. The eight-million-pound offer was reduced to 4.8 million. Lazio would show their good faith by paying out 750,000 pounds immediately and the rest in instalments, according to the player's progress. If Gascoigne *was* finished, the money would have to be repaid. For cash-strapped Tottenham, who had feared that the Italians would pull out altogether, a refusal was out of the question. After some dignified dithering they said yes—yes, please. And so far as Gascoigne's own deal was concerned, the original terms would have to be re-thought— although he would very likely still get the million he'd been promised.

Gazza's knee was now world-famous, the object of anxious scrutiny. Sports journalists were deep in *Gray's Anatomy*, discovering for the first time how the limbs they reported on each week actually functioned. John Browett, Gazza's surgeon at London's Princess Grace Hospital, explained to the cameras the full grisliness of the injury and showed, with the help of a plastic model, how he meant to put it right. He would reconstruct the ruptured ligament, he said, by cutting out the middle third of Gascoigne's patella tendon. To each end of this excised tendon he would attach a piece of bone, one piece grafted from Gazza's kneecap, the other from his thigh. He called this his 'little composite'. The composite would then, by keyhole surgery, be threaded into place behind the kneecap and held there with screws and staples. In effect, Gascoigne would be given a new cruciate ligament, stronger perhaps than the original, and would supply the parts himself. The surgeon stretched his little composite like an elastic band, as far as it would go: it didn't snap.

Most people doubted that the hyperactive Gascoigne would be able to endure the grim months of physiotherapy that lay ahead. When in July he was seen on crutches, sticking his tongue out at the cameras, firing his water-pistol at reporters, nobody laughed. Gazza seemed to be limping out of the headlines. There was a brief flare-up later that month when he was arrested outside a Newcastle nightclub for 'alleged assault'—he had fought with two men who were bothering his sister. The incident was chalked up as a black mark: what was the injured player doing outside a nightclub in the first place? Then in September came the story so many seemed to have been waiting for. Another nightclub, another fight, but this time Gazza landed on the floor, and smack on to his wounded knee. The kneecap broke. Five months of treatment appeared to have been thrown away.

DON'T CRY FOR GAZZA was the headline of a long *Sunday Times* investigation into the new knee-break. James Dalrymple was sent to Newcastle to be told by drinkers in the Half Moon in Bigg Market that, on the fateful day, Gascoigne was half-drunk by ten o'clock. 'He was about eight out of ten and rising. But with Gazza it's hard to tell. He looks as if he was born with five pints of a start.' Gazza, Five-Bellies Gardner and a handful of the lads from the Excelsior had begun drinking in Dunston that morning before setting off to watch the Newcastle–Derby game. 'They were just a bunch of lads off to the match on a Saturday afternoon. They weren't looking for no bother. Just a few beers and a laugh.' At the game, Gazza bought himself an 'Haway the Lads' hat, but he and his friends left at half-time 'and spent the next six hours trawling the pubs and wine bars of the city centre.' The trawl ended at Walker's Night Club where, said Gascoigne later on, 'I was on my best behaviour. I signed as many autographs as I could. I was friendly to everyone. Then someone just whacked us, y'know. He

just said "Gascoigne" and I thought he wanted an autograph. I
dunno why he did it . . . well, I do know—'cos he's a jealous
bastard, that's why.'

The intrepid Dalrymple was in no mood to be conned. His
painstaking reconstruction of events did not tally with the account
put out by Gazza. Gascoigne claimed that his assailant came at him
'outside the gents' toilet.' But the toilet was directly opposite the
bar. Surely someone would have noticed the North-East's biggest
celebrity being pummelled to the ground? There was evidence that
Gazza was 'unharmed' when he left the club that night. And why
was no one pressing for the police to get involved? Gazza's own
assault charge was coming up before the beak in three days' time.
Could this be of significance?

The *Sunday Times* verdict was that Gazza and his pards
pretty much deserved to be assaulted—and on a regular basis, if
that could be arranged. They went from club to club, from pub to
pub, with their shaved heads, their medallions, their T-shirts, their
earrings, their aggressive ribaldry, their Gazza. And Gazza himself
was a sort of Comus for the eighties, with his designer gear, his
wad of fifties, his Algarve-flush, his photograph-me grin. Said one
Dalrymple confidant: 'He moves at the centre of his pack of
minders and he tries it on with every girl who crosses his line of
sight. He thinks it's all good clean fun—but their boyfriends are
Geordie lads just like him, and don't take that sort of thing. The
result is trouble wherever he goes. He regards Newcastle as his
personal domain.'

The incident is worth dwelling on because it marks the end of
Gazza's 'one-of-the-lads' chapter. He seems to have finally sorted
out *why* the just-like-him Geordie boys could so readily turn into
jealous bastards. From where they were sitting, broke, on the
dole, with dire prospects, there was plenty to be jealous *of*—not
least, perhaps, the bright red, hand-made shoes that Gazza wore
to Walkers on the night that he got thumped. 'I think the penny's
got to drop,' he said. 'I can't go—I'm never going to a nightclub
in Newcastle again, you know, never. The thing is I've come to
realize that people outside football are not going to give us a
chance to be one of the lads. All I want is to be one of the local
lads, you know, and they're not giving me a chance. They're

Photo: Rex Features

Gascoigne being helped from Walker's Night Club, his kneecap broken.

jealous. Now I've come to realize that I can't *be* one of the lads.'

When Gascoigne talked like this the press sneered at his 'self-pity'. They'd heard it all before. How could he have imagined that it might be otherwise? Grow up. But in earlier laments, Gazza had been blustering, defiant. This time he sounded genuinely plaintive. People called him 'flash', he said, because he liked to 'stand my mates a drink or two, even if the bill is over the top. It's not me being flash. It's just that I would feel embarrassed in case people would think I was a tight bastard. You can't win. I get on a train and sit in second class and people think, "Tight bastard. Money he's got and he sits in second class." So I think "Fuck them" and go in first class and then they say "Look at that fucking flash bastard in first class." Where do I win?'

And in a *Sun* exclusive he defended the much-maligned Five-Bellies Gardner: 'A tower of strength. He would walk to the end of the world for me. He was crying about the last nightclub incident. He said, "Why couldn't it have been me?" . . . I can't go around not having friends all me life. I've had me friends since I was at Newcastle. I can't say, "Thanks very much. That's it, now I'm a star, sorry lads, you're nothing, now fuck off."'

The broken kneecap set back Gascoigne's recovery by about three months, but in medical terms it was not quite the disaster that it seemed. In spite of having sustained 'a tremendous trauma' the transplanted cruciate ligament was found to be intact. It would have been hard to have devised a sterner test. The surgeon denied that Gascoigne's kneecap broke because it had been weakened by the surgery he'd had. The two injuries, the doctor said, had no bearing on each other. But there must be no further risks. Gascoigne would be 'gated' for eight weeks.

According to all reports, Gascoigne's determination during those eight weeks could not be faulted: he did as he was told, which amounted to several hours of physiotherapy each day, early nights, no social life and not too many laughs. 'Paul's had a fright,' said one of the Spurs physios. 'He's different, still a lovable lad, but he's quietened down a lot. He had to.' He was not that quiet, though. According to John Browett, Gascoigne's 'motivation' was, if anything, 'too high—he has to be reined in.' And the journalist Rob Hughes remembers seeing him in action at the Tottenham training ground. The physios had told him he could run around a bit, 'but no kicking.' 'So Gazza grabs a couple of apprentices and takes them off to the training pitch. And there he was, blasting shots at goal and giving his own running commentary: "Gazza's gonna hit this—it'll be a fucking massive shot," and so on. When he finished I asked him, "Does your leg hurt?" and he says, "Why, aye, it does a bit." So I tell him, "Stupid cunt" and his face crumples.'

This was in April 1992. In February, Gazza's wires and staples had been removed, and he was taken to Rome to watch the Lazio–Roma derby game—really to be shown off to the fans. The reception was ecstatic. With great ceremony he was led into the arena and there read from the cue-card he'd been given: '*Arrivederchee al prossimo campianato*'—to which he added: '*Ciao*'. The crowd went wild: 'Gazza's boys are here/Shag women and drink beer.' 'Unbelievable,' said Gazza; 'It's nice to be wanted again.'

By March, he was running, cycling, even kicking. And he had

a new girlfriend, Sheryl Kyle—a married woman with two small children. 'He's had his fill of dolly birds,' the *People* was told by 'a friend': 'He wants to settle down. He likes Sheryl because she's stable, level-headed.' In April he played his first full practice match and performed reasonably well, though in slow motion. In May, Lazio were told that he was ready for inspection. The Italians sent a three-man delegation, and Gascoigne was subjected to six days of training-tests—sprints, jumps, twists and turns, five-a-side games and so on. He was then given the go-ahead for his final clinical examination in Rome. This was scheduled for late May, and Lazio had arranged for it to be conducted by an American sports-injury specialist, Jim Andrews. The transfer to Lazio would depend on Andrews's verdict.

The medical in Rome was an odd business. At first, Andrews announced that 'everything looks fine.' Then, having studied a scan of Gazza's knee, he said: 'It's fair to say we are undecided.' To which the Lazio doctor added: 'The images from the scan have underlined some problems.' This was on 25 May. Next day, the verdict was rewritten. At a press conference, Andrews declared that all was well. Stress tests had removed the doubts raised by the scan: in other words, the knee didn't look right but it worked. In fact, Andrews put it more buoyantly than that: 'Paul Gascoigne is quite simply a superman. A superman physically and a superman mentally.' If he continued to work hard at his exercises, 'He will be great. Not mediocre, great, perhaps the greatest.'

Some observers were puzzled. Why the change of mind? Lazio expected to raise about ten million pounds from season-ticket sales on the strength of Gascoigne's signing. In Lazio's shop, 'Go Gazza' T-shirts were already selling at ten pounds a time. The fans had been told to expect miracles. The club had had a sorry season, President Calleri had gone, and Dino Zoff, the coach, was having his car stoned. In this atmosphere, the *idea* of a Gascoigne could not lightly be abandoned. There were those who believed that Lazio would have bought him even if he *had* been crippled.

As it was, they were now able to hail him as 'the best player in the world,' 'the new Maradona,' and 'the saviour we've been waiting for.' When, on 27 May, Gascoigne at last signed for Lazio, the team manager Maurizio Manzini told the press: 'I feel like I did when I became a father for the first time. I've been waiting for the baby and it's finally arrived. And what a big baby it is!'

Actively Portly

When Ian Rush was asked to explain his failure to score goals for Juventus he replied that being in Italy was like being in a foreign country. And this rather happily summed up the attitude of at least fifty per cent of the British soccer stars who had taken the Italian plunge. In the words of Enzo Bearzot, the former Italian national team manager, Brits were notorious for '*i fallimenti, le fughe, i litigi, le sbronze*'—in other words, for reneging on contracts and for being quarrelsome and boozy. Not that liquor was a problem for Ian Rush: one of his chief gripes was that no one in Italy stocked his favourite brand of tea-biscuit.

Strange as it now seems, there are strong historical links between the football clubs of England and Italy. Genoa—the oldest Italian club—was started in 1893 by British immigrant workers and was originally called the Genoa Cricket and Athletic Club. The Italians were not allowed to join. They did turn up, though, to watch this peculiar new English game that used 'a ball as yet unseen in Italy, pumped full of air and kicked with the feet'—and they liked what they saw. They liked it very much. Within five years an Italian League was founded, with teams from Genoa, Milan and Turin, and some promising inter-city rivalries took root.

It was not long before every self-respecting Italian town had to have its own soccer club. If you wanted to be a mayor, or just an average big-shot, you were well-advised to look to the fortunes of your local side. The League's First Division grew so huge—at one point it had sixty-four members—that there was no chance of getting through the fixture list within a single season. In the 1910s, the structure was rationalized into something like its present shape—with promotion and relegation between small divisions— by the now-legendary Vittorio Pozzo. In 1929, Pozzo became national team manager and stayed in that post for twenty years. By the time he retired Italy was Europe's most admired footballing nation.

Pozzo, it was often noted by the English, learned everything he knew about 'calcio' on the terraces at Old Trafford. As a young man he worked for a few years as a language teacher in Lancashire. But in these early days, an English influence was something the Italian clubs took pride in: quite a few of them had English managers; one or two—including, to this day, Juventus— employed the suffix 'F.C.' (Football Club) rather than 'A.C.' (*Associazione Calcio*). And Genoa, in their centenary year, still use their English name, even though under Mussolini they were made to call themselves Genova.

In other words, we used to be such friends. This quasi-colonial relationship did not survive much beyond the 1920s. By then the Italians no longer needed us to tell them how to play, and we were making a performance out of standing aloof from the world stage. Now and again, the English national team would give the foreigners a thrashing, but through the 1930s we stoutly refused to take part in the so-called World Cup—which Italy won twice in that decade. The assumption was that we could easily win the thing if we thought it was worth winning.

And then came the Hungarians in 1953—a six-three defeat at Wembley, where we had never lost before, then seven-one in Budapest. From this year of shame, a new orthodoxy would dominate our thinking. The aliens had learned a few tricks which we, because of our climate, physique and stern island integrity, might never choose to learn. We decided to play to our strengths, our superior gifts of character and stamina, our will to win. In time, we would learn how to compete with the East Europeans, the Germans and the Dutch; we would learn how to win the European Cup with teams that were just a notch or two above the average. But Italy, although we beat them now and then, would always remain out of reach, the sinister, dark Other: a Brazil that was too close to home.

Whenever our standing in Europe was discussed, Italy was the principal yardstick by which we measured our own strengths and weaknesses. Italians were more passionate about the game than we were but they were also, or therefore, more corrupt. They had flamboyant skills, but they were sneaky with their fouls, their connings of the referee, their intimidation ploys and so on. Their clubs were richer than ours, their rivalries more vehement, but this was only because they were owned by industrial chieftains and political hustlers who were using the game to promote themselves, their businesses or their careers. Our soccer may be down-at-heel but at least it was what it seemed to be: a working-class Saturday diversion with no compromising attachments to the toffs and megalomaniacs who controlled our weekday lives. You would see no mink or cashmere at our footballing first nights. Aptly enough, the fiasco at Tottenham was the result of aping 'continental' methods.

A similar sort of double-think was evident when we talked about the actual players. In the 1950s, when many of our prejudices on the matter first took shape, the British player was seen as an honest artisan, pinned down by a maximum wage of twenty pounds a week, no richer and no grander than the fans who watched him play. By comparison, the Italian was the rich kid, deeply spoiled. We heard of back-handers, under-the-counter pay-offs, fixed cup-ties, referees who could be bought—horrors unimaginable in our decently feudal dispensation. Their players were better-looking than ours, we had to concede—but didn't they just *know* it? There was a sickening narcissism in the way they stroked the ball around so prettily. And why were they always passing it backwards, or sideways? Why were they so scared to lose?

An explicit falling-out between Italy and England came in the late 1950s. The Italians had lifted their ban on importing foreign players, and the English, whose maximum-wage limit was still—just about—in place, were obvious first targets. The Italian agent became a regular, and disconcerting, presence at our football grounds, and the papers were full of rumours that this or that star player was about to succumb to the 'lure of the lira.' Players who showed signs of being tempted were vilified as avaricious and disloyal, and there was much patriotic glee whenever one of them came skulking back, full of complaints about excessive club discipline, foul business on the field and the lack of basic human amenities—like tea-biscuits or warm beer. We heard less about John Charles and Gerry Hitchens, players who signed for teams in Italy and performed well, than we did about malcontents like Dennis Law, Joe Baker and Jimmy Greaves: each of these was reckoned by the Italians to be of '*carratere turbulento*'.

In the case of Joe Baker, there was the strange business of a wrecked Alfa Romeo; with Dennis Law, there were regular punch-ups with photographers. Most difficult of all was Jimmy Greaves, whose turbulence came across as a protracted sulk. He had signed for Milan 'for mercenary reasons'—5,000 pounds a year plus a 15,000-pound signing-on fee—but shortly after his transfer had gone through, the English maximum-wage limit was abolished. 'It was like a sick joke,' said Greaves, 'only I couldn't see the funny side.' He wanted to leave Milan even before he arrived, and most of his time in Italy was spent trying to break a three-year contract. He stayed for four months and when he returned, to sign for Spurs, he was like a man who had been let out of jail.

Apart from the money-vexation, Greaves's problem had been similar to that of Ian Rush—Italy was, irreparably, foreign. The Cockney sparrow had been sat on by the Italian eagle. In Milan, they couldn't make Greaves out: he seemed to them both dull and irresponsible. He objected to the club's system of '*ritiri*', by which players are taken off to a training camp for two nights before each game. Greaves wanted to stay at home with his wife. On other nights, though, he liked to be out on the town. His ale-house instincts were frowned on by his bosses and avidly scrutinized in the Italian soccer press. He was gated, suspended, fined, and, when he then asked to leave, the Milanese said no. In England we read about his plight with indignation: set our Jimmy free.

And when he did come back, his Italian saga was told and re-told, as an admonitory fable. With Law and Baker also set free, and with big money now on offer here at home, the Italians could be slandered without inhibition. It would be twenty years before the Anglo–Italian market re-opened for business. In the 1980s, there was another mini-exodus, but by then attitudes had changed, or were less stridently expressed. Graeme Souness, Trevor Francis, Liam Brady and Ray Wilkins were impressive on the field and sophisticated enough off it to make light of the tea-biscuit problem. They learned some rudimentary Italian—enough, anyway, to be described as 'fluent' in the English press—and were forthcoming with the Euro-chic.

When Gascoigne signed for Lazio, our most recent export to Italy had been David Platt. Platt had served a year with about-to-be-relegated Bari and had now joined Juventus for 1992-93. Some claimed that Juventus had bankrolled Platt's original transfer from Aston Villa and had arranged for him to serve an apprenticeship, or trial, at Bari. Similar rumours attached to Lazio's purchase of Paul Gascoigne, but they were always angrily denied in Rome.

In terms of image Platt was the opposite of Gazza. He was the clean-limbed head boy to Gascoigne's inky-thumbed delinquent. During his year at Bari, he had behaved flawlessly, praising the language, the weather, the people, the fashions. 'Armani, Valentino, even the names roll off the tongue,' he'd say, and the Italians loved it. He did not quite give off the sheen of an authentic *calcio*-celeb, and there was something rather badly wrong with his hairstyle, but he tried. 'Be it three or eight years, I wouldn't want to go back without saying I'd done more than just the football.'

At Juventus, known as the 'Old Lady' of Italian soccer, they set great store by what they called 'the Juventus Deportment'. In the words of their president: 'We conduct ourselves correctly. We set out to present an example of how to live in the sporting world.' Platt, always courteous, low-key and anxious to fit in, was clearly Juve material. Gascoigne, according to the evidence, was not. It was Gianni Agnelli, the owner of Juventus, who after the World Cup called Gazza 'a dog of war with the face of a child,' but Agnelli then listened to his advisers. The word was that Gascoigne's deportment was not all that it might be, that he would clash with referees, or with provocative opponents, and be given the reddest of red cards.

And this was pretty much the view in England. When Gascoigne set off for Italy, the sages queued up to prophesy the worst. John Sadler of the *Sun* warned Gazza that 'If you muck about, become side-tracked by temptation, the future that was salvaged in the operating theatre won't be worth three coins in a fountain. You've been given your chance. Again. Don't blow it. Again.' Even Terry Venables feared that if Gascoigne failed to approach Italy 'in the widest possible way' he would be 'eaten alive'. Venables wanted him to learn the language and 'become part of the life of the city. If he is left to himself and begins to look in rather than out, and just surrounds himself with his own English friends, it could be a disaster.' There were words too from Italy's most celebrated soccer hard-man, Claudio Gentile, now retired: 'If he uses the elbow on the pitch it will be the end of him . . . if he tries to make people look silly he will be seriously hurt. Italian defenders always get their revenge.'

Most specific of all, though, was the advice from Jimmy Greaves: 'If Gazza's experiences are going to be anything like mine, he will react to the iron discipline of Italian soccer by rebelling against the rule-makers. I turned into a rebel when A.C. Milan tried to restrict my private life, and I became expert at slipping past their bodyguards to sneak into local bars for a drink or three. I was disciplined enough not to get legless, but it was the pressures of Italian soccer that made me start drinking as a habit rather than a hobby.'

Gascoigne was leaving the green playing fields of England for the 'minefields' of Italian soccer; he had a mountain—an 'Italian Alp'—to climb; he was about to be thrown to 'the lions of Rome'. Even as the papers issued these warnings they found time to outline the rewards that lay in store. In *Today*, we were given—by the aptly-named Ben Bacon—a breakdown of Gazza's '£10 million Italian Job'. His basic salary, said Bacon, would be three million pounds over five years, 'but his total package from Lazio amounts to nearly £5 million.' And this would be doubled by 'world-wide endorsements'. The bonuses for playing well would be 'staggering'—90,000 pounds per man if Lazio qualified for the UEFA Cup; 200,000 pounds each if they won the Championship.

And this was just the money. Gazza's 'lifestyle' would be similarly 'swish': he would be getting a 'top-of-the-range Mercedes' and 'an elegant, exquisitely furnished villa' with 'a lake nearby where he can fish to escape the intolerable pressure he will be under.' Bacon had not himself laid eyes on this well-furnished villa but he was able to provide photographs of 'one of the villas Paul Gascoigne has seen' and of 'picturesque Formello', a suburb twenty kilometres from central Rome, and 'home to the rich and famous'—the captions read 'super-bia' and 'Rome sweet Rome'.

All this, in Bacon's view, might well prove too much for 'the kid who was brought up on brown ale in a working men's club in Dunston.' To help him cope, Gazza would have in residence his younger brother Carl, and once a month 'dad John will come out for a week to check on his boy.'

Gascoigne's pickings would indeed be rich, though not as rich as they would have been if he had not wrecked his knee. His 10,000 pounds a week was just over half of what he was originally offered. Des Walker had gone to Sampdoria for twice as much. And Villa Gazza, wherever it turned out to be, was not going to come cheap. Gascoigne would be 'making a contribution' to the rent. By Italian standards, said the *Independent*, his would be a 'journeyman's salary'. Ruud Gullitt of Milan was on a million pounds a year.

'This is Rome, right, but where's Lazio?' asked Gazza as he stood outside the Lazio club shop in Rome's Via Farini. His bodyguard Giovanni Zeqireya explained that 'Rome is city, Lazio is region.'

'But you're a Lazio supporter, right?'

'Oh, yes.' Zeqireya seemed to be an asset: six foot three in his shades, a karate champion and one-time protector of Madonna and Stallone, he also managed to look kindly and long-suffering. And he had undoubtedly taken to Gazza: 'The thing about Paul is that although he may look like a man, inside he is a boy.'

A dog of war with the face of a child. Perhaps this would turn out to be the key: this childishness that everyone at home was urging Gascoigne to outgrow. 'He loves children,' said Zeqireya. 'That is not just very important but to an Italian it says a lot about the person.' Poor Gazza: he always seemed to be on the lookout for adoptive parents, for wise uncles and stand-in older brothers, for shoulders he could cry on. In London Terry Venables and Mel Stein had fitted the bill, and in their different ways each would continue to look out for him, but they could no longer be on twenty-four-hour call. During his early negotiations with Lazio, Gascoigne had an agreement with Glenn Roeder, his former captain at Newcastle and always a shrewd and imperious presence

Photo: Syndication International

Opposite: Gascoigne arrives in Rome.

on the field, that he would move to Rome and serve as an all-purpose minder, a supplier of day-to-day 'maturity', but Roeder now had other plans. Brother Carl and dad John would bring with them an authentic whiff of Dunston, but to judge from appearances they would be looking to Gazza to take care of *them*.

Then there was girlfriend Sheryl, now in mid-divorce from her husband. The hacks had not quite made up their minds about Sheryl. Was she just another bimbo or was she middle class, a cut above? There was the estate-agent husband, the Hertfordshire semi, the children with fancy names—Mason and Bianca. For the moment, the papers decided to portray her as would-be genteel. When she and Gascoigne took a holiday in Florida before he flew to Rome, the *Sun* went too. Sheryl, they divined, had envisaged a romantic twosome. Alas, though, Gazza had turned up with his Dunston tribe: 'Dad John, mum Carol, brother Carl, two sisters and their boyfriends and drinking pal Five-bellies Gardner.' All the boys, including Gazza, had had their heads shaved, or re-shaved, for the trip and from day one they engaged enthusiastically with all the local spots: there were 'high-spirited' nights out in the 'British-run London Tavern' and 'boozy jaunts' to Disneyworld. Sheryl, according to a 'family friend', was an 'outsider' in all this and was 'getting the cold shoulder' from the lads. 'She didn't have a great time,' said the friend. 'She never expected to land up with five skinheads—it's not her scene.'

This being so, it was just as well that she did not attend Gascoigne's farewell 'do' in Dunston a week later. STRIP GIRLS WHIP GAZZA—SHOCK SCENES AT HIS FAREWELL was the *Sun*'s front-page exclusive on 5 July. Two hundred guests had gathered at the Excelsior to send Gazza on his way, and the organizers had thoughtfully laid on two kissogram girls. 'Gazza was lost for words' when 'scantily-clad six-footer' Lindsay Nesbitt removed her nurse's uniform to reveal 'just a black basque, stockings and suspenders.' 'He just looked around, really shy,' said one witness. 'Nothing like you'd expect.' But Lindsay had her way: 'She got him on his knees and made him twang her suspenders with his teeth. All his mates and family were cheering.' Then came the whipping: Gazza, Carl and Five-Bellies were 'each told to bend over and were then whipped ten times by a "roly-polygram."' Was this the girl or the instrument? We were not told. At the end, with everyone 'fairly drunk', Gazza gave his goodbye speech: 'I can't go to London or Italy to enjoy mesel. So I come here to Dunston and the Excelsior where nobody pesters me. I'm going away on Tuesday but I'll see you again at Christmas when I've done the business and taken the piss out of the Italians.' The speech was greeted with chants of 'Dunston! Dunston!'

When Gascoigne left England in July he was seriously overweight—actively portly, one might say. The Italians took one look and set to work. For the first time, the Lazio trainers and physios had sole charge of their expensive property. The season started on 6 September, and there was not much chance that Gazza would be ready. But even if he were to be ready, there was the question of how Lazio would use him. Under Italian rules, a club is allowed to field three foreigners, no more. Milan, for example, had half a dozen costly imports, at least three of whom—Papin? Boban? Savicevic? —would start the season on the bench. Lazio would also have to choose: in addition to Gascoigne, it had Karl-Heinz Riedle and Thomas Doll from Germany, and Aron Winter from Holland. Doll had been signed a year earlier, after Gazza's injury at Wembley, and Winter was recruited when it became clear that the Englishman's rehabilitation might run into the new season. Each was a distinguished international and had cost Lazio big money.

Italian commentators were already hinting that some unpleasantness could be expected. Thomas Doll was said to have declared that if he and Gascoigne played together, he would not surrender the number 8 shirt that he had worn the year before. Gascoigne could have the number 10. In 1991–92, Doll had been Lazio's star player. An East German, he was known to delight in his Italian celebrity and in all the consumer-goodies that went with it. It was said that his car was comically over-equipped with electronic gadgetry. He wore his blond hair long and wavy and he had a ready smile. One could guess that he might not be overjoyed by the arrival of a new messiah. Had he not served as the club's saviour for a year, a year in which Gascoigne—through his own folly—had been stretched out on the treatment table? Was it his fault that the club had finished tenth?

Not so long ago, Lazio would have been content with a mid-table slot in *Serie A*. In their ninety-two-year history, the club had only twice won major honours—the Cup in 1958, the Championship in 1974. They had served time in Italy's Division Two. In England they were barely known before the Gascoigne transfer. For most English fans, the name Lazio evoked vague memories of an ugly clash with Arsenal in the UEFA Cup some twenty years ago, when a punch-up developed at the post-match dinner, with players and officials piling in. 'Too much wine,' said Lazio's coach, who had been in the thick of the fighting. 'If my players go crazy it is not my fault.'

In Rome, the brawl with Arsenal would have surprised nobody. Of the city's two clubs, Lazio was known to be the home of rough-necks. And it had a guilty past. Its support came mainly from the rural areas around Rome and from what was left of the old fascist aristocracy. In smart Roman circles, no one would want to be caught preferring 'Mussolini's team' to their rivals, the newer and more successful A.S. Roma. Most of the slogans and obscenities that deface the city's walls and statues are pro-Lazio, and some have a racist slant. Several celebrate the *Ultras* or *Irriducibili*, Lazio's hooligan squads, would-be counterparts to the head-bangers of Millwall and West Ham. The term *Irriducibili* means 'the indomitables', or 'those who will not yield'.

Although Lazio and Roma play on alternate weeks at the same stadium—the Stadio Olympico—the Lazio bumpkins have more miles to travel than Roma's city slickers. Hence, maybe, the gang instinct, the feeling they seem to have that they are invading their own city, a city 'occupied' by A.S. Roma. For the *Irriducibili*, Gazza and his Geordie boys were kindred spirits, and they were ready to worship this *ragazzaccio*, or 'rude boy'. For them, tales of Gascoigne's indiscipline were welcomed as testimonials, and in their slogans and banners they were keen to let *Il Matto* know that, if he wanted rough company in Rome, he need look no further than the Curva Nord—the Olympico's North Bank.

This was not quite the image that Societa Sportiva Lazio itself had been fostering in recent years, and the new regime—under the presidency of Sergio Cragnotti, a merchant banker and packaging magnate—was seemingly rich enough to force the club up-market.

In the close season, a Lazio buying spree had brought in not just Gascoigne from England and Aron Winter from Holland but also a trio of Italian big-names: Roberto Cravero from Torino, Diego Fuser from Milan and Guiseppe Signori from Foggia. The coach, Dino Zoff, was Italy's captain and goalkeeper when they won the World Cup in '82. So far, Zoff's managerial career had not been much of a success—at Juventus he had won nothing, and Lazio, during his two years, had failed to break into the top half of the table. With his new signings, Zoff was expected to deliver—not this year, perhaps, but soon.

The fitness was of course what mattered most. It was over fifteen months now since Gascoigne had played competitive football. In two practice games, he had shown the old touch at odd moments, but he was blowing hard before the end and complaining of muscular twinges—not in the bad knee but here and there, mostly in the thigh. In one of the games, for Lazio's reserves against the first team, he scored a goal and then shortly afterwards almost crippled another of Zoff's new boys, the Under-21 international Guiseppe Favalli. Zoff, according to one report, gave Gazza a dressing-down 'in his best pidgin.'

When Lazio kicked off the new season against Sampdoria, Gascoigne did not attend the game: 'I get too upset just watching.'

'Where were you, Gazza?' asked the *Mirror*-man, 'out shopping?'

'No, I was at home, looking to make babies,' was the pert reply. Two days later, Gascoigne flew to Santander to join the England team in its preparation for a friendly against Spain. Graham Taylor wanted him to 're-acclimatize'. He also believed that Gazza's presence might give the lads a lift—a lift they badly needed after their dismal showing in the summer's European Nations Cup. This reunion in Spain was the English reporters' first chance of a Gazza close-up since he'd left for Italy two months before.

How was the leg? they asked.

It was just fine, except that 'the right leg doesn't bend as far as the left. It stretches a certain muscle in your leg, and the muscle has been very hard lately. Every time I kick a ball—it's three times now—I split the thigh. I can run. I can do everything, but I'm not kicking with my right foot at the moment.'

Most days he didn't think about the leg. 'All I know is that I want to give everything I have for England again.' He had thrown away his World Cup videos, he said. In the 'dark days' he would watch an England tape 'and upset meself all over again. I watched David Platt's last-minute winner against Belgium. I thought it might help. It didn't. Just made it worse. I've missed it all so much. English voices, the banter, the jokes. Yes, I have been lonely.'

What about Italy? How was he doing with the language?

'There was a dog barking outside my house. It kept on and on. I shouted at it in English but it kept on. So I went through my phrase book looking for something like "Shut up". I yelled out "*Silenzio, bastardo*" and it stopped.' In other words, no problem. The hacks were greatly charmed and next day they reported warmly on Gazza's impressive weight loss, his charisma, his new-found maturity. They had grown tired of Graham Taylor-bashing for the moment: a reborn Gascoigne would be more than welcome. But what *about* the knee?

Under a clause in Gascoigne's transfer deal, Lazio and Tottenham were committed to play two exhibition games, one in London, one in Rome. The Rome date had been twice postponed, since without Gascoigne the game would not have much point. It was now scheduled for 23 September, and after much further hesitation Lazio announced that this would now for certain be Gazza's '*giorno della verità*', his day of truth. In London, not long before, we had sat through a Channel 4 television film called *Gazza: The Fightback* in which we had watched the saw tearing at the kneebone, the scalpel scooping out the tissue. We had seen Gascoigne's X-certificate X-rays, his livid six-inch scar. We had seen him taking his first nervous steps after the wires and screws had been removed. The idea of this fragile reconstruction getting clattered by a first-division tackle made at least one of his fans shudder. Still, let it be remembered that the first tackle, when it came, would very likely be a *Spurs* tackle: it might not connect.

Finally Fit

On the day before the Spurs game, Gascoigne was being interviewed by Gordon Burn for an *Esquire* cover story—a story for which the magazine was asked to pay 5,000 pounds plus 3,000 pounds-worth of Armani gear. 'I want them to play that song,' Burn overheard Gascoigne tell Mel Stein before the match. 'Phil Collins. "I can feel it comin' in the air tonight . . . " Remember. Tell them.'

Burn did not get many other pearls in exchange for his, or *Esquire*'s, cash. As with most interviews with Gazza, the main drift was to do with how much Gazza hated giving interviews. And on this day he had a particular new grievance. An Italian magazine, *Eva Express*, had snapped a topless Sheryl Kyle sunbathing in the grounds of Villa Gazza. The pictures had been sold on to English tabloids. The Italians billed their exclusive feature '*Nudo nel "Ritiro" Privato*', but it was the English Gascoigne blamed: 'You expect that from the English. Who are they? What do they do? They're nothing. They get paid for writing crap, following people around and getting pissed up. That's all.'

Gordon Burn took this on the chin. He had, he reported, been pleasantly surprised by the new-style, Romanized Paul Gascoigne: 'I came half-expecting to see somebody spraying effluent from both ends, like some bloated grotesque in *Viz*.' For *Esquire*'s photo-shoot, Gazza was looking pretty good: 'composed, calm, muscles toned, jawline firm, almost languorous.' And he was proud of his trim figure, although, 'There's no way I was ever the size people thought. The English papers used to touch the pictures up to look fatter.'

At the Lazio training ground, Gazza's conduct was more reassuringly *Viz*-like. 'Yiz fifteen great poofs, yiz!' he bellowed at his team-mates as they limbered up. And he clearly preferred being photographed to being asked: 'Do you still believe that scoring a goal is more thrilling than "shooting your bolt"?'

'I've forgotten what scoring a goal is like,' was his reply.

The small concrete stand that overlooks the practice area was filled with English newsmen. When one was caught eavesdropping as Gascoigne spoke to Italian television, the player turned on him: 'I've told you,' he said, 'if you take notes now, I won't talk to you later.' This was petulant, but who could blame him? He recognized some of the faces in the stand. He knew that these men had come to bury him or praise him. He was on edge, under scrutiny. Dino Zoff was not happy with his player's pre-match mood: 'I hope it doesn't all become too exciting and emotional for him.'

On 23 September, *il giorno della verità*, Rome had its first rainfall for six weeks. On the day I arrived, just an hour before Lazio and Tottenham were scheduled to do battle, there was lightning and great rolls of thunder. By kick-off time there was a crowd of about 25,000 in the cavernous Stadio Olympico—a remarkable turnout, given that the national side was playing a Swiss team live on television at the same time. But few of us had thought to bring umbrellas. By eight-thirty, the rain was sheeting down, and the thunder and lightning seemed to be directly overhead. The police dogs around the track began to bark. Were lions whelping in the street? Had Gazza been *too* saucy with the gods?

Like Phil Collins, I too could feel it in the air tonight. And so too could the *Irriducibili*, massed on the Curva Nord, their Union Jacks grotesquely on display. The huge screens at each end of the ground showed gems from Gazza's past as well as his pop video, 'Fog on the Tyne', to which the *Irriducibili* gamely tried to sing along. More thunder. When the teams finally came running out, to an enormous cheer, there were some silent and anxious-looking spectators in the VIP box: dad John, mum Carol, brother Carl, Sheryl, Mel Stein and Lawrie McMenemy, England's assistant manager. And on the Spurs bench we could see Dave Butler and John Sheridan, the physios who for twelve months had worked on Gascoigne's knee. Sheridan was in tears before the game: it had been a long wait, he said, but he had never doubted that the day would come.

And there was Gazza, centre stage, the number 10, saluting the North Bank. Thomas Doll was wearing 8. Lazio's selection problem had been simplified by Aron Winter's absence, playing for Holland against Norway. As the players lined up for the start, we Spurs fans for the first time checked 'our' line-up. It was deeply unfamiliar. None of Gazza's best mates was in the team, apart from Steve Sedgley and the goalkeeper, Ian Walker. No Gary Mabbutt, no Paul Allen. And there was a sprinkling of kids we'd barely heard of: Nick Barmby, playing his first game for Tottenham; Ian Hendon; Andy Turner. We hoped that these teenagers knew what tonight was all about, that they wouldn't try too hard to cut a dash. In defence, Spurs had Ruddock and Cundy, two gorillas and, so far as we knew, no friends of Gazza: they had arrived at Spurs after he had left. We hoped that they too knew what was required of them: i.e. not very much.

As soon as play started, all eyes were on Gascoigne. He was running smoothly, that marvellous, high-chested run, and he was calling for the ball as if he really wanted it. It took him two minutes to get a touch, a neat lay-off, and seconds later he made a dart along the right wing and aimed a perfect cross to Stroppa, who headed into Walker's arms. A murmured '*Bella*, Gazza, *bella*' came from two rows back. Could we relax now, please? He was running, he could kick, his skill had not deserted him. And he seemed to be pacing himself sensibly, not moving forward every time Lazio attacked. During the first ten minutes he touched the ball eight times. Only once did he attempt a run at Tottenham's defence, and it was good to see Ruddock and Cundy respectfully backtracking. We could take about half an hour of this, we reckoned, and then Lazio could pull him off, point proved, no damage done. We might even settle down to watch the game.

And then Gascoigne, as if he'd sensed some slackening of terrace-tension, turned the screw. A cross from Doll missed Riedle and ran loose to Gazza, six yards out, with no one near him. He did a little skip as he ran on to it, to get in stride, and that was that: a goal in the eleventh minute of his comeback. Gazza kept running, and the crowd behind the goal heaved forward. 'The fans sucked me to them,' he said later, and that's how it looked. *En route*, pursued by a small posse of ball-boys, photographers and cameramen, he had to swerve to avoid the track's water-jump.

Overleaf: Gascoigne, following his goal in the Lazio–Tottenham friendly in Rome, 23 September 1992.

Photo (overleaf): Mike Hewitt (Allsport)

Five of his pursuers were less nimble and fell in. Back on the field, the Spurs team watched, all smiles, and in the VIP box there were hugs and tears. And we at last were able to sit back.

Or were we? When play resumed, Gascoigne was still beaming and his fists were clenched. The fear now was that he might think that this was all too easy and do something stupid. After a few minutes, though, he was positioning himself even more cautiously than at the start, as if he knew that the night's work was done, and done perfectly, and ought not to be spoiled. For the next half-hour, he made no real effort to keep up with play. Most of the time he hovered near the centre circle and waited for the ball to come to him. Just before the interval, as if fearing that perhaps his time was up, he tried one of his famous surges from midfield, holding off Jason Cundy and then Carl Tuttle, who grabbed at Gascoigne's shirt. The run ended with a weakish shot, and with both Tuttle and Gascoigne on the floor. But it was Tuttle who needed the trainer. As Gazza picked himself up, Riedle and Stroppa came across to remonstrate: don't push it, seemed to be the drift. Gazza pretended to look hangdog but as the teams came off at half-time he was looking, as he'd say, well chuffed. That late run was something that he'd *had* to try. And he had scored the only goal.

Zoff gave him twenty minutes of the second half, and Gazza made the most of them: an intelligent through-pass to Doll created Lazio's second goal, from Stroppa. But Gazza was looking sluggish now, worn out, and made no complaint when he was summoned to the bench. For the rest of the ninety minutes he horsed around with the thirty or so photographers who crowded round the dugout. Play went on uneventfully until near the end when the Italians got a third, and Gazza's antics were the focus of attention. He ran through his entire funny-man routine: the stuck-out tongue, the wincing-manic grin. He threw a flagon of water over a photographer who got too close, and this won him a huge cheer. And when the final whistle came, he was instantly back on the field, bear-hugging and arm-waving, shaking hands with everyone in sight. And then, to cap it all, he set off on a triumphal trot to the brink of a wildly-welcoming North Bank: *re per una notte*, as the papers said next day. King for a night.

'*Oh yes, à proprio Paul*' ('It's really Paul') was another Italian headline, and in England it was 'Emperor of Rome!' In theatrical terms, the night had been splendidly successful, and the reviews were suitably ecstatic. But everybody knew that the real test was yet to come. The Spurs game had been the friendliest of friendlies. On the following Sunday, Lazio would be facing Genoa at home. Should Gascoigne play? Cragnotti, the club's owner, had no doubts. He told reporters that 'It would be nice if Zoff could find a way to use Gazza even if it isn't for the full ninety minutes.' And then again, more forcefully: 'Surely Zoff will not waste the chance to play this new champion we have with us. It's very clear he wants to play and needs to play.'

The next day the champion himself announced that he felt 'ready to play' and that between now and Sunday he would be making cups of tea for Dino Zoff and cleaning all his shoes. Zoff was, as usual, poker-faced, not telling, but it was evident that, left to himself, he would hold Gascoigne back, at least for a few weeks. But Cragnotti had spoken, and Zoff had to reply. The problem was: who to leave out? Winter had been performing well, and Thomas Doll, when asked if he thought Gascoigne would play against Genoa, had simply said: '*I* play.'

Zoff tried to stall, saying that if Gascoigne missed the Genoa match, he would certainly be picked for the following week's fixture, against Parma. But this was not good enough, for Cragnotti, for the fans, or for the English pressmen who were hanging on in Rome. My own return ticket was a seven-day job. I had to stay in Rome. I might even get to look at a few buildings. Or I could make a trip to the Via Britannia in search of a bar that had been opened there in Gazza's honour by a consortium of aging Irreducibles. Rumour had it that Five-Bellies worked there as a barman—unpaid: he liked the atmosphere. The bar was called Wembley Park Station, and when I finally did seek it out, I had evidently chosen the wrong night—the place was empty. No Five-Bellies, no customers. On the walls there were pictures of unidentified English players of the 1950s, and hanging from the ceiling were scarves and rosettes of English clubs, from Preston to Notts County. These, too, were seriously out of date. The manager asked me if I knew anyone in London who might want to buy the joint, cut-price. I asked him if he thought Zoff should pick Gascoigne against Genoa. Oh yes, was the reply. Wembley Park Station badly needed a fit Gazza.

Gascoigne had now relaxed the policy of '*silenzio*' (not speaking to the press) which had been intermittently in force since his arrival. 'I would like to show the fans my best but I do need to get match-fit. The only way to do that is to play.' And so he played, at the expense of Winter, who did not protest.

For me, the ordeal of watching the Tottenham game was child's play compared to Lazio versus Genoa, just four days later. This time the opposition needed points and, so far as we knew, had no particular compassion for our wounded star. And Gascoigne's approach this time was likely to be different. Against Tottenham he had answered Question One: was he still able to play football? It was time now for Question Two. And sure enough, right from the start, he was striving to 'show the fans my best,' to let them know that he was special. He shuffled and dummied in tight corners; he made a couple of bold runs at the Genoa defence; and when he passed the ball, he opted always for the imaginative angle, now and then outsmarting his own colleagues.

None of it worked quite as Gazza would have wished, but in a way this didn't matter. The fans were afforded intimations of what a fully-fit Gascoigne might be like. They saw the body-swerve, the on-a-sixpence ninety-degree turn; they saw the acceleration and the power. In glimpses, maybe, but sufficient to ignite their fantasies. The crowd of 50,000 cheered everything he tried. And if his team-mates were aggrieved they did not show it. When a pass was over-hit or when Gazza juggled himself into trouble, none of them complained. Doll even put himself in the way of a tackle that was meant for Gascoigne.

Were the Genoa defenders giving the Englishman an inch or two in which to show his wares? In or near their own area they were unbending but once or twice in midfield or on the touchline they could have clobbered him but didn't. Or was this my anxious fancy? Just before the end of the first half, Gascoigne was caught from behind and went down, clutching at his knee. The stadium fell silent as the Lazio trainers and medics gathered round. Gazza had one hand across his eyes and with the other he was prodding at the

Photo: Press Association

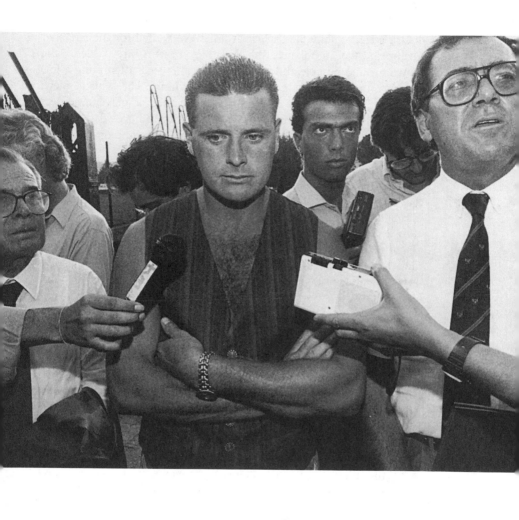

doctor's leg: to show him where it hurt. We waited for the stretcher to appear, the ambulance, the Wembley re-run, but suddenly the crowd around him cleared and he was on his feet, attempting a few experimental hops, then running, with a limp. The whistle blew: half-time. As the teams walked off, three Genoa players were at Gazza's side, as if to commiserate, and from the crowd there was an uncertain flutter of applause. He was still limping when he disappeared into the tunnel.

Gascoigne did not appear for the second half, but we thought we could see him on the bench. Lazio had two other light-haired players—Doll and Sclosa—but they were on the pitch. It had to be Gazza. If so, he was sitting very still. After the game, the Lazio club doctor announced that all was well, that we had had a false alarm: 'It wasn't a big accident. Paul was hit on the knee around the sciatic nerve, but there is no distortion of the knee joint. The impact deadened his leg for a moment. He was a little scared. But he will have to get accustomed to these kinds of kicks.'

Gascoigne refused to comment. He had reimposed his 'silenzio', he said later on television, because the papers had told lies about a 'quarrel' he had never had with Dino Zoff. 'It's the lies I canna stand,' he told Channel 4, to whom he was contracted. Even so, the papers contrived to get some quotes, of the 'he told friends' variety: 'I was scared for a moment but it's not serious. The thing I remember most was how quiet the crowd went. The lad who hit me came up at half-time and said he was sorry. He thought he'd only tapped me.'

By the following Tuesday, Gascoigne was back in training, and Zoff was hinting that he might pick him for Sunday's game against Parma. Zoff looked depressed when he said it, but Zoff always looked depressed. As Joe Lovejoy of the *Independent* wrote: 'The sighs of relief could be heard all the way from Lazio to Lancaster Gate.' Nonetheless, the incident was troubling. Two years ago such a tackle would probably not have found its mark: Gazza would have sensed it in advance and twisted clear. But he had lingered for a second, wholly focused on thed man in front of him. Then thwack—he was taken from behind. And, whatever he may be saying to his friends, he *had* been badly scared. This was his first competitive collision for almost eighteen months, and it had made his knee go numb. How could he not be scared? From now on, would his evasive instincts quicken or would his every move be tinged with apprehension? The two might amount to the same thing, of course, and anyway such questions were absurdly premature, but we too had had a nasty fright. Would watching Gazza always be like this? As the club doctor said, he would have to get used to the kicks, and so would we. But how?

Gascoigne did play against Parma and for thirty minutes he played well. He came off midway through the second half, triumphant and unscathed. And Lazio, who had drawn all their games so far, at last came good. They won five-two. Gazza helped to make two of the goals and he won a penalty from which Signori scored. For the penalty, he was rudely felled by Taffarel, the Parma goalie, but this time there was no deathly hush. Gazza cheerfully bounced to his feet. Indeed, throughout the game, his demeanour seemed determinedly bubbly and fear-free, as if he had become weary of our worries. And on the bench, after he was substituted, he was seen to be 'back to his old self'. NUTS, said the *Daily Mirror*, over a big picture of Gazza playfully cupping the bits and bobs of one of his Lazio team-mates: 'He's still a mischievous ball-boy at heart—Gazza's certainly getting to grips with Italian football.'

Gazza's high jinks may have been aimed at Graham Taylor, who was sitting in the stand. Taylor had missed the Spurs and Genoa games but—apart from the injury scare—he had had good reports from McMenemy. After the Parma match he was able to pronounce: 'For the first thirty minutes we had glimpses of the old Gazza.' Would he then think of picking Gascoigne for England's forthcoming game with Norway—a vital World Cup qualifier to be played in ten days' time? To general astonishment, Taylor did not rule it out, though he doubted that Gascoigne would last ninety minutes.

Taylor had developed a Bobby Robson-like habit of giving voice to his every indecision and dilemma. He had begun his reign with expansive talk about the need for a new openness, for a cordial give-and-take with the journalists who had hounded Robson out of office. At first, the press had gone along with this, although there was no real warmth in their response. Where Bobby Robson, in defeat, had had the good grace to look haggard and distraught, Taylor was invariably ready with some verbose explanation. After the event, he had a way of talking about defeat as though it were a victory for pragmatic common sense: 'Well, Sweden of course won because they play the English game.' And he would say this with a strange, condescending fervour. At press conferences he was like a headmaster on parents' day: there was a touch of the bogus in his bonhomie.

Some thought there was a touch of envy too in his dealings with star players, players he could not think of as his own. Waddle and Beardsley had been too eagerly discarded, and Taylor's treatment of Lineker in the match against Sweden was surely both petty and vindictive. It was Gary's last game for his country, he was one short of an all-time scoring record, and Taylor pulled him off with twenty minutes to go. Had he forgotten Lineker's last-minute goal against Poland, the goal that got us to Sweden in the first place? No, Taylor was not the straight-arrow nice guy that he liked to seem.

There were also questions about his competence. Post-Sweden, the feeling was that for all his coaching-manual glibness, Taylor was probably out of his depth. He was a tactical ditherer, switching from one system to another. At heart he was a long-ball man. As a club manager, his success had been built on by-passing the midfield. At international level, though, he was obliged to present himself as a wily, sophisticated strategist. No wonder his players often seemed confused.

Certainly Graham Taylor was not Gascoigne's sort of boss. He was more social worker than adoptive parent. There was something about Gazza that he badly wanted to sort out, once and for all. But this was no time for therapy. After the European Nations Cup fiasco in Sweden, where England had failed to win a game, Taylor's head was on the block. A defeat in the World Cup by Norway might well bring down the axe. For weeks he had been cooling the pro-Gascoigne fever, pronouncing wisely on the need for patience, pointing out that Gazza would need several full-length outings before he would be fit for the demands of the World Cup. 'I have to cut through the emotion,' he had said. 'I have to remember that the boy has not played for seventeen months, and no one, not even Paul Gascoigne, can make up for that.'

On the whole, the press had backed him: it would be mad to take the risk. By 13 October, though, most papers had already changed their tune. They had watched Gascoigne train at Bisham Abbey and declared him to be 'full of running again and back to peak fitness.' He had come out first in a short-sprint competition and had scored well in his lung-capacity tests. And there was more approving talk of his 'maturity', even after he replied: 'Fuck off, Norway,' to a television request for a message to that nation. This kind of conduct was, said Taylor, the 'downside' of Paul Gascoigne. 'His language at times! You think, "Oh, my God," but that's what makes these people . . . the Bothams, the Gascoignes. Most of us like to say the right thing, be diplomatic. He says what he feels.'

The news, finally, that Gazza would be playing at Wembley after all, added 30,000 to the gate, and on the morning of the game there were 'England Expects' war-cries in the tabloids: GIVE US BACK OUR PRIDE, GAZZA, said the *Mirror*; GO GET 'EM GAZZA said the *Sun*.

In the first half, Gazza did next to nothing—in fact, it was ten minutes before he got a kick. He had been given a 'free role', Taylor had told us, with the ferocious Ince and Batty detailed to protect him. Not much protection was required. For most of the time, Gazza was to be seen wandering in space a yard or two behind the front men, Wright and Shearer. England's passes from defence were high and inaccurate; rarely was it evident who they were meant for. The tall Norwegians had no trouble heading them back where they had come from. Time and again, Gascoigne was left standing as the ball flew over him, from end to end. He seemed to be under orders to stay forward; or at any rate not to seek the ball in his own half. In the first forty-five minutes, apart from one or two nice touches, his most notable contribution was to get booked for elbowing a Norwegian in the face.

By half-time, the England fans had stopped chanting Gascoigne's name and had settled into that old Wembley state of mind: a sort of placid discontent. The assumption was that Gazza would be substituted, that he had not after all been ready. But at least he was unharmed. There was a cheer, though, when he came out for the second half. If he had more to give, then so did we. And for eight minutes of that second half he delivered what we craved: a flashback to Italia '90. His control, his running with the ball, his passing were suddenly spot-on, and magisterial. He was upbraiding his team-mates when they made mistakes, snarling at the crowd for more support, demanding the ball whenever it came near. Play quickened and both teams looked springier, more urgent. And Gazza was red in the face, eyes popping, his neck-muscles at full pulse. For those few moments, we forgot the knee.

Gazza did not score the England goal, but it was his quick thinking that helped to set it up. The captain Stuart Pearce was shaping to take a free kick out near the right touch-line when Gascoigne yelled at him to wait. The foul had happened at least five yards further in. The ref agreed, the ball was moved forward and Pearce was now within range of Norway's goal. He unleashed one of his specials, Platt deflected it and England were one up. A minute later, Gazza planted a low, in-swinging corner-kick on Shearer's head, and it should have been two-nil.

By the time Ekdal equalized in the seventy-sixth minute, Gazza's fiesta had burned out. He played the last minutes at half-speed. But Taylor left him on until the end: his first full game since his return. And although England had dropped a vital point, perhaps *the* vital point, no one at the time seemed too concerned. The official man-of-the-match award, we heard as we trooped off into the night, had been given to Paul Gascoigne.

The following morning the papers were on a Gazzamanic high. Gascoigne's display had 'defied logic, medical opinion and shot to pieces any doubts about his ability to withstand the most intimidating challenges.' By the weekend, though, the plaudits for Gazza gave way to some pretty sour analyses of England's overall performance. Was Gascoigne really as wondrous as he seemed, or was it just that the men around him were so mediocre?

Hugh McIlvanney in the *Observer* was unillusioned: 'Have we been so institutionalised by the recent diet of workhouse gruel that we are prepared to burst into rapturous applause at the first taste of something more palatable?' Gascoigne was 'nothing less than a helping of caviare,' but even he—'every inch a player of the first rank'—had been ridiculously over-praised. There was that ugly foul to be remembered, as well as a need for 'that old bugbear, perspective.' If Bobby Charlton 'had done precisely the things that Gascoigne did on Wednesday he would not have been praised to anything like the same extent . . . Charlton had to perform in an era when failing to destroy the likes of Norway guaranteed a storm of disapproval.'

There was justice in McIlvanney's scorn. England had been inspired by Gazza for ten minutes but otherwise their play was unimpressive, both frantic and laborious—an unlikely combination but one for which the English are renowned. On the other hand, Gascoigne had shown—as in the World Cup—that team spirit could be lifted by the performance of one player. He had shown too that his own spirit could be lifted. The crowd's oaths and chants were familiar music to his ears; his team-mates revered him as their leader; the hype was in a language he could understand.

For McIlvanney, Gazza at Wembley was a 'rose among wallflowers'. If, just four days later, he had watched Lazio against Milan, his point would have been proved. Facing Milan's exotic line-up of world stars, our Gazza looked weedy. With Riedle injured, Doll played up front—or would have done if he had been allowed to. As it was, he was regularly forced back into a midfield already occupied by Winter and Gascoigne. Lazio thus had three play-makers with no one to play *to*—except Signori, who was repeatedly caught offside by Milan's robot-like back four. As a result, the three of them kept getting in each other's way. Lazio fought well, but the eventual score—five-three to Milan—made the game sound tighter than it was. At times, Milan's high-speed, one-touch interplay seemed telepathic. And most of it passed Gazza by.

But surely our expectations were absurd. He must be tired. On the morning after the Norway game, Gascoigne had caught a six a.m. flight to Perugia where he was paraded in a money-spinning friendly. From there, on the Friday, it was back to Rome for the pre-match *ritiro*, and then off to the San Siro to be met by Gullitt, van Basten, Panin, Baresi and 70,000 baying Milanese. Milan had won last year's championship without losing a game and in the close season had pushed out over twenty million pounds on new

91

players—including thirteen million for the raw Lentini from Torino. A.C. Milan's owner, the limitlessly rich media mogul Silvio Berlusconi, had worked out that the best way of weakening the opposition was to buy up *all* the talent that was going—no matter that it then languished on his bench. So far this season the team had yet to drop a point. I longed, of course, for Gazza to sparkle in this company, even merely to gain its respect. The word was that two years ago Milan had decided that he was not good enough for them. *Not good enough?* I'd spluttered at the time. It was sad, therefore, to see him so diminished, so peripheral. But surely they too must know that he was knackered.

Three days later, Gascoigne was back in London, for the return match against Tottenham at White Hart Lane. He played for fifty minutes, ineffectually, then took his bows. At the presentation afterwards, he raised a modest laugh by debagging Sclosa just as the Lazio captain was readying to hoist aloft the so-called Coppa della Capitali. For Spurs fans, it was a melancholy night. We had watched the Norway game with pride. We knew now that Gascoigne was fit again and would probably get fitter. But we also had to acknowledge, for the last time, that he was no longer ours. When he left the field, he saluted the terraces and they saluted him, but there was a weariness, an exasperation even, in the handclaps and the cheers—a sort of 'if you're going, *go*.' As so often, the *Spur* found the words:

> I still can't get used to seeing him in that pale blue Lazio shirt . . . he's like some bird that's chucked you. Your ex is out on the town with a new love, flaunting it, and not giving you a second thought. So you find someone else, and tell yourself you are happy and you're over it. I really thought, I really *really* thought I had got over Gazza.

Il Commento Gastrico

In the old days, when a British star went to Italy, he disappeared. There would be bulletins from time to time but these would be irregular and mostly scandalous and their import was likely to be reassuring: our favourite would soon be home. In the case of Gascoigne, though, we heard from him each week, on Channel 4's *Gazzetta Italia*, a Saturday morning compilation of Italian soccer news, 'presented by Paul Gascoigne.' And, when possible, the same channel would feature Lazio on their Sunday afternoon 'live match from *Serie A*.' Before we knew it, we were getting to be experts on Italian football: would Juve get their act together this year, had Fiorentina bought too many forwards, would Napoli survive the departure of Maradona to Seville? We knew about Vialli's head-shave, Roberto Baggio's pigtail, Daniel Fonseca's teeth. Channel 4's timing had been perfect. With Des Walker, David Platt and Gazza at three different *Serie A* clubs, there was always a good chance of a Brit slant, and the *Gazzetta* briefing allowed us to talk knowingly of Des's rivalry with Lanna or of Platt's with Andy Moller; it gave us the context and the gossip.

Gascoigne, we heard, was getting 1,000 pounds a week for his *Gazzetta* chores, and these were hardly onerous. He appeared briefly at the top of the show, saying something like: 'Hello, I've had a very interesting week. But more about that later. Now *this* . . .' and we would then be handed over to the voice of Kenneth ('They think it's all over!') Wolstenholme, which would lead us through the last week's clips. Then came James Richardson with a somewhat shrill resumé of the Italian soccer press. And then back to Gazza for two minutes of anodyne reflections on 'my week': 'As you can see I had a very tough match this week. The England match was very good but on Sunday people say I looked tired. It wasn't that I looked tired; it was because we were up against a very, very strong team in Milan—one of the best teams in the world.'

In addition, there were Gazza's Golden Goals—'They have a panel of guys who choose but I am asked my opinion'—and Gazza's prediction of next week's *Serie A* results: 'Ancona versus Parma. This will be a tough match. Zero-zero.' This sequence of the show was so nakedly unauthoritative that after a few weeks it was quietly dropped.

But after a few weeks the 'Gazza factor' was no longer reckoned to be crucial. A *Guardian* survey in December showed that Sunday afternoon Italian soccer was pulling audiences of over

2.5 million, compared to the 600,000 who watched BSkyB's exclusive coverage of all the most important English games. 'Different people will quote different figures to support their case,' said Neil Duncanson, head of sport at Chrysalis TV (the company that produced the Channel 4 coverage), 'but the one I like is the one that says that for the Sunday before last a hundred and sixteen thousand homes equipped with BSkyB were in fact watching our programme.'

At Sky, there was a feeling that someone had blundered: Sky had itself once held the rights to the Italian League but had relinquished them in the euphoria of being able to broadcast English premier division games exclusively. The reasoning seems to have been that British fans would never take to the Italians' sterile, defensive style of play. But Sky was not to know that in 1992–93 this style would change—not least because of the new rule prohibiting goalkeepers from handling deliberate back-passes. In the opening weeks of the Italian season, there had been results of three-three, four-nil, seven-three, five-three: figures unthinkable in the heyday of *catenaccio* (or 'bolt', as in 'I bolt the door'). The goals-average in 1992–93, so far, was 3.45 per game compared to 2.27 the year before.

Was it just the back-pass rule that had performed this miracle? Some observers believed that the influx of top foreign players was equally significant. Liam Brady told the *Independent*: 'Time and time again when I was playing there, in the mid-80s, you would just face a wall of ten players. You would get teams going away from home and just camping in their own half. The foreign players who play the game to see who can score most goals have changed the Italian mentality considerably.' It also helped that, under the three-foreigners rule, none of these imported stars could be certain of his place.

Lazio had had one or two goal-sprees but had also been on the receiving end—as in the game against Milan. They looked a good team going forward but in defence they had one or two day-dreamers. In this respect, they were a lot like Spurs: when the cockerels go two-up they change into peacocks and all of a sudden it's two-two. Lazio, in the first half-dozen games of the new season, had confirmed their reputation as Italy's draw specialists. Since their promotion to *Serie A* in 1988, they had drawn just over half their games—a record that was beginning to eat at the nerves of their supporters. Last season's anti-Zoff campaign had been revived, and by November the indications were that he was on probation. It was said that the Lazio–Roma derby game on 29 November would seal his fate, one way or the other. A draw in that game would be bearable. After all, Roma were looking good. A defeat, though, would bring down the roof.

Zoff had to hope that Gascoigne would come good before that date. The signs were promising: indeed, the month of November can now be viewed as the purple period of Gazza's first Italian year. The month began with an exhibition game in Spain, against Seville—a match billed as 'the battle of the number 10s—Gazza and Maradona face to face on the world stage for the first time.' The reason for the fixture, from the Spanish point of view, was to help fund Maradona's purchase from Napoli. A large part of his five-million-pound transfer fee was unpaid and overdue. And although Seville fans were unresponsive—only 1,500 turned up to watch the game—the screen-rights had been sold to Italian television.

Maradona's contribution to the game was sparing. He curled a free kick against the bar and delivered one superb overhead cross from a tight angle, and was happy enough to let these two moments serve as his credentials. Gascoigne played for only one half and seemed at first to be aping the Argentinian's haughtily negligent approach. After thirty minutes, though, he stirred himself and scored. A thirty-yard dash took him past three defenders, and two more were on top of him when he shot. The strike was low, angled and unstoppable. Afterwards, Maradona called him 'a great player' and hinted that Gazza might turn out to be his own worthy successor. 'I suppose that was nice of him,' said Gazza, 'But I still remember the hand of God. I tried to kick him for you, Peter [Peter Shilton].'

This patriotic postscript was for Channel 4 consumption and was no doubt aimed at the fans who turned out in force at Wembley a week later for England's World Cup game with Turkey.

Turkey, with San Marino, were the punch-bags of England's World Cup group. Before the game, Graham Taylor and others tried to build up the opposition, just in case: after all, were they not managed by the wily Sepp Piontek? Piontek, it was predicted, would have Gascoigne man-marked. It would be up to Paul Ince and Carlton Palmer to clear space for Gascoigne to shine in. As it turned out, he was gifted all the space he needed by the panicky, retreating Turks. And, majestically, he made the most of it. He scored two goals and made one in England's four-nil win. Against Norway his intervention had been critical but brief. In this match he was at his best throughout, superbly dominant in everything he did. His two goals were virtuoso-pieces: for the first he skipped between two floundering defenders; for the second he burst on to a lucky bounce in the Turks' area, dummied the goalkeeper, then more or less walked the ball into the net. And it was his elegant flick-on that set Wright free to cross for Shearer's diving header.

England's victory was hailed as comprehensive: by general consent, Gascoigne was reinstated as the nation's saviour. Graham Taylor, for one, could not conceal his gratitude: 'We have been ekeing out results without Gascoigne. I can't remember any player who has influenced a team so much.' For the first time since taking charge of England, he 'felt like a club manager again. There was a nice warm feeling in the dressing-room. A pity we can't play another game next week.' The players also paid tribute to Gascoigne's effect on their morale. 'Just to look at Gazza in the warm-up gives you a lift,' said Lee Dixon, 'Tony Adams winds people up shouting his head off, Stuart Pearce makes sensible points in his quiet way, but Gazza can just stand there and everyone thinks: "Here we go." He doesn't do anything specific or say anything specific—he is what he is.' What the players also admired was Gascoigne's commitment to the team; for all his fame, he had not become 'big-headed'. And they loved his sense of fun. Before the game Carlton Palmer had cut the toes off Gazza's socks: just for a joke, like. Did Gazza mind? Not a bit of it. Next time he'd be looking out for Carlton's shoes. Before returning to Rome, Gazza donated his 3,000-pound man-of-the-match award to the team 'pool'. 'My mates did a wonderful job,' he said, 'It was a team victory.'

'Please God don't let anything go wrong for this lad,' said Taylor at the post-match press conference.

Like what? he was asked.

'This fellow has got something about him which can still, if we're not careful, bring him down. You're on edge all of the time with him. He's probably at his most vulnerable now he's back playing. He has time to think about other things, and it could be that people may suggest he gets involved in all sorts of things.'

What sorts of things?

'Other human beings. He enjoys life to the full and might get sidetracked.'

And this was a cue for Taylor to be asked if he could now reveal why he had dropped Gazza for that Ireland game in 1990. His reply was characteristically teasing and obscure:

> I can never actually say everything about that decision. I was concerned about his health. It was my first experience of seeing somebody who looked quite glazed at times. Everybody always wants a bit of the boy, but I need him for England. That's the tightrope. The reasons to drop him were not tactical. There were certain incidents before the game. The boy was in a state and I was concerned about his health.

And that was as far as he would go. Which is to say, not very far—and yet too far. Gascoigne, we knew, disliked this kind of managerial speech-making—to the press, behind his back—but he said nothing. The subject would come up again, though, and was clearly at the crux of his relationship with Taylor.

Back in Rome, the Lazio–Roma conflict was at hand. On Channel 4, Gascoigne confided that he had never known a build-up so protracted and intense. 'For three months all the fans have been saying "win the derby, win the derby" or "don't lose the derby." For them, it's life or death.' After forty-eight minutes, death seemed the likelier outcome. When Giannini scored for Roma, the Curva Nord broke into chants of 'Dino, go!' and the Roma fans responded with 'Serie B! Serie B!'—all this to an accompaniment of smoke-bombs, fireworks, flares, even the odd bonfire here and there. Gazza looked drained and out of touch—rather as in the Milan game that had followed his triumph against Norway. But he had had two weeks to recover from the Turkey match, and for once Zoff decided to let him play the distance. 'In a match like this,' he said later, 'a player like Gascoigne, even when he's struggling, is still always going to make a difference.'

And so it proved, although the miracle came late. With three minutes to go, and with Roma sitting on their one-nil lead, Signori lifted a hopeful free kick into the box. Four players jumped for it, but it was Gascoigne who made contact. A powerful glancing header and Lazio were safe. One-one. It was Gazza's first league goal in Italy. His tearful dance of celebration lasted for two minutes and would have gone on longer if his team-mates had not dragged him back on to the field. He was booked for the delay but didn't notice. For the last seconds of the game he wandered free, muttering to himself, punch-praying with his fists, still choking back the sobs. 'Yes, it was the old waterworks again,' he said afterwards. 'I've never felt pressure like that, not even in the World Cup, because of what would have happened if we'd lost. Ever since I got clumped by that fella in the discothèque I'm still a bit frightened of supporters.' (It so happened that he *was* attacked by fans: three days after the game, Gazza was molested by a gang of nuns. 'I've never had anything like it, nuns, Roma supporters, giving us punches on the arms. I thought nuns were really nice. Incredible. Getting punched by nuns.')

The *Irriducibili* had put on a grateful show when Gazza scored but at the end they were still calling for Zoff's head. When some of the players threw their shirts into the crowd, the shirts were instantly thrown back. Next day, the press was scathing: the game had been a bore, they said, a contest of 'many nerves and little football.' In revenge for this, the Lazio squad announced an indefinite '*silenzio*', a media blackout. In England, though, nobody cared that the game had been no good, nor even that Gascoigne had played badly. It was HAIL CAESAR in the *Mirror* and HE CAME, HE SOARED, HE CONQUERED in the *Sun*. And the tears were, of course, lapped up: 'There they were—those tears of joy that have become his trademark. Yet again it was all too much for a kid who

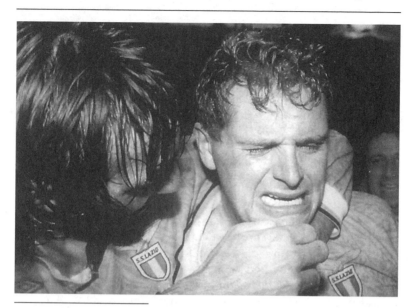

Gascoigne, in tears, following his goal against Roma.

has never really had time to grow up.'

A week later, Gazza scored his second goal for Lazio, against Pescara, and it was one of his best ever—a near-replica of the strike against Seville, but this time the defenders were not playing in a friendly, and the final shot was more spectacular, hit high and hard. It was Gascoigne's last game of 1992. He was substituted near the end with a 'thigh strain'. He then caught 'flu and missed Lazio's next game—a stirring three-one win over Inter Milan. But even in this match Gazza caught the eye: '*Divertendo tutti in tribuna, con scene di esultanza ad ogni gol della Lazio.*' In other words, he really got behind the lads. Or, as he put it: 'I saw the game from a supporter's point of view.'

The Lazio squad was required to report back from the Christmas break on 28 December. Their first game of the New Year would be against Ancona on 3 January. Gazza would not be playing. The rumours were as usual: a merry Christmas in Dunston had piled on the pounds. He was in need of 'special training' before he would be fit to play. And there were other vexations: while he was away his villa in Rome had been burgled, and in Newcastle his uncle Ian had got into trouble—attacked with a bottle, it was said, by some 'fucking nutter' who had just got out of jail. Uncle Ian would be 'recovering' at Villa Gazza. Gascoigne then had to break training and fly back to England to attend his father, who had fallen seriously ill.

It was 10 January before he was ready to turn out again for Lazio—more than a month since the game against Pescara. By this time the Italian press was offering mid-season breakdowns of '*il Gascoigne Italiano*', his performances in Italy so far, his '*infortuni, spettacoli, gol, botte e lacrime.*' The figures were none too impressive: nine games had been played, and in four of these he had been substituted. Three matches had been missed because of injury or illness or—in this latest case—'*il padre malato.*' Altogether Gascoigne had been on the field for 630 minutes. He had scored two goals (as many, it so happened, as Vialli) and had provided one 'assist'. He had 'procured' one penalty. And the match-by-match analysis revealed that his overall play had been erratic: in most games he had flitted in and out of the action. And he was right to believe, as he did, that the goal against Roma had been vital. Without it, the fans might now be beginning to pull faces, and so too might Dino Zoff. Lazio's official line was cryptic: Gascoigne, they said, was '*importante, ma non indispensabile.*' They were 'disappointed' that he had failed to keep in shape during the mid-season break.

So far, Zoff had not had to resolve his 'three foreigners' dilemma. Both Doll and Riedle had at separate times been injured, and only once or twice had the manager been forced to choose. Injuries can of course be invented, in order to save the face of an excluded star, and this might have been the case with Gascoigne's thigh-strain, or even with the 'flu that kept him on the sidelines against Inter. The Inter game was now regarded as a high point of Lazio's campaign so far, and had been seized on by some critics as a portent: perhaps the presence of Gascoigne, with his special status and his suspect stamina, his '*bizzarrie*', had inhibited the team. Without him, Lazio had seemed faster, fitter, more spontaneous. And this argument was strengthened by Gascoigne's current 'poor condition'. Cragnotti was heard to remark that 'without Gascoigne we had eleven Gascoignes.'

On Channel 4, Gazza replied to the soccer writers who were calling him 'stressed, overweight,' not worthy of his place. 'I'd like to see some of these guys, if their father has an operation, if their uncle has a slit throat, your house gets robbed, they take a helluva lot of stuff, then you come back and they expect you to be happy straight away . . . It's just a pity when you stop speaking to people they just go and cause more problems.' It was the familiar plaint: the press tell lies about you so you refuse to speak to them so they tell even bigger lies. What was a chap to do?

In the past, Gazza's most effective answers had been delivered on the field of play. During the first weeks of his comeback he had been fired up, he said, by a determination to 'prove people wrong,' and in his two games for England he had surely done just that. Was this defiant fire extinguished now? Was the adrenalin beginning to run low? After his Christmas knees-up in Newcastle, he was now faced with six months of heavy exile, of training twice a day and of lengthy *ritiri* with team-mates who, nice as they were, did not speak Geordie. His days off would be mainly spent behind the walls of his now-burgled Villa Gazza.

The domesticating influence of Sheryl and her children had, he attested, made him more settled and responsible. He had been smartened up. On a shopping trip with Sheryl he had bought 'Thirty thousand pounds-worth of designer clothes—in one go'— every bit of it, alas, now nicked, along with a wardrobeful of Sheryl's equally expensive gear. In Rome, his idea of a good time was to watch Postman Pat videos with little Mason and Bianca: 'I get a load of popcorn and bottles of Coke and settle down on the settee. I let the kids stay up so I can see the films.' But even Postman Pat could pall after a time, and so too perhaps could Mason and Bianca, although there was no doubting Gazza's devotion to the kids: 'I have always liked children. I could play with them all day. To Mason I am the only father he has ever known because he was six months old when I met Sheryl. When I am away he'll come to the phone and ask: "Daddy, are you playing football?" It gives me a real thrill to hear his voice.' In England, Colin Kyle, the children's father, had begun legal proceedings to prohibit Mason and Bianca from living abroad. The action was scheduled to be heard in early February.

With Riedle injured, Gascoigne returned to action against Brescia but was again substituted after a marginal display. The same thing happened a week later in the three-one defeat at Napoli. This time Gazza vehemently claimed that he had taken 'a nasty knock on me hip.' Lazio's next test would be at home against Juventus, who shared with them joint third place in the league. The Juve game was always an event and it was not often that Lazio faced the Turin side on equal terms. David Platt had a knee injury and was out of the Juventus team, but Gascoigne felt certain of his own place: certain enough to invite over a contingent of family and friends, a home from home. On the Friday before the match, though, Zoff told Gascoigne that he was dropped. By all accounts, he took it hard. Some stories have him refusing his reserve-team bib and exiting from the training ground, enraged. Others tell of him drowning his sorrows on the night before the game.

Most of these stories were to be heard, or overheard, in the bar of Rome's Foreign Press Club, where I was entertained by the *Guardian*'s Paddy Agnew, who also covers Italian football for *World Soccer*. Agnew, a Liam Brady fan, was fairly scornful about Gascoigne—not fit to lace the boots of Brady or of Best—and so too were the other journalists I spoke to. A chap from the *European* told of a press conference where he had put it to Gazza that one of his tackles might, perhaps should, have earned him a red card. 'Have you ever played football?' asked Gascoigne.

'Well, no, not really, not . . . '

'Well, fucking shut up then.'

Others weighed in with similar anecdotes, and when I told them that I was hoping to write a fan's portrait of the star, there was general incredulity. Why bother? Gascoigne, they said, thinks with his feet. But all of them were keen to know what I knew about Sheryl and about the daily routines of Villa Gazza. When I told them that I only knew what I read in the papers, *their* papers, incredulity softened into a sort of pitying contempt. 'If you could get one minute in his kitchen,' said Agnew, 'your story would be written. I mean, does anyone *cook* in that place?'

On Sunday, though, thanks to my contacts, I had access to the Olympico's press box and from where I sat I could see Gascoigne, next to David Platt, looking chirpy and spruced up in his Lazio club blazer. His mates, plus brother Carl and uncle Ian, were in the back row of the VIP area. They looked and no doubt felt conspicuous with their shaved heads, their tattoos, their ready-for-the-business bomber jackets. Surrounded by Italian toffs, they did their best to play it cool, but their cigarettes were kept well out of sight behind their backs, and their refreshments were demurely tucked beneath their seats. There was a blonde girl with them: was this Sheryl or was it Gazza's sister Anne-Marie? In the press box just behind them there was much consultation on this point. Somebody thought he recognized Anne-Marie's husband, a non-skinhead sitting to her left. It must be Anne-Marie. Did Sheryl ever go to Gazza's games?

The match ended in a one-one draw, but Lazio dominated in the second half and would have won if Riedle—back in action and replacing Gascoigne for this game—had not bungled a last-minute chance. Riedle, to everyone's surprise, was emerging as Lazio's 'fourth foreigner': it was he, and not Winter, who had made way when Gazza played, and there were reports that he would soon be transferred. Brought back for the Juventus game, he was too scurrying, too eager; even his famous headwork was awry. The watching Gascoigne knew that his own place in the team was guaranteed for Lazio's next fixture—a mid-week Cup-tie against Torino—because Thomas Doll would be suspended for that game, but in the long term it was Riedle's form that mattered.

In the car-park after the match, Gazza was in jovial mood. If there had not been a '*silenzio*', he might even have shared a few thoughts with the milling hacks. Lazio was now one of four *Serie A* teams to have announced a boycott of the press, and the scribblers, with three dailies to be filled with soccer-chat, were getting desperate. As it turned out, Gazza saved the day—indeed, he saved the week. Approached by an Italian television crew with a question about being excluded from the team, he grabbed the interviewer's microphone and released into it—a belch: nothing Falstaffian, more a side-of-the-mouth hiccup, but unmistakably non-verbal. The incident was shown that night, at peak time, on one of Italy's most popular shows, and next day the papers had plenty to report.

'*Il commento gastrico*', '*il rutto in stereofonia*': Gazza's belch was headline news, and not just in the sports press. In *Il Messagero* and *La Stampa*, there were deep-dish editorials on the meaning of Gascoigne's 'pure and spontaneous vulgarity'. What had happened, it was asked, to the manners of the English working class, to Orwell's miners, Kipling's soldiers? Did *they* belch on television? 'The next move must be made by society which cannot permit such lapses of taste.' And this was the view also of a neo-fascist M.P. Guilio Maceratini (a former member of the Lazio youth team). In parliament, Maceratini demanded an official inquiry into the affair; he wanted 'disciplinary measures . . . a lesson in civility for a champion who seems to ignore the most elementary rules of polite society.' Lazio, clearly embarrassed, tried to calm things down. Zoff admitted that Gazza's 'gesture' had not been at all 'pretty', and Cragnotti said, 'It's all right to do that when we are among ourselves, but not in public when you are wearing the Lazio uniform.' All the same, he said, 'I like Gascoigne very much and I desperately want him to do well.' 'The character,' he said, 'the will to win' was there for all to see. The 'dignity' would surely follow in good time.

In England, the inclination at first was to mock the po-faced Italians. The *Guardian* ran a jokey leader on international belching customs, and the tabloid sub-editors made merry: 'Belch Up', 'The Italian Yob'. Brian Glanville, who on a recent visit to Rome had felt the rough edge of Gascoigne's tongue, was pleased that the Italians were now seeing 'the real Gazza': 'Club president Cragnotti is said to feel "betrayed". What a silly fellow. Didn't the penny drop when, first meeting Gazza in his London office, he saw our hero shooting paper pellets from an elastic band? One dropped on Cragnotti's head.' Gascoigne, said Glanville, had the brain of a four-year-old, and it was all to the good that, with his belch, he had broken free 'from the hypocrisy and the smoke-screen which has surrounded him ever since he got to Rome. Free from the conspiracy of silence between Lazio and the Roman press which pictured him as a reformed character, belying the image he brought from England.'

Gascoigne's immediate advisers were divided on the matter of the belch. Jane Nottage, his day-to-day representative in Rome, admitted that it had been 'very unfortunate'. The Italians, she said, were 'always conscious of their image.' Ms Nottage, author of a spicy novel called *The Italians*, had her own problems coping with Gazza's whims and humours, as she had explained to me when I met her in London two months earlier. On that occasion she had been haughtily protective of Gazza-the-property: she told me my face was on the Gazza dartboard because of an article by Brian Glanville in *World Soccer*. Glanville had told Gazza to 'watch out, there's a poet about' and had made me out to be a highbrow sneerer. Nottage said that she might be able to help me with my Gazza studies, perhaps as a co-writer, but we never managed to arrive at an agreement. Her view of Gascoigne, it seemed to me, was rather more *de haut en bas* than mine could ever be. She was not, let's say, a totally committed fan.

On the matter of the belch, Nottage had to tread carefully; she had to stick up for her client without offending the Italians. Mel Stein, based in London, had rather less to lose, and was in any case unresponsive to the Italians' sense of style. Had he not first been seen in Rome wearing a floral beach shirt, shorts and shades, with sandals and brown socks? It was his view that 'the Italians have no sense of humour. It was just a joke. If Paul had done it in England everybody would have laughed.'

But in England the belch-story ran and ran, with mockery of Italian solemnity soon giving way to contemptuous reappraisals of the Gascoigne psyche. Belch-related feature articles appeared: the decline of English manners, the abuse of celebrity, the menace of the 'new Englishman' who was 'increasingly being seen as a brutish and leering figure with little or no right to respect.' This last treatise, by a professor of 'cultural studies' at Lancaster University, was adorned—in the *Daily Mail*—with good-old-days photographs of Stanley Matthews, Biggles, *Brief Encounter* and Phileas Fogg. On the facing page, there was Vinnie Jones, a frame from *Viz*, a *Spitting Image* puppet of Prince Charles and—most prominently—Gazza, in yob mode. A few days later and the gallery of virtuous old-timers would surely have included Bobby Moore. When Moore announced in mid-February that he was suffering from cancer and would shortly die, there were at least two newspaper articles contrasting his gentlemanly ways with the repellent gracelessness of Gazza.

Long before the English had settled into their moralizing plod, the Italians' indignation had burnt out. At the Lazio training ground two days after the belch, Gascoigne had a two-hour confrontation with Cragnotti. There was unconfirmed talk of a 9,000-pound club fine. Certainly Gazza got a talking-to. He was advised that Cragnotti saw him as 'team leader', as 'one of the crucial components of Lazio's future.' He must therefore 'show maximum commitment, seriousness and concentration.' In the end, his aim must be 'to show us all he knows about football, to show us his technique, but above all to show us the team leader.'

On the following day, Gascoigne recorded his 'my week' spot for *Gazzetta Italia* and asked forgiveness for his indiscretion. His demeanour was sheepish, naughty-boy. The stand at the training ground was filled with English journalists, and every so often he would glance up at it. He knew why some of these newsmen had been drawn to Rome. Rumours were abroad that Sheryl, with the children, had quit Villa Gazza, and that her flight back to England was perhaps connected to the belch and/or to the Villa's recent influx of house-guests.

The house-guests were in attendance now as Gascoigne said his piece to Channel 4. The group of them made for an odd spectacle: the celebrity in dandyish, bright yellow jacket and checked waistcoat; the lads, beer-bellied, vigilant, in functional T-shirts and jeans. The lads looked like bodyguards, except that now and again one of them would giggle. And what was the star saying to the cameras? 'I'm sorry for me little belch.' Half an hour later, as Gazza was being driven from the ground, his exit was blocked by a small crowd of Lazio *tifosi*—quite a few of them beer-bellied and skin-headed too. They vespa'd to the training ground each day, to watch and wait. There was no need for Gascoigne to apologize to *them*, and he knew it. He signed autographs then rode off, with a lordly wave.

I too was at the gate, the fan from home. I had got chatting with Gazza's brother-in-law, the non-skinhead in his entourage. He was more interested in discussing Oldham Athletic's chances of avoiding relegation than he was in talking about Gascoigne, or Lazio, or even Spurs, but he was amusing on the subject of Italian fans. At training grounds in England, he said, the spectators were mainly 'little kids'. In Italy, they were all teenagers and grown-ups. On one occasion he had seen a sixty-year-old Italian burst into tears when Gazza looked at him.

And on Thursday night, against Torino in the Cup, he was indeed '*Gascoigne, un Lord*', as the *Gazzetta dello Sport* would dub him on the Friday morning. This game against Torino was his finest hour—or half an hour—in Italy so far. For the first time, his whole repertoire was on display, and the Italians marvelled. And so too did the lads. Every time Gazza pulled one of his breath-taking stunts—a defence-destroying pass, a mesmerizing run, a spot-on cross—he would turn to the VIP box and salute his skinhead troops, as if to say: That was for you, for us. And they'd be on their feet, punching the air, no longer conscious of the toffs. The toffs, anyway, were cheering too. Then Gazza would be off again: another pass, another run, another victory salute.

It was, at last, an Italian Gazza-show, more impressive even than his exhibition against Turkey. The Torino back four were not used to being treated with such high disdain, and a quarter-full Olympico was not the same as Wembley. But Gazza once again had things to prove. For four days he and his friends had been held up to ridicule. They had been mocked for their crudity and lectured about 'style'. Very well then, his performance seemed to say: *this* is my style. When Gazza walked off at half-time, his team-mates lined up to shake his hand.

At that point the score was two-one to Lazio, but it could, should have been five-nil. Gascoigne had set up both of his team's goals and had created several openings that might have been made more of. He himself had been thwarted by an acrobatic save by Marchegiani. And then, just before half-time, an error in the Lazio defence had let Torino in. In the second half, Gazza was spent. He puffed and strained but had nothing left, and Zoff pulled him off with half an hour to go. He left the field, arms held aloft, and the crowd rose to him, respectfully—there were more claps than cheers.

Torino equalized in the last minute when Lazio's goalkeeper, the oft-maligned Fiori, let a soft free kick squirm through his legs, but afterwards the talk was all of Gazza. And one moment in particular stayed in the mind. Halfway through the first half, a high-speed shuffle of the feet had taken him through a ruck of four defenders. It was the shuffle, a kind of feint or jinking quick-step, that captured the Italian imagination. Gazza's manoeuvre, it was said, had a distinguished name—'*il passo doppio*', derived from the 'paso doble' dance-step—and it also had an ancient history. Invented in the 1930s by a Bologna player called Amadeo Bavati, it had over the years often been attempted. Never before tonight, though, had it been executed with the speed and flair of the original. The papers the next day had cartoons and diagrams to show how the move worked, together with photographs of the esteemed Bavati. In 1939, playing for Italy against England, Bavati had employed the '*passo doppio*' to bewilder the Inglese full-back Habgood (sic). And there were columns of awed homage to the reinventive artistry of Gazza:

> The 'passo doppio' of Gascoigne blossomed at the Olympico under a light rain. A ballet improvised and seductive, it caused the pleasure of enchantment to gush forth. Gascoigne on the bathed field achieved something rare and incandescent. This unconstrained lunatic Gascoigne has exhumed an ancient and musical movement which has the rare beauty of a valuable relic. The 'passo doppio' is of the history of football. It is as precious as the miniature lettering of an antique manuscript . . . And it adds beauty to the chiaroscuro of the situation that this pearl has an heretic for a father . . . On Thursday Paul, in a game of pure elegance, has redeemed his recent pig-like belch, worthy of Gargantua. He has restored the magic of a tapestry. With beauty he has confounded the critics. He has given the game the dignity of the dance and he has transformed the field into a drumskin.

Well, that's roughly what it said. And whatever we may think of its author, one Claudio Gregori, he's a world away from Harry Harris.

Did Gascoigne *know* that he had so redeemed himself? If so, he made short work of his halo. Two weeks later, in Turin for the return leg of the Cup-tie, he was in the news again. A distinguished *Il Messagero* journalist called Maurizio Saticchioli approached him in a hotel lobby: 'I went up to him and said "good evening",' said Saticchioli. 'He got up, signalled for silence, lifted his leg and broke wind. He tried to fob off the blame for his performance on the kit man, who was sitting next to him. But the kit man denied it and everyone knew it was Gascoigne. Then he started laughing. Everyone else was extremely embarrassed. This Gazza is clearly a real gentleman.' On the plane back to Rome, after the *Il Messagero* story had appeared, Gascoigne berated the reporter for his breach of confidence: 'Fuck off,' he is said to have said. 'I fart whenever I want to.'

Portly Again?

'English football's most precocious and precious talent is evaporating into the skies over Italy like the fading flares of a half-spent Roman candle. Somebody, somewhere, has to be brave enough and rich enough to say, Gazza Come Home.'

This was the *Sun* on 18 February, the day after England's World Cup match with San Marino. England had won the game six-nil, but this was not reckoned to be much of a result. Had not Norway recently put ten past these postmen and bus-drivers, these *Serie B* rejects? For days the English press had been predicting a double-figure massacre, with bags of goals for Gazza. On the night, though, England laboured, and four of the six goals arrived late in the game. By then the crowd had remembered the words of 'Wot a Load of Rubbish' and had taken to booing John Barnes every time he touched the ball. Poor Barnes, just back after a bad injury, had played as he always plays for England, abstractedly, but he had made one of the goals and had done some nice things now and then. Why the yob nastiness? Some observers believed that the crowd's exasperation had more to do with Gascoigne than with Barnes. Gazza had struggled from the start. He had been jittery, ill-tempered, slow. After Noway and Turkey, this match was meant to be a Gazza-fest, but the star of the show looked as if he wished he wasn't there. The hype-crazed fans had been let down—but how could they boo Gazza?

In fact, Gascoigne was by no means the feeblest England man on view. Nobody played well and the full backs, Dixon and Dorigo, probably had most to answer for; with no forwards running at them they should have been romping down the wings—getting to the byline, getting crosses in. Actually they did romp down the wings, but the crosses kept landing in the crowd behind the goal. Still, that was the way it was with Dixon and Dorigo: what did anyone expect? At one point, after Dorigo had been grounded with concussion, the England trainer told Graham Taylor: 'Tony's hurt—he doesn't know who he is.' To which Taylor is supposed to have replied: 'Tell him he's Ray Wilson.' With Gascoigne the difficulty was that he was 'not himself', and most of the post-match analysis centred on this issue: what had gone wrong with our messiah?

Taylor, needless to say, was both gnomic and expansive. The lad was 'having a struggle with himself.' He was unfit, overweight. He had perhaps peaked in the games against Norway and Turkey: 'In his mind he had won the battle to prove us all wrong and get back on the pitch.' Since Turkey, 'his fitness has slipped away.' If it continued to slip, 'Crikey, we may not be able to get fifteen minutes out of him.' So were the Italians to blame for not having kept Gascoigne up to scratch? On this, Taylor put on his diplomatic face; his relations with Lazio were excellent. What was it then; who *was* to blame? 'He is a very emotional boy. He seems unhappy with himself and within himself. His eating habits go with the moods. When he's unhappy, he finds solace that way.'

There was plenty to get stuck into here. 'Unhappiness' surely had to do with what the hacks, off-duty, referred to as 'the great divorce'. Since leaving Italy in January, Sheryl had been holed up in Hertfordshire, saying nothing, but her mother had been telling the press plenty. Sheryl's life in Italy, it seemed, had been a lonely

Opposite: Sheryl Kyle and Paul Gascoigne, arriving at Heathrow from Rome.

Photo: Syndication International

Terminal 1 arrivals

yawn. The girl 'hated football'; she missed the discos and the bright lights, '*la dolce vita*' of Dobbs Weir. When Gascoigne was off for days on end, in *ritiro* with the team, she spent her evenings on the telephone to mother. In Rome she could not go shopping without the paparazzi on her heels; she had no social life; she could not speak the language. And she found it hard to cope with Gazza's frequent house-guests—especially his mum, Carol. Even so, she still loved him, and there was no doubt that he loved her, although snaps taken of the pair in restaurants and airports always showed Sheryl looking cross and Gazza looking contrite and bewildered. When Jane Nottage later told all to the *Sunday Mirror*, this impression was confirmed: Sheryl, said Nottage, was the stronger of the two and something of a shrew. 'He seems totally obsessed by this woman. She obviously has something he needs. When he's with Sheryl, he gets uptight and nervy. They quarrel constantly when you're with them. It's like the Battle of Waterloo. Paul is a sweetie when he's on his own. It's pathetic. Paul's family are his rock, his stability. I think he should look very carefully at his relationships, and ask if he is really happy.'

For Gascoigne, the week before the San Marino game had been packed with Sheryl-incident. Her husband, Colin Kyle, had won his court injunction: if she wanted custody of Mason and Bianca, she would have to live in England. Colin, we read, was a bankrupt and therefore unable to make trips to Rome. Although Sheryl had unsuccessfully appealed against the ruling—there was a court hearing in Cambridge on the day before the Fart—pressmen privately figured that she rather welcomed its constraints. From now on, she would visit Rome alone, stay in a hotel and enjoy city-nights with Paul: no more Villa Gazza, no Carol, no Five-Bellies, no four-day *ritiri*. For Gazza, of course, all this meant no more Postman Pat.

Sheryl's first visit to Rome since the 'divorce' had been a week before the San Marino game and had ended chaotically. She and Gazza were in a restaurant, staging a lucrative reunion-with-Sheryl photo-shoot, when some lensmen from a rival newspaper happened to appear. Fisticuffs ensued. Five photographers ended up in jail, and Sheryl headed—'grim-faced'—for the airport. Sheryl was now perpetually, almost officially, 'grim-faced'. Gascoigne, it was thought, had had further words with her before the Wembley match. And in between these meetings, if Graham Taylor's hints had been correctly understood, the player's head was in the fridge.

In Italy, when Taylor's comments were decoded, there was understandable resentment. It had never been Dino Zoff's policy to push Gascoigne hard during his first year with Lazio: the 'pain barrier' could wait. He wanted to bring him along gently, both as a player who had been seriously injured and as a personality whose culture-shock would necessarily be difficult to manage. Zoff had several times said that only next year—1993–94—would he expect the 'real Gascoigne' to emerge. Hence the substitutions, the rest-periods, the tolerant approach to Gazza's conduct off the field. And Cragnotti, although more impetuous and star-struck than the coach, took a similarly patient line: 'Of course you cannot go around belching and farting, but I honestly don't think that these last two incidents were the real Gazza. I think he's an intelligent man who likes to wind people up. Paul is very important to us and it is up to the club to help him as much as we can. He can stay as he is—like a clown—and that clowning could complete his image as a great player. I expect to see the real Gazza at the end of this season, and eventually the Lazio team will form around him.'

Graham Taylor could not afford to be patient. He wanted the real Gazza now. As a club manager, Taylor had been affably paternalistic: the players who worked for him were *his*. He knew when to cuddle them, he claimed, and when to kick their backsides. Not so with England. In the international set-up, 'his' players actually belonged to Alex Ferguson, or Terry Venables, or Dino Zoff. Even John Barnes, his one-time Watford favourite, had other masters now. And with Gascoigne, Taylor's control was most painfully tenuous. He could not get at Zoff through the English Football Association, as he could with any recalcitrant club manager in England. Indeed he had to be careful not to tread on the Italians' toes. In Italy, players really are owned by their clubs, and why should Lazio trouble themselves with England's World Cup woes?

So far Lazio's interests had roughly coincided with Taylor's. Each wanted Gascoigne revived as a world figure: Taylor for obvious reasons and Lazio because much of the club's income came from exhibition games, starring the 'new Maradona'. But should there be a falling-out, Taylor had more to lose than Zoff. And the San Marino game neatly illustrated the underlying differences between the two of them. Gascoigne was clearly not fit to play a ninety-minute international. He had been involved in four matches during the eleven days leading up to San Marino, and off the field he'd been having a rough time. At Wembley, if Dino Zoff had been in charge, Gazza would have been pulled off after sixty minutes, if not long before. Taylor kept him on. But why? If he had replaced him, he said, 'it would have destroyed the lad.' Kindly considerations of this sort had not influenced Taylor's treatment of Lineker in Sweden. Was the manager afraid? Afraid of the crowd-reaction, the press, of Gascoigne's wrath—which, on that night, was surely on the boil? Or was he simply waiting and hoping, as we were, that something miraculous would happen, and that tomorrow's headlines would speak not of a ponderous, heavy-weather victory over sub-standard opposition, but of a Gazza-inspired goal-blitz? Managers are also fans: they fantasize. And they can have their ugly moods. From Gascoigne, Taylor needed a Norway and a Turkey *every* time, just as we all did. With San Marino it was a fit of fan-exasperation that led the manager to inflate an off-day into an existential crisis. But what of the burden on Gascoigne, the burden of not knowing *how* to 'turn it on?' After Taylor's provocative post-match soliloquoy, Lawrie McMenemy did his best to head off the 'Gazza Come Home' school of psychotherapy. He suggested that perhaps Gazza's unhappiness was more to do with his art than with his life: 'His unhappiness comes from the frustration of a person with such great natural ability who is wondering why he is unable to produce it as much as he would like. It is nothing other than that. It is not a personal problem, it is not about living in Italy. It is about a lad who is searching for the answers himself and wanting to sort it all out.'

McMenemy's hunch was that Gascoigne was better off in Italy than he would have been had he stayed on in England. And, all things considered, we bereft Gazzamanes were beginning to agree. In England, there was an essential hostility to Gazza: a class-fear, a culture-dread. Here he could be *placed*: on the terraces or on the rampage, down the pub or up before the beak. If we were to meet him, we'd be ill at ease—both awed and condescending, with the condescension somehow managing to win the day. When Gazza speaks on television, the English—or most of them—mock his *Auf Weidersehen Pet* accent and his all-over-the-place syntax. But in Italy, most people think he's speaking proper Inglese, or that his dialect is interestingly regional. In England the belch was seen as no more than you'd expect from such as he. In Italy, it was thought to be out of line but idiosyncratic. And the Italians were not in the least disconcerted by other, to us off-putting, aspects of his physicality: his huggings and kissings of colleagues, his patting of bald heads, even his sniffing of opponents' armpits. They saw him as generously tactile: we saw him as over-the-top, gross. In England, all but one or two of Gazza's mentors wanted him to change, to grow up, to become more like David Platt. In Italy, as Cragnotti testified, they regarded the nuttiness as an important aspect of his gift—and the gift was what mattered above all. 'In many ways,' said Jane Nottage, 'Paul's character fits into the mentality of the Italian people very well. He has a genial side and a dark, self-destructive side, which is very Roman.'

The conventional wisdom about English players in Italy is that success comes only to those who 'learn the language'. Repeatedly, on television and in the press, Linguaphone veterans like Ray Wilkins and Liam Brady painted a grim picture of what life for Gazza would be like should he fail to make an effort on this front. We heard that he was taking Italian lessons twice a week, but few really expected him to persevere, or to get much beyond the basics. As Mel Stein once pointed out, he was not a lessons sort of guy. With his Lazio team-mates he rubbed along, but comically, by monosyllable and mime—and the comedy, by all accounts, was helpful. Not speaking the lingo, Gazza was free to be pure clown. According to Ms Nottage, 'the rest of the team might speak Geordie before Paul speaks Italian.' Most Lazio players could now swear in fluent Tyneside.

Watching the team training, I found it hard to detect rivalries or tensions. The Italian players seem mightily amused by Gascoigne and are both indulgent and protective—parent-like, in fact. And he is, of course, remorselessly bubbly and prankish, and always on the move: one moment teaching the Italians how to make authentic British V-signs, the next demonstrating his kung-fu expertise. And in five-a-side games he does more than his fair share of Euro-yelling. All in all, the atmosphere seems boyish, a bit silly, but OK.

But tensions and rivalries were there. When, at the end of February, Lazio lifted their media embargo, both Riedle and Doll had lots to say. In their view, Gascoigne was getting preferential treatment. Why was it always one of the two Germans who got dropped? Riedle said: 'We are just fed up that he does what he likes and is still guaranteed a game every Sunday.' And when Doll was left out for the 28 February fixture against Genoa, he too made his displeasure known: he resented Zoff's last-minute methods of selection; he never knew until the Saturday who would be in the team next day. Gascoigne, of course, always knew.

Throughout February and March, 'Gazza Come Home' stories continued to appear in England. There was a possessiveness in these stories: Look what they're doing to our lad. But there was also a rebuke: Look what our lad has done to them. Blackburn Rovers were said to have offered Lazio four million pounds for Gazza. In Italy such rumours were dismissed and Mel Stein said that we could take his word for it that Gascoigne would see out his five-year contract. On the field, Gazza continued to perform fitfully and was usually substituted after an hour's play. He seemed to see the sense of Lazio's gradualist policy, and to know that his stamina was not yet what it was.

Against Genoa on 28 February, though, his removal from the arena was on the orders of the referee. The oft-predicted red card had finally been shown. But the surprise here was that most Italian observers were surprised. The particular offence was relatively minor—the bad-tempered elbowing of a too-adhesive marker—but even this was thought to be untypical, or 'out of character'. Since his arrival in Italy, Gascoigne had built up a reputation for good-humoured resilience in the face of enemy attack. There had been moments of petulance—he had to date chalked up two bookings—but on the whole he had been a model of restraint: he made a point of shaking hands with opponents who had fouled him, or whom he had fouled, and for smiling matily at referees when they scolded him.

There was an amusing moment in Lazio's home game against Sampdoria. Gazza, irked by a decision, ran to the referee as if to register a protest. The ref reached into his pocket and took out not a yellow card but a much smaller object, which he handed to Gascoigne. It turned out to be chewing-gum. Gazza popped the gift into his mouth and ran off, twinkling. And the referee looked happy too. I was not certain that I approved of this new Gazza, spreader of sunshine: it all seemed too calculated, too self-consciously compliant, and—although of course we thoroughly abhorred foul play and the questioning of referees' decisions—I worried that by blunting the player's Northern belligerence these genial Mediterraneans might also be blunting his resolve. With Gazza, the balance had to be just right.

After Gascoigne got his marching orders against Genoa, he ran around shaking hands with his opponents—including the one he had tangled with (Bartolozzi; he who chopped Gazza down on his Lazio debut). What was our rude boy up to *now*? Was he *apologizing* for his own wrongful dismissal? Or was he secretly taking the piss? Gascoigne's 'outrage turned to a smile,' said the *Gazzetta dello Sport*. 'Boyish, perhaps, but Gascoigne is his own man—no aloof aristocrat but prepared to give himself to his public and make us laugh, or at least smile. What more can we ask in these hard days?'

Gazza's hand-shaking act paid off. He was suspended for one match instead of the anticipated two. And this meant that he was well-rested for Lazio's home game against Milan, on 14 March. For Gascoigne, this meeting had assumed a large significance. The last time he had faced up to the Italian champions, he had been cruelly overshadowed, overawed. His pretensions to world-status had been called into question: Gascoigne looks good against the likes of Turkey but put him in with the big boys and he is instantly dwarfed. This was the whisper back in October, and it hurt. Gazza, we hoped, would be in one of his 'something to prove' moods.

And for Lazio as a team there was more at stake in this encounter than mere points. Four days earlier, Roma had beaten the champions two-nil: in the Cup, admittedly, and there was a second leg to come, but even so. Milan had gone forty games without defeat, and it had been Lazio's despised rivals who had been the first to cut them down. Lazio fans, who might in other circumstances have settled for a respectable defeat, now wanted blood: whatever A.S. Roma could do, Lazio could do better, or—at worst—just as well. And it so happened, anyway, that Lazio might never get a better chance of conquering Milan: the red-and-blacks were fielding a much-weakened team—none of their three Dutchmen would be playing, and their goalkeeper, Rossi, had a patched-up shoulder. Against Roma, as Lazio kept pointing out, Milan had had a seventeen-year-old between the posts.

In the event, Lazio drew with Milan two-two, but it could have been much worse. They had come back from two-nil down and had controlled the play for most of the second half. And Gascoigne it was who pulled the strings. After a tentative first quarter of an hour, he gradually emerged as the game's dominating presence, with Baresi and Co. looking unusually anxious whenever he was on the ball. In the October fixture, the midfield was like a war zone, and Milan were the gung-ho aggressors. At the Olympico, two-one up and intent on salvaging two points, they backed off and relied on their offside trap to nullify the dash of Fuser and Signori. Gascoigne, lying deep, had room from which he could direct the forward play. His through-balls to the front men had to be varied and accurate, and so they were—all the more so as his confidence grew into a mild cockiness. Before long he was making a few forward runs himself. For the record, he scored one goal (a tap-in from two yards) and assisted in two or three glorious near-misses. But this was no triumphalist occasion. It was an almost cerebral affair, a matter more of self-respect, of 'How good am I, really?' than of wishing to prove others wrong. Dino Zoff called it 'Paul's best game, considering the quality of the opposition.'

Gazza did not repeat the triumph in the 1992–93 season. Indeed, the Milan game turned out to be the climax of his year. For myself, I am inclined to wish that the season *had* ended that day. Two weeks later, playing for England against Turkey in Izmir, Gascoigne was marked out of the game and only a smart headed goal in England's two-nil win prevented a re-run of Graham Taylor's San Marino speech. With Lazio, he had little more success.

In the April derby against Roma—a neurotic nil-nil draw—he was peculiarly disengaged, even before a knee injury forced his withdrawal from the game. A *knee* injury! At first it did look bad— Gazza suddenly pulled up in mid-stride and clutched at his scar, the scar that by now I'd half-forgotten. In the end, a muscle-strain was diagnosed, but for the few days leading up to Gazza's next game—England's Wembley World Cup match against Holland— the old anxieties resurfaced. I had occasion to reflect on just how far Gascoigne had travelled since he had first taken the field against Tottenham in Rome. On that night I had winced every time anyone came near him. Now, when some bloodthirsty Turk spent ninety minutes hacking at his legs, I found myself wondering if he still had the power, the verve, to cope with a man-marker.

On the day before the Holland match, Ruud Gullitt—via the *Daily Mirror*—told Gazza that 'You'll *Never* be the Same Again': he, Gullitt, had taken a year-and-a-half to come back from his knee operations and the worst part had been having to accept, when he was fit again, that it was 'not possible to do again what you have done before.' In his prime, before the injuries, he used to make fifty-yard runs to deep positions; nowadays he could manage only twenty. 'But it's important that when you do it those twenty times, they are done well.' Gazza should follow his example: accept his limitations, alter his style of play and settle into a new, mature phase of his career. Gullitt was now thirty-one: Gazza had just turned twenty-six. Was this a pre-match 'psych'?

At Wembley on 28 April, the Gullitt-Gascoigne confrontation turned out to be a flop. Gazza, elbowed in the face by Wouters, was taken off in the first half with a broken cheek-bone, and Ruud was eventually substituted: a tactical move that resulted in Holland's equalizing goal. Gazza, and England, had looked good in the first half, but the loss of a home point meant that their end-of-season away fixtures against Poland and Norway were no longer games that England could afford to lose.

Gascoigne would be needed for those games. On 1 May, he had an operation 'to strengthen a depressed fracture of the cheek-bone.' He would be out of action for perhaps three weeks. England were scheduled to face Poland on 29 May, Norway on 2 June. With luck Gazza would make it, or—in the *Sun*'s words—NORWAY WILL

OP STOP ME The player seemed to welcome the respite: he was at once off to Eurodisney with Sheryl and the kids. And when he reappeared on 16 May, playing for Lazio against Ancona, he wore a funfair look: a yellow carbon fibre mask had been prescribed, as protection for his damaged cheek. Gazza was delighted with this new accessory; in a way, it was what he'd always wanted. 'I told the lads I was the Phantom of the Opera,' he said. 'I don't think they'd ever heard of it. They have now—and so has all of Italy.' In a five-nil win that took Lazio to within two points of qualifying for the UEFA Cup, he was in clownish mood, but deadly. He set up two of the five goals. The first of these, tapped in by Riedle, was the climax of an extraordinary Gazza run. He set off from his own half, ran fifty yards and left four Ancona defenders on the floor, outpaced and looking dizzy. He could have scored himself but, at the last second, he rolled the ball across goal to his German rival: a magnanimous touch for which he later took full credit. 'Beauty in a Mask' was the Italian press response. Two days later, a burglar broke into the Lazio training ground and made off with just one item: Gazza's now-celebrated facewear. The police were not sure that the matter ought to be pursued: it was a crime, they said, 'for love of Gascoigne.'

'I think I'll wear it all the time,' said Gazza, when a replacement was procured, and he took the mask with him to Poland and to Norway. We all know what happened next: a lucky draw against the Poles and in Oslo a defeat that had the press shrieking for Graham Taylor's resignation. These results meant that England would probably not qualify for the World Cup finals in America next summer. The hacks' vacation plans may have to be revised. One paper featured a pile of horse-manure on its back page. Gascoigne, mask and all, had looked weary, out of sorts. After the Poland match, Taylor singled him out for special criticism. The whole team had performed like 'headless chickens', but it was Gascoigne's performance that had annoyed Taylor most of all. It was the San Marino script, but read with more vehemence, more rancour. It was all very well, he said, for Gascoigne to claim that he trained hard in Italy; 'It's a matter of how you feed and refuel

Opposite: Gascoigne with his lawyer and adviser Mel Stein.

yourself between training sessions. This is something Paul has to come to terms with.'

'Refuel'? Did this mean food, or drink, or—dare the word be mentioned—drugs? Taylor would not be drawn, and Gascoigne made light of the whole business. Drugs could be ruled out: had not Gazza recently spoken out against Caniggia, the A.S. Roma player now serving a hefty suspension for cocaine abuse? Well yes, he had, sort of. He'd said: 'It's a shame on sport, but it's his life, he can do what he wants. If he gets caught there are problems. I don't know what cocaine does for you before a game but he has been scoring some good goals lately.' The food we knew about: the Fat Boy pigged out when under stress, and sometimes when not under stress—he liked pizza, pasta, mozzarella cheese, steak, chips and *see*-food ('That's when I eat everything I see'). It had to be the drink. And here Gazza confessed that he did have a problem: *what* should he be drinking, beer or wine? 'The doctor at Lazio told me I should be drinking wine because it would be good for me. When I did, he had one look at me and said, You'd better go back on the beer.' He promised that he would put things right against Norway. And we believed him: he usually came through when it mattered. In that disastrous game, though, he looked even more sluggish than he did against the Poles. And much the same could be said of the whole team. The jubilant Norwegian coach declared: 'They gave up in the last fifteen minutes. I've never seen an England team do that before.'

Gazza went back to Rome, disgraced. From there, he tried to be generous to Taylor: 'I felt sorry for him. We all let him down.' But he was clearly riled that, once again, he had been singled out. 'Don't forget,' he said, 'There's eleven players on the field and I cannot—these people expect me to do it week in, week out, and I cannot.' As usual, he didn't need the press (or, he might have said, the manager) to lecture him: 'I know exactly where I'm going wrong and what I've got to do to put it right.' He had been accused of over-eating, over-drinking—well, sometimes he played *better* when he was 'a little overweight'. This was a new one, but worth pondering: if it was true that Gascoigne spent the day before the Norway match in a sauna, trying to 'get fit', perhaps the whole matter of his podginess ought to be re-thought. He was looking forward, he said tauntingly, to a close-season of 'pizzas and beer'.

Gazza made little or no contribution to Lazio's last game of the season—a four-one thrashing at Juventus—but nobody seemed to mind. Lazio had qualified for the UEFA Cup for the first time in seventeen years. All in all, it was reckoned that 1992–93—and Gazza—had gone well: next year would be the year. Meanwhile England, in close-season 'Americas Cup', were being hammered by the USA. For Gascoigne there was news of other hammerings. Mel Stein, indicted for fraud in a Louisiana court, and now under threat of extradition, had placed himself in psychiatric care. Jane Nottage, Gazza's on-the-spot Rome gofer, had turned traitor: fired by Gascoigne in the wake of some Sheryl-related rumpus, Nottage was selling her *Paul Gascoigne—the Inside Story* to the Sunday press—a story in which Gazza would be portrayed as a bulimic booze-hound, with Sheryl as his devil-woman aide. (When Nottage's memoir appeared in book form in September, there was more in it about money and Nottage's personal grievances than there was about Gascoigne the player, and even the low gossip seemed to have been padded out, but there was one 'revelation' I will particularly treasure. It turns out that Gazza *is a poet*! Or, as Nottage puts it, he now and again savours 'the joys of dabbling in poetry-writing.' Before the Lazio–Roma derby, he penned the following, in Nottage's note-pad:

Blue is the colour
Lazio is the name
I am the other
Football is the game
Now never mind the league
Or the bastard cup
Because when we play the derby
We will fuck them up.)

And at Spurs, Terry Venables—the manager who 'took me from a boy to a good class player'—had mysteriously been sacked. Spurs had an option to buy Gazza back if Lazio should ever wish to sell. With Venables gone, there was 'no way' that Gascoigne would return.

He did return, but briefly, at the beginning of this season, in a competition for something called the Makita Trophy. Two teams from England—Spurs and Chelsea—were up against Ajax of Amsterdam and Lazio, in a four-match knockout. For the Spurs fan, this two-day tournament was an ordeal of divided or stretched loyalties. We didn't know which way to turn. Terry Venables had been banned from White Hart Lane by Alan Sugar, but sitting in his place was Ossie Ardiles, another of our all-time greats. And Glenn Hoddle was now a player-manager for Chelsea. Then there was Gazza, in Lazio's light blue. What we should have wanted was for Tottenham to crush Lazio and for Chelsea to be crushed by Ajax who in turn Tottenham would crush. We should have been yelling for Anderton, Barmby and Sheringham to show the door to these oldies and exiles, these ex-Spurs.

In our hearts, we yearned for something else. At least, we snowy-haired ones did. We yearned to see Hoddle up against Gazza —not up against, but on the same field, just once. We wanted to see them marvelling, gaping at each other's gifts. We wanted them to swap shirts at the end, like Moore and Pele. Or better still, they could throw away those peculiar blue vests they wore and call for new ones—white ones, with a cockerel on the chest. And then the two of them might do a lap of honour, to the strains perhaps of 'Ossie's going to Wembley/His knees have gone all trembly.' Do you remember 1981? And, since it was party-time, perhaps a few others could join in. Ardiles *and* Venables, for sure, with Stevie Perryman in tow. And Steve Archibald, maybe, and Crooks, and Dave Mackay and Jimmy Greaves and Blanchflower, and even the now-dead John White, the one they used to call 'The Ghost'.

The 'nothing-tournament' in fact ended with Chelsea beating us four-nil and with Hoddle masterminding our humiliation. At the end we had to listen to Chelsea fans chorusing Glenn's name—at White Hart Lane. And we also had to listen to Gazza getting booed. He took a dive, the yobbos thought, to win a penalty for Lazio.

But still, it wasn't a *bad* day. Gascoigne scored a brilliant goal, albeit against Spurs. And there was even talk afterwards of Glenn being 'recalled to the England team', with an admiring, fully-fit, sober and sensible, mad and mischievous Paul Gascoigne at his side, and with Venables as manager. Just to get us through the next two games, you understand, the Poland and the Holland, just to put us back where we belong.

Photo: Colorsport

GRANTA

JONATHAN RABAN
MISSISSIPPI WATER

Flying to Minneapolis from the West, you see it as a theological problem.

The great flat farms of Minnesota are laid out in a ruled grid, as empty of surprises as a sheet of graph paper. Every gravelled path, every ditch has been projected along the latitude and longitude lines of the township-and-range-survey system. The farms are square, the fields are square, the houses are square; if you could pluck their roofs off from over people's heads, you'd see families sitting at square tables in the dead centre of square rooms. Nature has been stripped, shaven, drilled, punished and repressed in this right-angled, right-thinking Lutheran country. It makes you ache for the sight of a rebellious curve or the irregular, dappled colour of a field where a careless farmer has allowed corn and soybeans to cohabit.

But there are no careless farmers on this flight path. The landscape is open to your inspection—as to God's—as an enormous advertisement for the awful rectitude of the people. There are no funny goings-on down here, it says; we are plain upright folk, fit candidates for heaven.

Then the river enters the picture—a broad serpentine shadow that sprawls unconformably across the checkerboard. Deviously winding, riddled with black sloughs and green cigar-shaped islands, the Mississippi looks as if it had been put here to teach the god-fearing Midwest a lesson about stubborn and unregenerate nature. Like John Calvin's bad temper, it presents itself as the wild beast in the heart of the heartland.

When people who live on the river attribute a gender to the Mississippi, they do so without whimsy, and nearly always they give it their own sex. 'You better respect the river, or he'll do you in,' growls the lockmaster. 'She's mean—she's had a lot of people from round here,' says the waitress at the lunch counter. When Eliot wrote that the river is within us (as the sea is all about us), he was nailing something true in an everyday way about the Mississippi. People do see its muddy turmoil as a bodying-forth of their own turbulent inner selves. When they boast to strangers about their river's wantonness, its appetite for trouble and destruction, its floods and drownings, there's a note in their voices that says, *I have it in me to do that . . . I know how it feels.*

I went down the Mississippi in a small boat in 1979, and met a woman, born in 1880, who'd grown up in the town of Milliken's Bend, a name I couldn't place. 'Nothing left of the town now,' Miss Lily said. 'The River took it.' She spoke as if it were common knowledge that you had to feed whole towns to the Mississippi every so often to placate it. Within her memory, the river had sluiced many places clean off the map, as it had taken chunks of Illinois and moved them over to Missouri and left busy grain ports high and dry in the cornfields. It had drowned a score of Miss Lily's friends and relations. She began to tick them off on her fingers for me, but lost count. She grinned—new teeth in an old alligator face. 'In a boat, huh? Well just *you* take care,' she said.

When the Mississippi climbed out of its banks last summer, I felt a surge of vicarious pride as it spread like a stain over Iowa and Illinois and tangled with the swollen Missouri river in the suburbs of St Charles and St Louis. The television pictures showed a power of darkness on the loose as the Mississippi rolled a trailer home over, squashed a summer cottage flat against the hull of a moored barge, liberated caskets from a graveyard, filled a restaurant kitchen with a moving tide of sludge, got up streets and inside marriages.

Ignoring the calls of hypocrite television reporters for 'gawkers' to stay home and not get in the way of the troops and the sandbaggers, I flew to Minneapolis, rented a car and followed the river downstream for a thousand miles.

Up in Minnesota the flood was in its infancy, the river only just out of its banks; yet even this far north the Mississippi had grown enormously since I'd last seen it, and it was hard to get my bearings. There should have been sandbars—there were none. All that was left of the islands I remembered were some sprigs of green shivering in the current. There should have been a towboat coming round the bend, pushing a fleet of shovel-fronted barges, but the river was empty of boats of any kind. The sunlit water was a yellowy purple, the colour of a ripe bruise, and it sounded like fire as it crackled through a nearby wood.

Out in the channel, the river wrestled a navigation buoy underwater—a big red can, about five feet in diameter, and no easy pushover. Inch by inch, this barrel full of air sank into the

Mississippi and disappeared for a full minute. Then it splashed back. The struggles of the buoy, as it weaved and shuddered on its chain, gave a fair idea of what this current might do to something altogether less resilient, like a grain elevator, or a house.

The upper Mississippi is supposed to be a staircase of artificial lakes, with only a trickle of current between them. From St Paul, Minnesota, to Alton, Illinois (just upstream of St Louis), there are twenty-six locks-and-dams, built by the US Army Corps of Engineers in the late 1930s and early '40s. In normal times, these enormous military installations, each with a lock chamber big enough to hold a multi-storey apartment block, lord it over the river like castles. Every twenty-five or thirty miles, you see them looming in the distance; blocky and turreted. This river has been conquered, they assert; it's under Army control.

Not any more. At Lock and Dam 7, near La Crosse, Wisconsin, the great roller-gates of the dam had been cranked up, to hang clear of the water, and the Mississippi was pouring through unhindered. 'It's just cruising right on by,' the lockmaster said. 'It's what we call open river right now. The gates are as high as they can go. It's been like that since March.'

Below where the dam should have been, the river seethed, a noisy shambles of steep pyramidical waves and quaking scud. One had to shout to make oneself heard over its hiss and rumble.

'How fast is the river moving?'

'Normally this time of year you'd expect anything between twenty thousand and thirty thousand cubic feet a second. Latest figure we have, it's coming through here at about a hundred and thirty thousand, nine hundred cubic feet a second.'

About? I looked at the drifting chaos of the Mississippi and tried to make it fit that nigglingly precise figure: it wouldn't go.

The flood was breeding its own obsessive numerology. The more nature got out of control, the more people measured it. Across the enormous drainage area of the Mississippi and Missouri rivers, people were stationed with rain gauges, rulers, hygrometers, knotmeters, probes. In the cities of St Paul, Rock Island and St Louis, people fed the data into computers. Each day at noon, the Corps of Engineers faxed out a new sheet of numbers. The sheet would tell you—among many other things—that the Mississippi was due to crest at Hannibal, Missouri on Thursday at one-thirty p.m., at a height of 31.4 feet.

Each day, these sheets were posted up in city halls and riverside bars. They were treated exactly as opinion polls are treated in a neck-and-neck political campaign. Spin-doctors interpreted them. Strategies were changed by them. 'Thirty-one point-four!' people said, and the number alone would excite fear or relief.

At noon next day, the number would be revised, by a foot or more—and it wouldn't be Thursday, it would be Saturday or Tuesday. Yet still people clung to it. 'Twenty-nine point-six!' they said, as if the prediction was itself a victory worth celebrating.

I asked the lockmaster how much warning he'd been given. Had he known about the flood for ages before it arrived?

'They didn't forecast it until it happened,' he said.

In March the river was high with normal spring run-off after the melting of the northern snows. One by one, the dams were raised—as usual—to give the Mississippi a free run to the Gulf of Mexico. Then the rain began.

'It just kept on coming and coming. It was unreal. In April, they were saying it would be all over by May. In May, things were getting real tight, but they said we'd be dry by June. And all through June, it rained and rained. And rained.'

As we spoke, five inches of rain had just been forecast for Nebraska; four or more in South Dakota; it was due to rain tomorrow in Minnesota, Wisconsin, Iowa, Illinois and Missouri. A *disaster* is a disorder in the heavens: *dis* + *astrum*, an unfavourable aspect of the stars or planets. Few 'disasters' are really *disasters*, but this one was—in 1993, the heavens were all to hell.

The road south crossed a dozen swollen creeks, and with the addition of each creek to the main stream, the infant flood grew stronger. It was on the boil now, moving in big greasy rolls and swirls. As the flood rose, the towns got emptier. 'It's not this bad in *January*,' said the waitress in Lansing, Iowa. There were no cars, no tourists, no fishermen, no houseboaters. Shops were closed; roads were closed; and in the café where I remembered a merry breakfast crowd on my last visit, four Iowa ancients in plastic baseball caps sat silently in line, staring out at the Mississippi. The river unscrolled like a movie: in the middle distance, an uprooted tree sailed slowly past from left to right. It was followed by an oil-drum, a tractor-trailer wheel, another tree. The ancients watched closely, awaiting the next twist in the plot—a vagrant skiff, an outhouse, an interesting box. For half an hour, I watched them watch the river. Something over 235,620,000 cubic feet of Mississippi water slid past the window, bearing nothing worth the bother of salvaging it.

I spent the night at a motel in Prairie Du Chien, on the Wisconsin side, and had just fallen asleep when I was woken by thunder—a series of grumbling explosions directly overhead that made the second-floor room shake and waver in its flimsy timber frame. I found the switch on the bedside lamp, but the lamp was dead. The sound of thunder gave way to that of rain on the parking lot outside, like gravel pouring from a long chute. I groped my way to the window, from where I watched bursts of sheet lightning flicker over the roofs of the darkened town. My watch said that it was eight-fifty.

Soaked to the skin by a ten-yard dash to the car, I drove round to the candlelit motel office. The woman at the desk took my key and checked her ledger by flashlight to make sure that I'd paid. 'Come back and see us sometime,' she said, indifferently. 'Have a nice day.' No mention of the storm, the lightning, the power outage, the candles at mid-morning. This was evidently how summer days usually began in the year of the Deluge.

The roads were awash. A truck cruised slowly down US 18 like a clipper ship with a bone in its teeth. On the car radio, a tiresomely upbeat, top-of-the-morning announcer was enjoying himself, reading out flash-flood warnings for Crawford, Grant, Clayton and Allamakee counties. 'Seek higher ground,' he said, as I crossed the river back into Iowa and struck out south on a low-lying minor road that kept close company with the Mississippi. Having told everyone to run for the mountains, he then told them to head for the Free Sweet Corn Boil at Johnson market. 'Go on!' he urged, 'brave the rain! Take the kids! It's going to be a whole lot of fun!' If we were thinking of spending the day in Illinois, he said, we must be sure to dial a 1-800 number: 'They'll tell you if your favourite tourist destination is underwater.'

By ten a.m. the rain was thinning, and the sky took on the appearance of a wintry dawn. The Mississippi was like an enormous sheet of dirty gauze, spread flat across the landscape. It was now impossible to guess where its banks might have been, and hard to tell where the river left off and the unflooded land began. Fields of short corn ('knee-high by the fourth of July') brimmed like ponds, and as the Mississippi rose to meet them, there was a kind of fluid commingling between this river full of earth and this earth full of water.

I stopped for breakfast at a grocery store on a low hill, a mile or two inland, and was shocked by the heat of the day as I stepped out of the car. It looked like November, but the temperature was over ninety degrees, and the rain on my scalp was warm as sweat. The same four ancients, first seen in Lansing, or their four cousins, were seated at the breakfast counter.

From them I learned—slowly and with some difficulty—that:

The floods were caused by paving. *Paving?* Parking lots. Malls. Condo blocks. Community colleges. People from the cities were covering the land with concrete and there was nowhere for the rain to go.

The water-table was rising. It was now so close to the surface that crops were rotting from the roots up.

Things were going to get worse. Much worse.

'You think it's bad now, you better come back next year. Then you'll see floods. I'm telling you. What we got now—that's nothing to what's coming. You wait till the year two thousand. Where they've got cities now, there'll be just swamps then. Levees won't hold the river in, not with the water-table where it's at—no way.' He looked as if he was going to make damned certain that he stayed alive until the year 2000, if only for the sour pleasure of seeing his prophecy come true.

When I went back to the car, the rain had turned to steam. Visibility was down to less than half a mile. The river smoked, the bluffs were shrouded in hot fog. The road ran along the edge of the flood, which had recently dropped a little, exposing a margin, ten or twelve feet wide, of shiny black goo—a compound of

Map: Line & Line

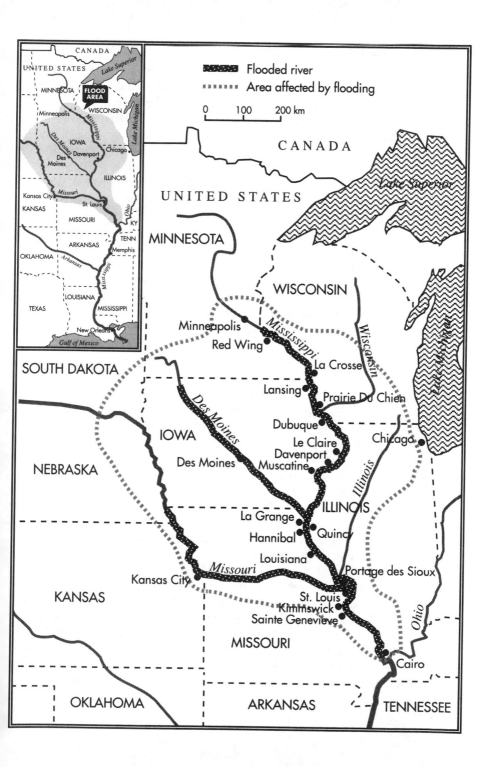

Flooded river
Area affected by flooding

0   100   200 km

CANADA

UNITED STATES

MINNESOTA

WISCONSIN

Minneapolis

Red Wing

Mississippi

La Crosse

Lansing

Prairie Du Chien

Des Moines

Dubuque

SOUTH DAKOTA

IOWA

Le Claire

Davenport

Muscatine

Chicago

Des Moines

Wisconsin

NEBRASKA

Illinois

ILLINOIS

La Grange

Hannibal

Quincy

Louisiana

KANSAS

Missouri

Kansas City

Portage des Sioux

St. Louis

Kimmswick

Sainte Genevieve

Ohio

MISSOURI

OKLAHOMA

ARKANSAS

TENNESSEE

Cairo

Inset map:

CANADA

UNITED STATES

Lake Superior

MINNESOTA

FLOOD AREA

WISCONSIN

Lake Michigan

Minneapolis

Mississippi

Des Moines

IOWA

Davenport

Chicago

Des Moines

ILLINOIS

Missouri

Kansas City

KANSAS

St. Louis

MISSOURI

Ohio

KY

ARKANSAS

TENN

Memphis

OKLAHOMA

Arkansas

Mississippi

LOUISIANA

TEXAS

MISSISSIPPI

New Orleans

Gulf of Mexico

rotting grass and corn-stalks, drain-water, fertilizers, oil and dead fish. The smell was of the sort that glows in the dark.

The mayflies were doing well in it. A huge hatch was in progress, and the big clumsy flies pasted themselves against my windscreen, hundreds at a time. The wipers made a crunching sound and were caked solid with bits of wing and thorax. The stink, the insects, the bubbly, sewagey look of the uncovered ground, were the result of a drop of just a few inches in the level of the river. When the Mississippi really went down, it would leave a margin of fetid slime, miles wide on either side.

In 1979, an Iowa farmer, Harvey Schwartz, showed me the precious soil of his bottomlands farm between Davenport and Muscatine. He powdered it between his forefinger and thumb, and made me do the same. It was soft, brown, moist and pungent—almost as rich in nutrients as dung itself.

'Taste it,' said Harvey Schwartz.

I parked a few grains on the tip of my tongue.

'That's some of the richest soil in the whole world,' he said, as if the grains were caviare.

Now the river was only doing what rivers are supposed to do with their flood-plains: enrich the soil with the long, slow work of regular flood, siltation and decomposition, coating the fields with smelly glop. At present, all the talk was of how the Mississippi had 'devastated' the land around it. Actually it was nourishing it, though with scant respect for the barns sunk to their eaves, or the farmers' homes where the river was now in possession of the bedrooms on the second floor. When Governor Branstad of Iowa spoke on the radio of the tragedy that had befallen his state, with eight million acres of land under water, he might have added that most of this land was being improved by the experience. When the flood finally went down, there would be a foot or more of fresh topsoil on the 'bottoms'—a fine-sifted mulch in which the wheat would stand as thickly as the bristles on a brush.

At Le Claire, I spotted a fisherman sitting in the picnic gazebo in the centre of a children's playground. I waded across to talk to him on his island. He'd brought sandwiches, Gatorade and a transistor radio to while the day away. He watched his rod tip. His bait, a plump nite-crawler, had been cast far out; it lay between the slide and the swings.

'Ain't nothing doing,' he said. 'I don't know why. I think it's because the fish don't like the river going down. Beginning of the week, when it was coming up, the fishing was real good—right over the road there . . . ' He pointed to where I'd parked the car.

'Catfish?'

'*Big* catfish. And perch. And croppies. It was good fishing.' He reeled in. His worm hung in a limp *U* from the hook. It looked stressed-out by the heat and the humidity. He took a fresh one from the can, threaded it past the barb, and flicked it out towards the jungle-gym.

His radio, on the picnic table, was full of advice and instructions. Volunteer sandbaggers were being issued with assembly points. They were told to bring plenty of mosquito-repellent and to swab down thoroughly afterwards. 'Remember,' the announcer said, 'this is tough, hot, smelly work.' For about seven seconds, I toyed with the idea of becoming a volunteer sandbagger in Des Moines—a two-and-a-half-hour drive to the west—but the only thing that I could seriously imagine doing out in the open air was steaming asparagus in it.

As the Mississippi spilled untidily southwards, it added more and more new rivers to the flow. There were the Wisconsin river, the Rock river, the Iowa river, the Des Moines river and—before the Mississippi reached St Louis—it was also joined by the Illinois river and the Missouri river. There were Indian rivers: the Maquoketa, the Wapsipinicon, the Kickapoo. There were animal rivers: the Turkey, the Fox, the Bear, the Skunk, the Buffalo. There were the Apple and Plum, the Cedar and Root, and smaller rivers, by the dozen and the score, piling into the Mississippi—and all the rivers were in flood.

According to the Corps of Engineers and their current meters, the Mississippi was moving at a speed and volume of 130,900 cubic feet per second at La Crosse; 400,000 cubic feet per second at Rock Island; 1,000,000 cubic feet per second at St Louis. Over the same stretch of river, the current was quickening from about three knots to about ten knots.

These figures make it sound as if the Mississippi was travelling

137

downstream with the concentrated energy of a locomotive on a track, when its actual motion was more like that of the suds in a washing-machine. It spun and tumbled, gyre on whirling gyre, water rubbing against water. The friction generated strings of whirlpools, some big enough to trouble, if not quite swallow, a boat.

Wherever one looked, the water was moving in coils and wreaths, like smoke. The dead mayflies on its surface were drifting every which way on the turbulence. They raced, dawdled, described long lazy *S*s, revolved in dizzy pirouettes. I focused on a single fly, one veined wing standing proud of the water like a windsurfer's sail. It would . . . but it didn't. It feinted, sashayed, zig-zagged, confounding my predictions over every inch of the course.

From Davenport on down, the cities began to take to the waters in earnest. Muscatine and Port Madison were in the river up to their middles. Their downtown shopping streets had become canals. Parking meters had turned into convenient mooring-posts for the aluminium skiffs that served as gondolas in these new Venetian times. The boats moved silently. There was a ban on the use of outboards, whose wake might have toppled the sandbag walls, so people rowed and punted, as if they were doing it for the scenery and the exercise on this broiling Saturday afternoon. It's said that a change is as good as a rest, and most of the flood victims were in a larky holiday mood.

'Start your own business! Be your own boss! Fax machines! Answerphones . . .' sang out one jolly ferryman over the water, as he paddled a cargo of office equipment to higher ground.

The bottom end of each town petered out into a semiotic playground of signifiers, divorced from their referents, sticking out of the flood. TURN RIGHT FOR US 61. STOP. RAILROAD CROSSING. BUSINESS LOOP. NO PARKING. NO LEFT TURN. STRAIGHT AHEAD FOR THE MUSEUM. ONE WAY. YIELD. EXIT ONLY. Some of the signs had been knocked sideways by the Mississippi and leaned at forty-five-degree angles to the water. Some were completely submerged. The river ran placidly through the slough of antediluvian messages, the current making braids around every post.

All the shutterbugs in town were out with cameras, and the jumble of signs was everybody's favourite subject. Pictures of the signs would become one of the two or three key images of the

Great Flood. They're happy pictures. They show the river making monkeys of City Hall, the Highway Department and the rest. They show authority wittily subverted by the water, which has robbed every imperious command of its meaning. They catch something important, about which little was said at the time: the glee that people felt as the river came up and played this gigantic practical joke on their world.

In Port Madison at dusk, with the mosquitoes beginning to sound like a string band, I was loitering at the edge of a flooded street, watching a line of sandbaggers build a wall around a threatened gas station. An elderly woman with a camera stood nearby, her Oxford shoes islanded. She was waving the bugs away with a handkerchief, and smiling, hugely. When she saw me see her smile, she felt called on to explain it. 'Well,' she said, 'everybody's got to look at the water, haven't they?'

On Sunday morning, I crossed the Iowa–Misssouri state line. Now things looked like a war. Each tributary river ran higher and faster than the last. Big creosoted barns were pasted flat against trees, like stoved-in cardboard boxes. Lines of oddly foreshortened telephone poles led out to isolated farms that were sunk to their roof beams. From a distance, they looked like bivouacs, pitched on the water. Things were so bad in towns like La Grange that even the National Bank was in the river. US 61, the main highway to the west of the Mississippi, led down a hill and ran slap into the flood. At every turn, soldiers, in battle fatigues and camouflaged armoured cars, manned roadblocks and talked importantly into antique two-way radios. With the sodden fields, the National Guardsmen and the pensioned-off military equipment, it looked as if one had stumbled into the making of a movie set in Vietnam, *circa* 1968.

The National Guard was there to deter looters and turn sightseers away. But the sightseers were locals—farm families, still dressed for church; shrunken grandpa-figures in straw hats and oversize pick-ups—and the soldiers shrugged and let them through. Me, too. At one checkpoint, I pulled up and prepared to spin a story, but the sergeant in charge said only, 'We're going to have to start charging for tickets of admission soon.'

The families formed a slow promenade in the heat, leaving

139

their cars to walk out to the end of a gravelled road that was now a pier. The sheet of water ahead, dotted here and there with roofs and treetops, stretched to the horizon, an inland sea. People said very little. There was some nervous joking among the adults, some rough-house capers from the kids, but the prevailing atmosphere was that of the church that most of them had just left. We squinted at the flood in silence.

Water not only finds its own level; it makes itself perfectly at home. The winding contour-line of the edge of the flood had the natural authority of any coast. It looked so *right*. It was not the water that was in the wrong place, but the strange, angular things that poked impertinently out of it. Wherever the water impinged on the man-made—on a road or a city parking-lot—it resulted in a sweet curve across a surface that one would previously have thought of as flat. The flood redefined the land, and the dangerous thought came, unbidden, that the work of the flood was a beauty and a wonder.

Driving south through Missouri, as close to the water as I could manage, I had to brake several times for lumbering racoons. There were many dead, but all the bodies lay on the right hand side of the road. They looked like cuddly toys from an infant's crib—dead opossums, racoons, coyotes, chipmunks, fawns. They had all fled west to get out of the way of the rising river; racing to escape nature, they'd been felled by technology.

But on the whole, nature was doing well out of the flood. The fish were thriving, and the birds that ate the fish, like herons and ducks, were everywhere. People said they couldn't remember a time when so many birds were in residence on the river. The mosquitoes were in heaven, and the lower orders—viruses like *e coli* and tetanus—were enjoying a rare taste of freedom from the constraints of civilization, breeding by the billions in the stagnant swampy water on the fringes of the flood. For the wandering tribes of freshwater plankton on whom the whole ecosystem of the Mississippi depended, life had never been better than in the summer of '93.

The flood was making many humans happy too. Door-to-door insurance salesmen were working round the clock, selling dubious policies to frightened home-owners in low-lying areas. On the

Chicago stock market, commodity traders were making a killing on wheat and soybean futures. In St Louis, panhandlers were putting on their best clothes and representing themselves as charities collecting for flood-victims.

It was a wonderful time for prophets.

On the car radio, Randall Terry of Operation Rescue, the anti-abortion outfit, was being interviewed by Terry Gross of NPR's 'Fresh Air'. The floods in the Midwest were, he said, 'The first Call. The first Blast of the Trumpet.' There was a triumphant I-told-you-so squeak in his voice, and his tone was that of the mad lounge-bar logician who can prove that the moon-landings never took place and that Richard Nixon was a communist spy. We had, according to Randall Terry, seen nothing yet. 'God has a *hundred* hurricanes, a *hundred* droughts, a *hundred* floods . . . ' And in His wrath over abortion, He would bowl them at America one by one.

Terry Gross pointed out that God's choice of the Midwest as the locus of His vengeance seemed a little unfair: had He not picked on the most god-fearing region in the whole United States? Why was He so punishing His own home team?

'When God judges a nation, innocent people suffer,' said Randall Terry, with frank relish. 'Innocent people suffer—for the sins of the child-killers, and for the sins of the homosexuals . . . '

A few days later, CNN financed a poll which found that one in five Americans—the same percentage as had voted for Ross Perot in the Presidential election—believed that the floods were God's judgement on the sins of the people of the US.

At Louisiana, Missouri, that Sunday evening, a Free Supper for Flood Victims was advertised on the noticeboard of the Masonic Temple. The feast was being scoffed by six perspiring National Guardsmen, each attended by a Mason's wife, looming with another dish.

I was barely inside the door before I was fending off an avalanche of ribs and wings. I explained that I hadn't come to eat, but that I would like to meet a flood victim, if any of the flood victims would care to talk to a stranger.

'There aren't too many flood victims here right now, but you *must* try these cookies.'

Photo overleaf: Philip Mosier

141

'Are you a vegetarian? We could make you up a special plate—'

I could see why the Masons themselves were all men of impressive substance, whose most noticeable clothing-items were their belts and suspenders. One man wore a particularly fine belt of strange devices proclaiming him to be a member of the Ancient Arabic Order of Nobles of the Mystic Shrine.

'You have to be in the photograph—' he said, and I was hustled into the group of waiting brethren. The picture was for a forthcoming issue of a Masonic magazine. In it, the Shriner and I have our arms around each other's shoulders; I am grinning weakly and billed, I fear, as a visiting Knight Templar from London, England. The reason for the picture is that we have all been helping flood victims.

When the photography was done, I asked the Shriner about the flood victims.

'Those people,' he said. 'Most of 'em, they just don't want to be helped.'

How many people had been washed out by the flood here?

'Oh, not too many. Down in the flats . . . must be about thirty families, maybe?'

How were they coping?

'Oh, those people, they cope pretty good. They're used to it. They're the same people got flooded out in '73. They just move right back in: hang out the carpets to dry, hose down the furniture, and they're back in there, happy as clams.'

'Are these people—black?'

'Oh, no; some of 'em are—it's pretty much of an even mixture, down there in the flats. Between you, me and the gatepost, most blacks in this town have got more sense than to live there. The smart ones all live up on the bluff, as far away from the river as they can get. And good luck to 'em!'

The Masons' wives began, reluctantly, to shroud the bowls of food with Seranwrap, while the Masons folded up the tables, and the guardsmen returned to their roadblock on the flats.

I went for a stroll in the dusk. The cabins of the flats-people were deep in the river. The current spiralled through bedroom windows that had been smashed by floating railroad ties. At the corner of Alabama and 6th, a catfish was rootling down the centre of the street, its progress marked by the bursts of small bubbles that it sent up at steady intervals. Further down, where someone's yard shelved steeply into the river, I spotted what appeared to be a large pale halibut. It turned out—disappointingly—to be a submerged satellite dish.

The flats were on a back-eddy of the Mississippi, a natural assembly-point for drifting junk, and wherever the river touched dry land, it returned a broad selection of objects to the civilization from which they had been thrown away. On the little beach at the end of one quite narrow street, I counted more than twenty car tyres, a propane cylinder, a torn-out car headlight, a fishing float, a fifty-gallon oil drum, a glove, several super-economy sized detergent bottles, numerous soft-drink cans, some lightbulbs, a clutch of aerosols, a toddler's yellow plastic tricycle, badly mauled and encrusted in gobs of tar, some broken honeycombs of polystyrene packing, and enough baulks of lumber with which to build at least one new cabin on the flats.

In the Downtown Lounge, a spry black man in his seventies was half-telling, half-miming, a flood story to an audience of two younger white men.

'And Duval—you know Duval—has that purple house down there? Duval's up on the levee, takin' pictures . . . ' The storyteller was being Duval; prancing on tiptoe, his right hand curled into the shape of a viewfinder, while his left hand cranked on the imaginary handle of an old-fashioned movie camera. His head jerked to one side; he'd been interrupted in his filming. '"Oh, I ain't baggin'," says Duval, "I'm too busy takin' pictures of the water—". They're piling up the sandbags, fast as they can go, but Duval's *busy*. He's walking round his house, round and round, taking *pictures*. "I ain't baggin',"'—the storyteller was wheezing with laughter. '"I ain't baggin'."' He stopped to sip his beer. 'And the river, he's *rising*, right around Duval's purple house. The river's through the door. Duval, he didn't get *nothing* out of there; he's taking pictures on the levee. And when it's too late, and the water's come right up, you shoulda heard him! "My TV! My couch! My rug! My clothes!" That Duval!'

145

He returned to his stool and hoisted himself up on it, shoulders shaking.

' "I ain't baggin'!" '

I asked the storyteller if his own house was safe. Did he live down by the river?

'Where's my house? Oh, my house is fine. I live *way* up the hill.'

At St Charles—in normal times—the Missouri river briefly runs parallel to the Mississippi, tucking behind a wide and leisurely bend of it. For more than twenty-five miles, the two rivers swing in consort, first north, then east, then south, before they tangle violently with one another, twelve miles before St Louis. But now they did not run parallel; their separate floods had met and washed across a flatland of industrial estates, trailer parks, farms and townships—a hazy shimmer of water, the same colour and texture as the sky.

I had wanted to reach Portage des Sioux, once on the Mississippi, now ten miles out across the lake, but still, just, connected to the mainland by a road that was only a few inches under water. I was turned back at the first roadblock: only residents and emergency workers were allowed to tackle this amphibious route, where jumbo pick-ups crawled like a line of ants traversing a mirror.

People here looked mugged.

In the small towns where I'd been stopping, people knew each other, knew the Mississippi, and had found in the flood a cause of anarchic Blitz humour. It was different in the Greater St Louis suburbs, where the river is normally little more than a glint of brown water with a towboat on it, seen out of the corner of one's eye from a car on the expressway. Tourists, doing the Gateway Arch thing, saw more of the Mississippi than most native St Louisans, for whom the river lay on the far edge of the known world, a convenient barrier between St Louis proper and the desperate no-go area of East St Louis over in Illinois. You could live in St Louis without giving the river a second thought from one year's end to the next; you might not even be aware that you had a river on your doorstep at all.

So when the Missouri, the Mississippi and the little Des Peres ganged up and moved into the suburbs, their arrival was a horrible surprise to people who had no memory or mythology to help them cope with the flood. The little one was the nastiest of the three. The Des Peres had backed up from its junction with the Mississippi, burst through its earthen levees and made itself at home in the middle of residential South St Louis. Headline writers renamed it the Despair.

I passed over the Des Peres on a freeway bridge. The river was being escorted through evacuated streets on a leaky aqueduct of sandbags and plastic sheeting; the area was surrounded by troops. Meanwhile, policemen were unrolling a floppy orange screen along the side of the freeway bridge to deter motorists from slowing for the view. The sight of a nice, quiet neighbourhood spectacularly ruined by the flood was bringing rush-hour traffic to a standstill.

The region around St Louis was suffering from another inundation, of journalists. The world's television crews had set up command-positions in all the best hotels, and were fanning out across the countryside in search of stories. At Kimmswick, on the Mississippi, I reached the roadblock in time to catch the tail end of an altercation between *Time* magazine, the Houston *Post* and a captain of the National Guard. No one, said the captain, was to be allowed through: orders of the mayor.

'What about *Good Morning America*?' said *Time*. 'You let *Good Morning America* through.'

The captain allowed that an exception had been made for *Good Morning America*.

'It's typical,' said the Houston *Post*, 'this is what we're finding everywhere—discrimination against the print media. The breakfast shows are reporting from the levee, while national newspapers have to put up with "briefings" in the City Hall—and here we can't even get to City Hall.'

'It's not me,' said the captain. 'I'm here to carry out the instructions of the mayor. And that's what she says. No journalists beyond this point.'

'I want to speak to the mayor,' said *Time*.

The captain spoke into his radio. The message from downtown was that the mayor was out of her office and would not be back until the evening.

'But we have to file our stories by six,' said the *Post*, 'in the print media.'

'And they know that,' *Time* said, 'that's why she's out of her office. Can we reach her at home?'

The best that the captain could do, he said, was to report that the newspapermen had filed an urgent request for access. He spoke into his radio again. 'I've got *Time* magazine and the Houston *Post* and—' he turned to me: 'who are you with?'

'Oh, I'm not exactly . . . *Granta*,' I said.

For a moment, the captain looked at me with a flicker of significant interest.

'That's *Time*, Houston *Post* and Greta,' he said.

Sainte Genevieve, Missouri, was lapped in a cloud of hot grey dust. This dust was everywhere: it turned the grass grey and greyed the faces of the people on the streets. In the town centre, the high school yard had become a sandbag factory, where dozens of small squads of volunteers were shovelling dust among the mounds. Dotted about the yard were more small squads, of cameramen and reporters, filming the sandbag brigade.

The dust was from the local lime-producing plants, whose trucks rolled through town on their way to the levees. The noise of their passage blended nicely with the sound of an enormous orchestra of two-stroke pumps. From end to end, Sainte Genevieve rumbled, coughed and snuffled in the dusty air, while the river drifted past, just overhead.

The Mississippi had already taken a large slice of the town, but a winding line of inner levees had so far stopped it from swamping the antique heart of the place—a pretty grid, five streets by five, of freshly-painted antebellum houses, gift shops, restaurants and hotels. The river was on the rise. The water was now within a very few inches of the top of the sandbag-parapet, and it was coming up from below, puddling the streets and making ominous dark stains on the dry ground.

That day, Sainte Genevieve was where the story was. CNN were in town, with ITN and Swedish television hard on their heels, followed by a brilliant rabble of scribes and photographers, conspicuous in their Florida beach-vacation wear. Along the balcony of one old hotel had been strung a banner—STE. GENEVIEVE—DOING IT AGAIN BEATING OLE MAN RIVER—and the TV reporters were taking turns being filmed in front of it as they delivered their to-camera pieces about historic-town's-heroic-cliff-hanger-battle-with-mighty-Mississippi. Up on the levee, cameras slowly panned from the rooftop-islands in the river to the sweating sandbaggers. *They fight a foot at a time. They fight a day at a time. They fight with grit and determination . . .* And you could almost see the levee bulge and quake as the river threatened to sweep away this precious, candy-coloured piece of early Americana in a tide of foaming slurry.

It was a good image, and a valuable one. Sainte Genevieve had always wanted a 'federal levee'—a top-of-the-range model, built by the Corps of Engineers, with a solid clay core encased in layers of earth and rock. When the river eventually went down, there would be a tremendous contest between the flooded towns for federal money. In Sainte Genevieve, whose experience in the tourist industry had equipped it with more worldly cynicism than most towns of its size, it was thought that the money would flow naturally to those places that had been most prominently pictured on the evening news and on the breakfast shows.

Trying to catch the attention of senators and congressmen, Sainte Genevieve went fishing for journalists. Its little city hall was like the headquarters of a political campaign; in fact it was the headquarters of a political campaign. Under the slogan WE CAN DO IT the walls were decorated with factoids, written out in a big, round hand: '40,000 Sandbags Are Needed Every Day'; 'Number Of Sandbags Used So Far—800,000'; 'Ste. G. Annual Budget, $1.4m—Estimated Flood Expenses, $15.3m And Rising.' Every journalist was supplied with a map and a fact sheet, which proved, beyond any journalist's reasonable doubt, that floods in Ste Genevieve, Mo. were usually caused and always exacerbated by the construction, in the 1940s, of federal levees on the Illinois side of the river.

The city had appointed a Media Coordinator—Jean Rissover, a local woman who had once been editor of the Ste Genevieve *Herald* and now ran her own PR firm—and it was hard to figure out quite how Ste Genevieve had managed to contain Ms Rissover before the flood. She had the metropolitan knack of being able to maintain efficiently three conversations at once; she knew how to hobnob with purpose; she smoked; and she nourished the story of Ste Genevieve, as it was told on the networks and in the national press, adding just enough to it each day to keep it alive for many days on end. If there was a weak spot on a farm levee, or a dip in production at the sandbag factory, the fact—and the name Ste Genevieve—would appear on the ten o'clock news and in next morning's *New York Times*. Given the geographical extent of the floods and the intense competition for time on television and space in papers, it was extraordinary how Ste Genevieve managed to keep itself in the public eye. That was Ms Rissover's work.

Under her direction, the National Guard took the journalists off on helicopter rides, and the Coast Guard ferried them around in boats. She kept a team of local historians at the ready, to brief the journalists on the unique nature of the national treasure that was threatened by the flood. For Swedish television, she found a Swedish-speaking local historian.

Ms Rissover thumb-tacked newspaper stories datelined *Ste. Genevieve, Mo.* to the wall around her desk. They hung there in fat bunches of wilting newsprint, and the wall was fast growing too small for them. Some day soon, the City Administrator would cash them, for a correspondingly thick pile of tax-dollars and a new federal levee.

For *Granta*, Ms Rissover (who took the democratic line that a medium was a medium was a medium) laid on a boat trip. In the company of a photographer from FEMA, the Federal Emergency Management Agency, and another from the A.P. wire service, I got afloat on the flood, in an aluminium dory piloted by two Coast Guard reservists.

The current was running fast, even though we were two miles from where the map said the Mississippi was. Though there was no wind, the treetops shook as if in the grip of a gale, and a street lamp oscillated wildly on its stalk.

'Dancing light-pole,' said Petty Officer Mobley.

The boat gained slowly on the current, the fifty horse-power motor on tickover. If Mobley made a wake, he risked knocking sandbags off the levee. He was also navigating without a chart and without local knowledge, for the Coast Guard detachment assigned to Sainte Genevieve came from Louisville, Kentucky, and neither Mobley nor his crew, Able Seaman Felicia Berba, who sat up front with a five-foot boat-hook, had ever visited Sainte Genevieve before the flood. So we moved gingerly, in doubtful water, over foul ground, with the A.B. sounding for chimney-pots, parking-meters, heating vents, rock gardens, sheds, power-lines, trailers. Though there were plenty of roofs and utility poles in view, it was surprisingly hard to make out the safe, deep channel of a street.

The current, spooling through the shallows of an orchard, made the boat slew.

'Lot of eddies here,' FEMA said.

'By the time you get the current figured out—forget it,' said Mobley, weaving the dory between a gable-end and a submarine garage. 'Snake . . . ' he called out. 'Snake in the water.' It moved like a spring, in quick spasms. A.B. Berba, sitting next to me, screwed up her face in pantomime disgust.

'What sort of snake is that?' I said. 'It's not a water-moccasin—'

'They got more snakes in this river than I ever heard of,' said Berba, 'and any kind of snake's a bad snake to me.'

'Snake . . . ' said Mobley. 'Snake in the tree.' It was dangling from a branch, apparently trying to make up its mind as to whether to take the plunge. It plopped neatly into the water as we went past, ten feet clear.

After a few minutes of this, Mobley stopped alerting us to snakes; it was like shouting 'Fly!' on a warm evening in a barnyard. There were a lot of snakes. The mammals, ousted from their homes on the islands and wooded river banks, had fled inland, but the snakes were happy with any dry lodging they could find—a window-sill or chimney did nicely; an upstairs deck was snake heaven. So the flooded half of town had filled with copperheads, cottonmouths, rattlers. There were snakes sunning themselves on roofs, snakes on couches, in drawers and closets, in beds. The snakes—so sinuous and riverine in shape—were natural emblems of the Mississippi itself, and nothing so well represented people's sense

151

of being violated by the river as the image of the cottonmouth in the child's crib. When people talked about going back to their houses after the flood, it was the snakes they mentioned first, and with good reason. The snakes were real, deadly and in residence.

Pacing the current, Mobley opened the throttle and immediately the boat ran into something soft and substantial. It reared, slid sideways over the obstruction, and nearly tipped Associated Press into the snake-infested river.

'I never hit that before,' Mobley said.

Berba, leaning over the bow, prodded about with the boat-hook, but it went cleanly down into deep water.

'It wasn't hard enough for a shed,' Berba said.

'It felt something like a dead cow,' I said.

'The things people have in their yards.'

The levee, seen from the perspective of the river, was only a shallow rim, no more than six inches high in places, of grey sandbags and torn plastic sheeting. We coasted to its edge and looked over at the flimsy streets below—at the pumps, the limestone piles, the dark wet patches on the ground. It was as if someone had tried to patch Holland together overnight.

We ducked to clear the telephone lines and nosed out into open water, skinning a couple of shingles from a roof. As we headed for the main channel, Mobley ran the motor on full thrust, and the dory began to kick up a steep and curling wake. It slammed and bounced on the water as it climbed on to the plane, but the fringe of trees alongside barely moved. The engine roared, the wake streamed in a white V behind us, the boat pounded, but the land remained obstinately still.

We skidded from boil to boil as the Mississippi poured southwards under our feet. The surface of the river was a lacework of rips and swirls: oily mushroom-heads, a hundred feet or so across, bloomed and spun; little whirlpools raced away on private zig-zag tracks; everywhere the water was dividing, folding in on itself, spilling, breaking, spitting and sucking.

It was only when the down-draft from its rotor blades began to disrupt the patterns of the current that I saw the National Guard helicopter overhead. Associated Press was photographing it. I could see the picture he was taking, and it was a good one:

the coastguard afloat, alone, on the raging flood; and, over his left shoulder, a military chopper on a rescue mission.

'Oh—' said A.P., and put his camera down. 'It's full of journalists.'

At the same time, the 'copter, having spotted the same problem, wheeled away into the sky.

'People taking pictures of people taking pictures,' said P.O. Mobley.

I was on the levee, making a sketch of how the river moved as it tried to flow through the middle of someone's house, when a small, raw-boned man in sun-glasses approached me. 'Got all your notes?' he said, and put out his hand. His handshake was of the kind that people go to evening classes to learn. There was a lot of technique in it—the modulated pressure of the thumb; the palm to palm interface; the finger-lock; the terminal wrist-flip. It was a prolonged and multi-layered assertion of confidence, frankness, solicitude and firmness of intent.

'John Kasky,' the man said, with an intimate cough.

I took him for a travelling evangelist, and noticed that his limp moustache was interestingly out of character with the powerful handshake.

'R. & H. Service & Supply.'

He was a pump salesman. He was shortly going to demonstrate a pump to the city administrator; in the meantime, he rehearsed his patter on me. The pump stood at the bottom of the levee, and looked like a shiny red tractor.

These were flush times. Mr Kasky could not recall exactly how many pumps he'd sold in the last three weeks, but it was over thirty. These were not tin-pot two-stroke jobs, but big industrial pumps, costing from 20,000 to 50,000 dollars apiece, and Mr Kasky was selling them, on commission, to cities up and down the river. The excitement of all these done deals had worked on him like speed. He was elated and twitchy.

This particular pump was a Godwin Dri-Prime 6-inch 65-horsepower model, with a throughput of 2.1 MGD>.

'Million gallons a day,' said Mr Kasky.

'That's a lot of water.'

'Oh, we go way up. Take a twelve-inch pump, for instance. That'll give you a throughput of nine MGD—and that *is* a lot of water.'

I was curious to find out how much water had to be pumped out of Sainte Genevieve every day.

'You'd be talking hundreds of millions. Close on a billion. But don't quote me.'

He snapped open his briefcase and got out the literature on the Godwin. 'We just took on this line a little while back. Pretty fair timing . . . ' He gazed appreciatively over the levee and its lines of pumps, each with a hose poking over the top of the sandbags, spewing dirty water back into the flood. Beside the spanking new Godwin, they looked a sorry collection of rustbuckets.

Mr Kasky explained to me the poetry of the dry-prime system. A wet-prime pump—he flagged his hand dismissively at the hardware nearby—is a source of never-ending tribulation. It must be constantly tended. If you allow your wet-prime pump to suck dry, it will probably break its seals. With broken seals, it won't pump. And in any case, you'll have to reprime it.

On the other hand, suppose you go the extra mile and invest in something like the Godwin Dri-Prime? When there's water to suck, it sucks. When there's no water to suck, it quietly hums along, waiting for the next leak to spring. It requires no adjustment and no priming. **Its seals** don't break. If you wish, you may go away on vacation to Hawaii, leaving your trusty pump to do its work unattended in your absence. Everybody should have one.

'And it's made in England.' He read the name of the place, with some difficulty, from the promotional sheet: 'Cirencester, United Kingdom.'

'How much?'

'Twenty-three, just shy of twenty-four thousand dollars.'

I was still puzzled as to why, in this drowning and pump-hungry city, Mr Kasky had chosen to spend time selling his shiny red tractor to me.

'You're the media. It's like everything else—you need to get media coverage in this business if you're going to succeed. You never know: you could be doing yourself a favour if you work in a reference in your article to the Godwin Dri-Prime Pump.'

I have done my best.

I hung around for the demo. The pump worked. I saw water coming out of the other end. The city bought it.

At his house on South Gabouri Street, Mr Ish Scher had fifteen pumps, and they all ran out of gas at different times, so Mr Scher spent the day going from pump to pump with a two-gallon gasoline can. It was hard enough to keep the pumps supplied with fuel, but they were old and temperamental, and every day at least one pump would cough and die, and the water would begin to climb. Even when all the pumps were smoothly churring, the basement of the Scher house was ankle-deep in flood water, and a bit of muck in an impeller would bring the level to knee-height in a few minutes. If one stood in the sopping basement, the river was just above one's head; held off by a home-built wall of sandbags. Water dripped and bubbled through the cracks between the bags, and the bigger leaks were miniature cascades.

'It's a beautiful house,' said Mr Scher. 'It used to be.'

Over the din of the pumps there was the sound of purling mountain streams. The wallpaper had slid from the walls, and so had much of the plaster, exposing bricks that were black with wetness.

'The city told us to evacuate. But I couldn't do that—not when we're so near the end.'

Did he mean the end of life or the end of the flood? Perhaps both. Mr Scher was in his late seventies; his wife, a woman with vague, shocked eyes, was a few years younger, but looked older. 'Elaine's taken this very hard. She gets no sleep. She's in a bad state. But I'm fine—just fine.' His voice was southernly soft, and he smiled, out of polite habit, when he spoke. Trudging from pump to pump with his gasoline can, while the Mississippi leaned against his house and forced its way in, Mr Scher seemed at home with the flood: he might have been pottering in his garden on any sleepy summer afternoon.

His left arm ended in a bare stump below the elbow; his fortyish son was blind.

'We've been so lucky with our friends—I can't tell you. If it hadn't been for our friends, we'd have lost this house long ago.

155

They've been so good to us—'

The Schers were defending a line about thirty yards long. Their sandbag wall, over which the river was now so nearly spilling that the removal of one bag could easily have caused the whole wall to give way, stretched round the side and back of the house and across the yard, where it was shored up by the side of a trailer home. Sandbagging is a skilled craft, like dry-stone-walling, and the nine-foot wall had been built by several sandbaggers in several styles. The good bits were dry; the bad bits sagged and dribbled.

In the trench at the foot of the wall, the water was the colour of beef bouillon; its surface was wrinkled and shivering in the contest between the leaks and the pumps. Measured against the coarse weave of a fallen sandbag, it was up a thread, down a thread, up two threads . . . *winning—losing—winning—losing—losing*.

In City Hall I found Mr Kasky. The deal was done. He had the contract in his hand.

'I've found you a great media opportunity,' I said, and told him about the Schers. 'You could get on network television . . . ' I stressed how the story of one deserving family, saved in the nick of time by a pump salesman with a heart, would carry more weight than the loss or salvation of a whole suburb. I came as close as I dared to suggesting that Mr Kasky's face might make the cover of *Time*.

'I'm with you, I'm with you . . . It is a good idea,' said Mr Kasky. 'But what a shame you didn't come up with it this morning. If you'd come to me then, I could have helped them out, no problem. Now, though,' he shook his head and chewed on his moustache. 'I haven't got a pump. I've sold it to the city.'

'You could get one by tomorrow.'

'That would be tricky.'

'Please—'

Mr Kasky consulted his watch and made a great show of being astounded by what he saw there. 'Sorry!' he said: 'I got to go!' And he was gone, the rat.

Jean Rissover was smoking on the loggia. When I told her about the Schers, she went off to talk with the city administrator, but came back with the news that there were no spare pumps of

the right size for the job.
'Isn't there any way in which the Schers could make the city change its mind on that?'
'Oh, they *could*. But they'd need to get media coverage. If Mr Scher could go on a radio show and tell his story there . . . '

Next morning, the river was still only shin-deep in the Scher basement. The previous evening, 1,400 new sandbags had been added to the wall around the house. Half-a-dozen neighbours had turned out to form a chain, and we'd spent three hours slinging the bags up to an expert sandbagger on the top of the wall; some of the worst leaks were now staunched, though new ones had started overnight, and another pump—a hefty one, with a four horse-power motor—was on the blink.

'It's looking good,' Mr Scher said. 'And the flood seems to be going down.'

It was, too. Up the street from the house, the river had found a new shoreline. There was a seven- or eight-inch margin of wet gravel, like an outgoing tide. A wooden stake in the water now showed a distinct dark band. As I watched, a whiskery splinter on the stake popped clear.

Suddenly there were a dozen people in the street, raptly, fondly watching the water as it exposed—first one crumb of gravel, then another, and another. We were witnessing a miracle.

'They were forecasting a rise—'

'What do they know?' said a woman with an exhausted face and a wild laugh. 'They've been wrong about everything.'

In ten minutes, the level of the water dropped by a full inch.

A uniformed coastguard, with a quacking VHF set holstered to his hip, arrived by bicycle. Half an hour ago, the levee at Kaskaskia Island, twelve miles downstream, had burst. Sainte Genevieve's few inches of remission were someone else's misfortune: thousands of acres had gone under; even now, the Mississippi was fanning out through the corn in a great wave.

'They're saying it's real bad down there,' the coastguard said.

'Excuse me!' said the woman with the laugh. 'My house is half underwater, and you're telling me to feel sorry for a *field*?'

157

Every time a levee went, it relieved the pressure of the river, for a few hours at least, on the towns nearby. This was tempting knowledge. In Quincy, Illinois, the breaching of the levee was said to be sabotage, and there was some unofficial talk of other levees that had burst with help and encouragement from the neighbours. Townspeople were prone to blame the farmers for unfairly constricting the river, as Missourians were inclined to blame the people of Illinois for flooding Missouri with their great federal levee.

It didn't take much to cause a breach. It was night-work, but easy to do, given a half-hour or so of privacy. You'd need to shift a dozen sandbags to create a good strong waterspout, and the river would do the rest. In no time at all, the hole in the levee would be big enough to float a barge through it. Then the whole soggy wall of softened earth would give way, and the river would swallow the long flat miles of flood-plain, as it was always meant to do.

The river dropped four inches, then began to rise again. It crept back across the gravel until it was an inch or two further into town than it had been before it took Kaskaskia Island. The excitement and the ensuing lurch of disappointment of the morning had tired people, made them cranky and strange. I spoke to a woman whose basement had the usual assortment of pipes and hoses leading out from it to the river.

'How are things holding up in your house?'

'We've got everything in there but the alligators,' she said. 'Everything but the alligators!' she repeated. 'Everything but the alligators!'

A boy of eight or nine came out of the house next door. 'Did you hear the noise, mister?'

'What noise?'

'A weird noise. I was out here earlier. I heard it. It was weird.'

'What kind of weird?'

'Kind of like a frog-noise. But much louder. And weirder.'

We listened together. There was just the drone of the pumps in the heat and dust. The boy drifted away, his head full of monsters.

Out on the levee, I met a telephone engineer, working for Southwest Bell, whose job it was to visit a long string of river towns, inspecting their phone equipment for flood damage.

'It's interesting,' he said. 'Every town reacts differently. Some towns, it's just like what people say it is on TV: everybody pulling together, neighbour helping neighbour, all that. You can see that in Dutchtown—it's real cohesive. But there's the flipside: towns where people sit on the hill, watching television and saying, "Why do I have to lift a finger to help those dumb-asses down by the river?" A lot of towns are like that. I don't know what it is. Maybe it's in their history. But it seems that whatever was in that town before, the flood finds it and brings it out. It's bringing out a heap of meanness, a heap of resentment, a heap of pettiness. Have you been down to St Mary?'

'No.'

'You ought to. There's no National Guard there, and no media. It's just a town that was flooded, and nobody paid any attention. When folks from St Mary see Sainte Genevieve on the evening news, they'll tell you: they're *bitter*—'

He was interrupted by a mud-spattered farm pick-up, which jounced up the levee. From the driver, there were salutations for the telephone engineer and an irritable growl for me.

'*Repawdah?*'

'Sort of.'

The farmer and the engineer grunted laconically at each other for a while, then fell to gazing at the water. Silence. The river flowed over shunting yards and through a factory. It was a placid floodscape; the ravelling whorls of current, the signs and telephone poles moored to their reflections. People might well come here with paint-boxes and easels.

'Repawdahs.' The farmer stared into the shining middle distance. Water chuckled under the eaves of a sunken house. The pumps grumbled and spat. 'They're making it out to be a whole lot worse than it is.' He put the truck into reverse and backed off the levee before I could say that I knew what he meant.

200 YEARS OF ATTITUDE

CONDUCT UNBECOMING:
GAYS & LESBIANS IN THE U.S. MILITARY

RANDY SHILTS

FROM THE AUTHOR OF *AND THE BAND PLAYED ON* COMES THE
SHOCKING EXPOSURE OF THE HYPOCRISY AND PERSECUTION WITHIN
THE US MILITARY, BASED ON OVER 1000 INTERVIEWS WITH GAY
SERVICE PEOPLE OVER THE LAST FIVE YEARS.

'ENGROSSING, ENTERTAINING AND OPTIMISTIC'
LOS ANGELES TIMES

'HISTORY-MAKING AND HISTORY-CHANGING'
SAN FRANCISCO CHRONICLE

£12.00

ETHAN CANIN
BATORSAG AND SZERELEM

In January of 1973, the year everything changed in our family, my older brother Clive competed for the mathematics championship of William Howard Taft High School in Shaker Heights, Ohio. The championship was held in the gym, where Clive and three other finalists sat at metal desks arranged around the painted Taft Tiger at center-court, working a sheet of problems. I sat in the bleachers with our parents, watching him.

Our parents had insisted I come. Clive's best friend Elliot was also there, and at our mother's request we chose a spot ten rows back in the pine bleachers, which was close enough to see Clive's progress on the answer sheet but high enough to be out of his line of sight in case he glanced up. Clive kept his head down. He worked his feet in his sandals, while next to me, holding her breath for long stretches, our mother did the same in hers. We watched Clive's answer sheet darken with neat diagrams and equations, only the +s and =s clearly visible. Ten rows below us, Sandra Sorento, his girlfriend, leaned forward and fixed her gaze on him from where she sat, alone on the first bench. Our mother's eyes kept wandering down to her, then snapping back up to Clive. Even from a distance, I could tell Clive was doing well. He answered twice as fast as the boy on his left, and he erased only once, just before he handed in his test.

Then he came up into the bleachers to sit with us, and in a few moments Sandra ambled across the gym to the water fountain, pretended to get a drink and then came up, too. Clive didn't say anything to her, so I tried to smile for both of us. She smiled back weakly. Then she moved over and stood next to Clive, who was showing our parents one of the problems, set in the middle of a sheet of ditto paper in smudged, purple type:

> LANCELOT and GAWAIN each antes a dollar. Then each competes for the antes by writing down a sealed bid. When the bids are revealed, the high bidder wins the antes and pays the low bidder the amount of his low bid. If the bids are equal, LANCELOT and GAWAIN split the pot. How much do you bid, LANCELOT?

Our mother beamed. Elliot whistled and shook his head. Sandra touched Clive's shoulder. I looked at the problem and pretended to

163

think about it for a while, although I did not understand what it was asking. Our father took it into his lap and said, 'Elementary, my dear Watson.' He began filling in diagrams and crossing them out, tapping his feet and scratching his ears, until, a half hour later, the buzzer rang and the other contestants turned in their papers.

Later, after Clive was declared the winner, our mother asked him where he wanted to go to celebrate. From the back seat of our Plymouth station wagon, Clive said something that sounded like *Bayosh ahdj*. Elliot grinned.

'Pardon, honey?' said our mother.

Clive said the same thing again, Elliot stifled a laugh and finally Sandra said, 'How about the House of Pancakes, Mrs Messerman?'

We always suspected that something was wrong with Clive, but our suspicions were muddled, especially in those days, by his brilliance. He didn't talk much, and when he did, he used words like 'azygous' and 'chemism'. That afternoon, when our mother's electric blender went dead three hours before her dinner party, he repaired it using her iron and a piece of wire from our father's old short-wave radio, then went around muttering, 'liquefy, blend, purée, pulverize, frappe.' He sang it like a little guitar lick, all the way down to the end—'grind, grate, chop'—even while our neighbours from Throckmorton Street, the Goldmans and the Cubanos, sat around the dining-room table with us. Clive didn't seem to know he was embarrassing himself; in the kitchen, where our mother had asked me to help serve the soup, she suggested I point it out to him.

In the old days, our parents' dinner parties had been quiet affairs that Clive and I listened to from the top of the stairs, but now we took part in them. We sat with the guests and were encouraged to talk with them, and before our mother served the first course we would all join hands over the quilted tablecloth to close our eyes and say a prayer for peace. We were supposed to bow our heads, but that night I caught our father looking at Mrs Cubano, and he winked at me. I winked back. Our father had a retired navy friend, Colonel Byzantian, who now vinted his own wines in California and sent them to us, and when the Goldmans and the Cubanos had looked up from the prayer, our father took

out the Colonel's most recent note and read it aloud. 'A wistful elegy of a zinfandel,' he said, deepening his voice, 'a nearly human longing in a grape.' He chuckled and filled the glasses. Then, while the Cubanos and the Goldmans laughed, raised their wine and leaned back in their chairs, I told a story about how my friend Billy DeSalz had sent the same love letter to three different girls from three different schools. Mr Cubano laughed aloud suddenly, and his wife, who I thought was exquisitely beautiful, glanced at him. I went on: but these girls, it turned out, happened to attend the same church. Now Mrs Cubano laughed out loud, and the story began to take shape in my mind. I lifted my glass of apple juice, leaned forward over the table and went further and further with my tale, searching for a plot that would take me to the end, turning to the Goldmans and then the Cubanos, and every now and then to my brother who was silently eating his roast.

Later, after everyone had gone home our mother sat on my bed and asked me questions about Clive. She asked me why he was always silent at dinner and what the girls at Taft thought of a boy who knew why mica acted as an electric diode; she asked me if at school he and Elliot ever spoke the strange language they spoke in our house. Then, touching her temple, she asked me to multiply 3768, our address on Throckmorton, by 216, our area code. 'You can't do that, right?' she said, her eyebrows raised, as if there were a real possibility I could. 'It's not normal to be able to do that without pencil and paper, is it?' She tilted her head to look at me, and when I shook my own she smiled.

'Mom,' I said, 'I made up most of that business about Billy DeSalz.'

She looked at me quizzically. 'I know that, honey,' she whispered. 'But at least *you* talk to girls in English.'

It was not that Clive was mean, or dangerous, or particularly delinquent; it was just that he didn't know how to act like the other kids. As a junior, he had scored two 800s on his SATs, while as a senior, when it counted, Mr Sherwood called to say that he had scored two 200s. 'It takes a profusion of intelligence to answer every question *incorrectly*,' Clive said that night to our father, who stood in the kitchen slapping the Education Testing Service envelope against the counter. By then, our parents had become used to calls from the Principal. One day that same year, Clive had stood still in the hamburger line at William Howard Taft, weeping, while the crowd of students parted around him.

The next night, while I was working on a plaster-of-Paris replica of Michelangelo's *Pièta* for my honors history class, I discovered Clive's secret. I was in the basement, molding my statuette on a piece of plywood behind our father's ping-pong table, copying the form from *Art Through the Ages*, when I looked up and noticed a sliver of light behind the Philco refrigerator box next to the furnace. When I looked up again, the light was gone. I wet down the furled skirts of my Mary, walked to the corner, pulled back the refrigerator box and found, in the small space behind it, a cot and a candle and, dangling from hangers on the electrical conduit, girl's clothing. The cardboard box from our old TV moved, and Sandra Sorento stepped out from behind it.

'Quiet,' she whispered.

She stood before me in a yellow halter top and a spangled maroon skirt that went to the floor, narrowing at the knees and spreading again at the ankles so that it looked like the bottom half of a mermaid; the halter revealed a cream-colored slice of her waist. Things were wrong at her house, I knew.

'Well, nosey,' she said, 'now you know.' She sat down on the cot.

'Were you watching me?' I asked.

'A little.'

'I didn't do anything weird, did I?'

'Nope.'

'Sometimes I do,' I said.

'Well, you didn't this time.' She smiled. 'You're so cute,' she said finally. 'You're so serious.' She touched her earrings, one, then the other. Then she said, 'Come here, little brother,' and slid over on the cot. She lowered her voice. 'I *had* to move here,' she said. 'It was my only choice.'

I nodded. 'I hear you,' I said. This was a phrase of Clive's.

She looked at me. 'You do, don't you?'

I nodded again. Her skirt was threadbare at the knees, and I remembered that her parents were divorced.

'You know,' she said. 'I'll tell you a secret.' She pulled back her hair, then let it fall again. 'I like you, little brother.' She smiled at me. 'That's the secret. You and me, we have this connection, because you know more than everybody thinks.'

'I can bring you food, Sandra.'

She let out her breath. 'That would be really cool,' she said. 'You know?' She stood, slid open the small clouded window next to her, shook a Virginia Slims from the pack and lit it. 'I wish Clive was as cool as you.' She set the cigarette in an ashtray on the sill so that the smoke lifted out into the yard. 'I wish,' she said.

'I'm not that cool.'

'Yes, you are.'

'Maybe,' I said.

She dragged on the cigarette again. 'Question,' she said. She exhaled. 'Does Elliot ever bug you?'

'Me?'

She looked around. 'Who did you think I was talking to?'

'I don't know,' I said. 'Not really. Sometimes.'

'Well, he bugs *me*.'

'Is that right?'

'Yeah, Clive is so superior to him. Clive's a genius, and Elliot's the last thing from one.' She thought for a moment. 'There's probably a word for what Elliot is.'

'I hear you,' I said.

She dragged on her cigarette and offered it to me. 'By the way,' she said, exhaling, 'did Clive ever tell you about us?'

I pretended to inhale. 'About who?'

'About me and him.'

'No.'

'He didn't?'

I exhaled. 'No.'

'You're not going to tell your parents about me, right?'

'No way.'

'All right,' she said, 'then I'll tell you.' She met my eyes. Then she blew a smoke ring, and as it rose above her, she pierced it with another, smaller, whirling one. 'I'm Clive's lover,' she whispered. The smoke rings spun up toward the ceiling like galaxies. 'It's a big secret,' she whispered, 'but now you know.'

167

It was the year the Vietnam War ended, Spiro Agnew resigned and the Indians took over Wounded Knee. It was the year lines formed at gas stations, and Henry Kissinger won the Nobel Peace Prize. It was the year our parents forsook their religion, the designated hitter stepped up to the plate, abortion became legal and our father wore bell bottoms and purple ties. It was the year my brother spoke in his own language; the year he won championship after championship and began drifting away from us, until we all began to fear that one day, like a branch in a storm, he would snap off completely.

Our parents were now Quakers. Our father came from a line of conservative Jews in Chicago, and our mother from Zionist farmers who had emigrated to Cleveland from the Negev desert, but now my parents went together two nights a week to Friends' meetings. They had spent so much time adapting to the changes that were coming at them from every quarter, that the world at home sometimes seemed utterly different from what it had been only a few years before. They had forbidden Clive and me from watching anything except the news on television, but one night that summer they came home from a peace march to find us watching *Mannix* and they took us both downtown and made Clive hand the television set to a bum in a doorwell.

We listened to radio news instead. That year, it was bad. Gunmen with black stockings over their faces appeared at the Olympic Games. Israel was invaded. George McGovern, whom our parents walked for, door to door, won in Massachusetts and nowhere else. In Paris there was a long debate over the shape of the peace negotiations table. The day the negotiations started, one of the vocational students, Vincent Jump, punched Clive in the ear, making him bleed, and our mother, who kept a map of Vietnam on her dresser, invited Vincent over to have our own peace conference. It was the third time that Clive had been beaten up, and she wanted to know why. Clive and Vincent sat at our rectangular kitchen table, glasses of grapefruit juice and a bowl of wholewheat pretzels between them, while our mother and Mrs Jump watched from the living-room. 'I can't figure out what he does to them,' she said to me that night, sitting at the edge of my bed again. 'Why do Americans hate a boy just for being smart?'

Our mother was never quite an American. On weekends, her anti-Nixon placards rolled into her hand, she waited in long lines of activists for the Greyhound to take them to peace marches in Columbus, only to shove the person in front of her to get on. She was damp-eyed, moral and stubborn, and she felt the world deeply. Once, in the A&P, she had browbeaten a soldier in dress uniform, pushing him up against the stand-up freezer and calling him *Chazer!* and *Gonef!* in a loud voice—a voice, I realized with embarrassment, that had become accented with Hebrew—while I hid among the newspaper stands, and the soldier stood blinking before her.

But she was devoted to my brother and me. In supermarket lines and at parent assemblies, to people she barely knew, she called us her two geniuses. Even in 1973, when the evidence about me began to come in, she insisted. We were the only kids at school who didn't know the *Partridge Family* plots, and the only ones who could distinguish Cambodia from Laos. There were bookshelves in both our bathrooms, a fact that also embarrassed me, and Clive and I were required to read at least one magazine each week. I read *US News and World Report* and on Saturday mornings talked with our mother about what I read, eating wheatgerm while she tried—I see in retrospect—to show me the bias of the reporting. Clive read *High Times*, which contained advertisements for pipes and rolling papers and long articles about how to grow marijuana in the closet. He clipped the centerfolds, which were pictures of cubes of hashish or plates of diced up psychedelic mushrooms, and kept them in his desk drawer with his guitar picks, his roach clips and his collection of metal cigarette lighters. Our mother tried buying him a subscription to *Scientific American* instead, and sometimes she sat on the couch and watched him read it. Now and then in an article he would smile, and, after a moment, she would, too. She liked to call him 'cerebral' instead of 'smart', which to me made his intelligence sound like an overgrowth, like a vine that would one day pull down a tree.

That week, I tried to forget about Sandra in our basement, but I felt a relentless force urging me to confess. So that I would not mention her, I told our mother instead about the malt liquor I had bought recently from the Sicilian grocer behind the Busy Bee market; I told our father about Kelly Reed, whom I had kissed in the back of the leather-seated Cadillac DeVille we had taken one night from Billy DeSalz's parents' garage—Billy was in the front seat, his head lowered like a chauffeur, and later that night we taught ourselves to fishtail on the wide, unlit road around the lime quarry; I told Clive about the things I had stolen that semester, candy bars and beer, mostly, and now and then a record. But what I really wanted to say, what took all my discipline not to blurt out, was that I had found his girlfriend, dressed in glitter, hiding in the basement of our house.

Instead, I tried to get Clive to talk about it. He had always lived an entire, secret life that he would never discuss, but I did my best to put him in a confessional mood. It was difficult. He never talked about anything, about the senior parties he went to or the bands he played in in his friends' garages; he never gave me advice, the way other brothers did, about girls or dressing or mixed drinks. Every night that week, I washed the pots and pans with him after dinner, and every night, standing next to me with drooping shoulders and tapping out-turned feet, he dried them without speaking; hunched over the sink next to him, I could feel the familiar ease that passed between us, like radar; it was a love, really, as calm as I would ever know, and I tried to let it wash over us so that he would talk. Yet in him it only brought out silence. Between pots, he would rest his knee against mine and tap out guitar fret-work on the towel, but he would not say anything; I would plunge my hands into the steaming water and tell the half-invented story of my friends training a telescope from the roof of the gym through the one, unclouded, topmost window of the girls' locker room, into their shower, or about cheating on our multiple-choice geometry test by placing our feet on specific colored tiles on the math-room floor. I told stories and looked into his eyes; I told them and looked out the window; but no matter what I did, no matter how much I talked or how silent I tried to keep myself, I could not entice him to talk about Sandra.

'Lover,' I said softly at the sink. Next to me, I sensed Clive's little twists and nods. Of course, he and Sandra were boyfriend and girlfriend, but *lover* was a word I had never heard in conversation before, a word I could not imagine our parents, nor my brother, nor anybody I knew, ever using. It made it seem as if that was *all* they did. I let the hot water run until it steamed the windows. Then I said it again, *lover*, with a little French accent, but Clive didn't answer.

After dinner I watched our father drinking coffee, our mother leaning over the counter, Clive pouring unfiltered apple juice, but these actions did not distract me; they only made my secret more exquisite. I felt my chest expanding, like helium, urging me to confess. Clive picked at some apple pie: I almost told him then that I knew. Our mother read her *Friends' News* on the living-room couch: there, I almost told her. Our father went back to his office to check on his accounts. Our parents moved about the house, doing their chores, oblivious to Sandra hidden downstairs like a body oblivious to its beating heart.

Finally, late that night, I went into our father's office and asked him to play ping-pong. 'I just feel like playing,' I said. We walked down to the basement, where he screwed on the light-bulb, took the paddles from the bin where they'd lain for months and dusted them on his pant leg. With the arm of his sweater, he dusted the ping-pong table.

'I'm not sure what's got into you, sailor,' he said, patting me on the shoulder, 'but I sure am glad to see it.'

Again I almost told him. Instead, I held the ball in my open palm for a moment, listening to the click of the furnace and the squeaks of the ceiling joists where our mother walked above us in the kitchen, and then I said, 'Service.' I hit a slice that he slapped back hard into the corner for the point. The ball bounced underneath the stairs and I retrieved it. 'One-zero,' I said. 'What do you think of Clive?' I asked.

'Zero-*one*, sailor. What do you mean, what do I think of Clive?'

'He's been acting strange, that's all.'

'Is that supposed to be a news flash?'

'I just thought I'd tell you.' I showed him the ball again. 'Service.'

He laughed and returned it to the same spot in the corner for the point. 'Thanks, sailor,' he said. Then he hit another past my backhand.

171

'What about Elliot?' I said.

'Elliot's a fine kid, why? Is there something I should know about?'

I served while he was looking me in the eyes and surprised him. 'No, I'm just talking. Three-one.'

'One-three.'

'What about Sandra?' I said.

'What about her?'

I waited a moment. 'What do you think of her?'

He crouched to receive my serve, his paddle held from the back of his hand the way the Chinese players had held it that year in the Olympics, and behind the refrigerator box I heard the flex of Sandra's cot. 'She's his belle,' he said as I served, 'if that's what you mean, but he'll get over her.'

After he won the point, the only sounds in the basement were our father's breathing and the soft rush of the furnace pilot. Then, behind the box, I heard the cot flex. 'I'm not sure he will,' I said.

He laughed.

'I think she's kind of pretty,' I said.

'Pretty, William?' He shook his head. 'Maybe so, but it's a cheap kind of pretty. It's the kind of pretty that won't last. I guarantee it, sailor. Serve.'

I waited a moment. Then I said loudly, 'I'm sorry.'

'About what?' said our father.

Walking by Clive's room one afternoon, I noticed a cold draft coming from beneath his door. There was no answer when I knocked, and when I entered I found him and Elliot sitting on the windowsill with the windows wide open. Their shirts and pants were off, and they sat cross-legged in their underwear, like Indians, facing out into the snowy yard. Their faces were blank, and neither of them moved when I entered. Icicles hung from the eave.

'Excuse me,' I said. 'Uh, Pocahantas?'

Elliot looked at me, then turned to the open window again. His chest and arms were pale from the cold, and the black hairs on his legs stood up.

'Um, is this a physics experiment?'

'Shhh,' Clive said. He didn't move.

'I get it. You're freeze-drying yourselves.'

Elliot raised his hand and examined it. It was yellow-white, as though all the blood had disappeared, and I could see the tendons contracted inside. He dropped it back into his lap, where it made a sound like wood.

Later, they told me they were practising what certain monks knew. These monks, Clive said, lived by discipline. They were capable of sitting like that, expressionless, without clothing, in the Himalayan winter, until they froze to death.

Clive's language had started out with a few words. One evening when our parents were out, I had come into his room while he and Elliot were playing Hendrix riffs with the volume turned up. Sandra was lying on the bed examining the palm of her hand. Clive was going off on a solo, bending his head up to the ceiling and contorting his face whenever the fingering took him high up on the bridge of his Stratocaster. He pulled his mouth tight when the shrillest, warbled notes came bending out of the Heath Kit speakers on the bookshelf. His features, ordinarily thin, grew even thinner in musical rapture, and his hair bounced about his shoulders like a mop. To keep his eyes clear he wore a headband, like Hendrix himself. Elliot—like all bass players—stood impassively, leaning back with his eyes closed as he plucked out the deep harmony.

'Clive,' I said from the doorway. Sandra let her hand fall. 'Clive, could you turn that lower, please?'

I came into the room. Only Sandra looked at me. 'Clive,' I said, 'I'm doing homework.'

The guitar stopped, and after a few more bars, so did the bass. 'Could you play a little softer, please?'

Clive touched Elliot on the neck. '*Aideshen sereti*,' I think he said, and they both laughed. Then Elliot said something like, '*maiz*,' and they laughed again.

Sandra shrugged. I looked hard at her. 'Don't ask me,' she mouthed.

But soon they were speaking it more and more, at school and in the car and on the telephone, strange words that rose up suddenly out of their English conversation like jagged prehistoric

173

rocks. '*Kirahy*,' I heard, and '*zenay*' and '*birkahoosh.*' One day in the bathroom at William Howard Taft, I heard some of the voc-ed kids talking about Clive. I was in the stall. 'That Messerman kid,' one of them said, opening the shut hot-water valves with his Allen wrench, 'He's a genius. I hear he invented his own foreign language.'

But when I told our mother about this, she wrinkled her forehead. 'Is this what a genius does?' she said the next afternoon when she lifted the end of Clive's mattress, and an opium pipe and a bottle of vaseline rolled on to the floor. 'Is this the start of Albert Einstein's day?' she whispered, pulling open the window shades so that Clive finally stirred in the bright light and blinked open his eyes. '*Edj perts moolvah*,' he said.

I waited as long as I could. Finally, two nights later, I went downstairs and knocked lightly on the Philco refrigerator box.

'I've been expecting you,' she said.

'I brought some oranges.'

'William of Oranges.'

'They're tangerines, actually.'

'William of Tangerines.'

She laughed, so I did, too, although I didn't understand. I took the tangerines from my pockets, set them on the windowsill and watched her shake a Virginia Slims from the pack. 'So,' she said. 'William.'

I could feel myself blushing. 'Sorry about what my Dad said, Sandra. I thought it would turn out funny.'

'It didn't.'

'I know.'

She closed her eyes, held them shut for a moment, then opened them again and looked at me. 'It's all right,' she said. 'We have the kind of love your father doesn't understand, that's all.' She smiled. 'Tell me, William.'

'Tell you what?'

She leaned towards me and tapped her finger on my wrist. 'Just tell me.'

'There's more tangerines where these came from.'

'That's not what I was thinking of.'

'I didn't think it was.'

'I know what you want to tell me. I'm just waiting for you.'
She looked at me and smiled. 'I'm clairvoyant,' she said.

'Clive's going to win the City's,' I said.

'That's not what I was thinking of, either.'

'He could win the whole state if he wanted.'

'*William.*'

'What do you want me to say?'

She turned and looked out the window into the dusty,
spider-webbed recess below our deck. With her back to me, she
said, 'Is it true you really think I'm beautiful?'

Our parents were trying to change with the times. During
World War Two, our father had been stationed on the
aircraft carrier *Wisconsin* in the Pacific, but now, one evening, he
brought Clive and me to stand with him on the Carnegie Bridge
and throw his old service revolver into the Cuyahoga. He used to
tend his insurance business in the dining-room, but now that we
had lost our television, he tended it in the den at the back of the
house, listening to radio broadcasts of the Cleveland Symphony.
Our mother didn't want insurance forms in our living-room any
more. Stored away in our old TV cabinet in a black, steel box
that locked with a combination, he kept cards on all his clients,
and more than once, when our mother was out, he had brought
me in, tapped its sides and told me not to forget that this was our
house, our family, our everything—that this was twenty years. In
1973 he was forced to talk about insurance all the time.

'People *do* have to be protected,' he said that evening, rubbing
his sideburns as we sat in the kitchen with the Cubanos again.
They had come to celebrate Clive's victory at the Taft mathematics
championship and his upcoming entry in the City's. 'Insurance is
primarily a service we're providing, and *secondarily* a task for
profit.'

'Why lie to your family?' Clive suddenly asked.

Our mother looked up from her Caesar's salad. 'It's true,
Simon,' she said. 'We all know what's going on with the military-
industrial complex.'

Our father set down his fork. 'Since when,' he said, 'since

175

what day exactly has an insurance salesman been part of the military-industrial complex?'

Our parents had had this argument before, and now the Cubanos looked down at their salad plates. Across the table, Clive mumbled, 'Grind, grate, chop, liquefy, purify.'

Finally, our father smiled. 'Anchovies!' he said, slapping his thigh and digging his fork into the salad.

'It's delicious, Rose,' said Mrs Cubano.

'It's a Caesar,' said our mother.

'Anchovies,' said our father, 'are—if I am not mistaken—a dollar-sixty a tin.' He looked around the table, feigning surprise. 'Thank you, Ohio Mutual.'

Mr Cubano laughed. Our mother stood up. 'We could have eaten plain salad,' she said.

'Right on,' said Clive.

'What did you say, young man?'

Clive looked at me and nodded.

'Either part of the solution, Dad,' I said, shrugging at my brother, 'or part of the problem.'

'Or dissolved in the solution,' said Clive.

Our father studied him, then me and finally said, 'Insurance is about protecting the average person.'

'Insurance is about corporate profit,' said our mother.

The Cubanos looked at each other. Our father stood from the table, went to the window and looked out into the yard. Clive hummed a lick and shook his pick hand near his waist. Our mother poured lemonade into all our glasses, then sat again, smoothed her pants suit and composed her expression. 'Clive,' she said at last, 'William tells me they're pretty impressed with you at school.'

'Hear! Hear!' said Mr Cubano, holding up his lemonade. 'To the champion!'

'I heard that some boys said you were a genius,' said our mother.

'They know one when they see one,' said Mrs Cubano.

'*Dweebs*,' said Clive.

'They were voc-ed kids, Mom,' I said. I waited a beat. 'Everything's relative.'

'It certainly is not,' said our mother. 'My two geniuses,' she whispered, smiling at us. I looked to see if the Cubanos had heard her.

'Nobody said anything about William,' said my brother.

'Clive, apologize to your brother for that.'

'Sorry, William.'

Our mother set her jaw. She swept her hand out over the kitchen, and her eyes watered. 'Genius is one per cent inspiration,' she said, 'and ninety-nine per cent perspiration.'

'Thomas Edison,' said our father. He turned around from the window to look at her, then came back to the table, where he put his hand on her leg. 'Geniuses *invent*,' he said, fishing an anchovy from his salad and holding it out over the table on his fork. 'That's the important thing. A genius isn't just someone who's learned something well. A genius is someone who's looked at the world everyone else has looked at, and he sees a new way.'

'Or *she*,' said Mrs Cubano.

'Or she,' said our father.

'A genius has to reinvent the world,' said our mother.

'That's right,' said Clive, 'you can't teach a genius anything.'

'Now wait a moment,' said Mrs Cubano, 'that's certainly not the point.'

'Geniuses study just like everybody else, young man,' said Mr Cubano. He sold tractors for John Deere.

'*Dweebs*,' said Clive.

'What does that mean?' said our mother.

'*Diznaw*,' he said.

She looked at me. 'And what does that mean?'

'Good salad, Mom.'

'Thank you, William. We're having macaroni after.' She thought for a moment. 'Though I still say we could have done without the anchovies.'

'Anchovies are brain food,' said Clive.

'The point is that we didn't,' said our father. 'The point is that we did not do without the anchovies.'

'What's brain food?' I said.

'Something you haven't been eating, little brother,' Clive answered, and then he winked at me.

177

That fall, since it was the first year Clive and I had gone to the same school, our mother had taken me aside. 'You and Clive are different,' she said to me one day as were tie-dying T-shirts in the bathroom. 'You don't have to do the things Clive did.' She dunked the knotted shirt in her mixing bowl, which was filled with yellow dye.

'How do you mean?'

'Clive's unusual,' she said. 'I just want you to know that. I'm sure your friends at Taft will be different from his. Your brother does some unusual things.'

'Which ones do you mean?'

'Maybe we should use some magenta here,' she said. 'What do you think?'

I watched her wring the yellow from the cloth. 'Which ones?' I said.

'Oh, ones we wouldn't be proud of. Things *you* wouldn't do. You know what I mean.'

'No, I don't.'

We filled the bathtub and hung the knotted shirts on a line above it, while she filled the mixing bowl with dye. I watched the yellow drip from the shirts and spread through the water.

'You and your brother are different,' she said quietly. 'That's all.'

I tied up another shirt. 'A lot of my friends shoplift,' I said with my back turned to her. 'Billy DeSalz got caught once.'

In February, the Cleveland championship was held, and our parents drove Sandra and me to the city library to watch Clive. The room turned out to be too small for spectators, and we had to sit on plastic chairs in a hallway in the library basement. Behind a metal door that had a small window in it, Clive and six other students worked at a long conference table. Our mother stood at the window, looking in, until the door opened and the proctor had a word with her. Then she sat back down in her chair next to our father. 'Why have a window if you can't look in?' she said. She looked at Sandra and me. 'Why don't you two run along for a while?' she said to Sandra.

Sandra and I wandered through the basement of the library.

The rooms were small and musty, each one furnished with a long metal table and folding chairs, like the ones Clive and his rivals now sat in. Some rooms held no books at all, others were crammed full. Sandra went into one lined with rows of identical volumes in dull green bindings, and I followed. She gazed at one of the books, so I gazed at another, a thick volume called *Thermodynamics of Liquid-Gas Phase Change* by Walter Y. Chang. I pulled it from the shelf and looked inside.

From the corner, I could smell the flowery scent of her perfume. I skimmed through the book, which had not even been type-set, merely typed, with a wide margin at the binding and the page numbers written out in words at the top, but I couldn't understand any of it. On some pages only two or three sentences were written and the rest was equations, full of symbols I had never seen. Sandra sighed. She said, 'Wow,' and a drift of her scent reached me again. 'Think of Clive out there,' she whispered, 'doing stuff like this.'

'Some of these equations are wrong, Sandra.'

'What?'

'Some of these calculations are incorrect.'

'Come on.'

'They *are*.'

'Don't tell me *you* understand this stuff, too, William.'

I closed my book. 'It's not that hard,' I said, 'if you know the equations.'

She smiled at me and closed her book, then looked at me a long time. 'My two geniuses,' she said finally. Then she laughed and disappeared into the corridor.

I waited a minute, then sauntered after her. The hallway was empty, and I moved along it, striding purposefully into each room, glancing around inside, then going on to the next. Finally, as I neared the main corridor—at the end of which sat our parents, waiting, and Clive, calculating—the lights went off in one of the rooms.

'Genius!' Sandra whispered from inside.

I peeked in. 'What?'

'Come in here.'

'Where are you?'

'Close the door. Do you see me?'

'It's pitch black in here, Sandra.'

'I see *you*, William.'

I strained into the dark.

'Try to find me, William.'

I stepped forward, imagining where the long table lay, struggling to see the pale shapes of the chairs. 'I mean, Sandra, I just found a few small errors in some of the equations, that's all. Probably typos.'

'Do you really think I'm beautiful, William?'

I steadied myself on the table. 'Yes.'

'How beautiful?'

'Very,' I said. 'Extremely.'

'You can't even see me.'

'Doesn't matter.'

'You didn't really understand that stuff, William.'

'Yes, I did.' I moved another step. 'OK,' I said, 'you're right. I didn't. I pretended I did. I don't like thinking about that stuff.'

'What stuff?'

'Equations. The things Clive thinks about.'

She was silent for a moment. 'Did you lie about anything else?'

'Like what?'

She didn't answer.

'Like, that you're pretty, you mean?'

'Yeah.'

I felt to the side for the wall. 'No way,' I said, 'not about that.'

Now there was no sound, and I waited for my eyes to adjust to the dark. 'How am I doing?' I said, stepping forward again.

'You're getting warmer.'

'You're under the table, aren't you?'

'Nope. Colder, genius. Good, warmer.'

'You're up on the shelves.'

She giggled. 'What *do* you like thinking about, William.?'

'You must be around the *S*s.'

'Warmer. Hot.'

I slid toward the wall in the dark, my hands out in front of me. When I reached the shelves, I felt for their crosspiece and held on to it, listening to her quiet breaths, just above me and to the left, like a panther in a tree. Then I said, 'I like thinking about *you*, Sandra.'

There was a flurry of motion, the soft hop of her landing on the carpet, and then, from behind me, the creak of the door.

When I found her, she was sitting with Clive and our parents, waiting for the other contestants to finish. Her knee rested against his. Clive was telling them that at the Cuyahoga County championships, which were going to be held in two weeks, there would be an audience, and it would be given the problems as well.

'We'll come watch,' I said, looking at Sandra.

'William can look for mistakes,' she said.

'The County's won't be anything,' said Clive. 'It's the State's I'm worried about. Sheshevsky will be at the State's.'

'Who's Sheshevsky?' asked our mother.

'He's some smart kid,' said Clive, 'that's all.'

'His father's a physics professor,' I said. 'He's supposed to be a genius.'

'That makes two of you,' said Sandra.

'Three,' said our mother.

Clive looked around. 'Sheshevsky'll be trouble,' he said, 'but I won't see him till the State's.'

'Assuming *you* get there,' said our father.

Our mother and Sandra laughed. So did Clive, and, finally, so did I.

'Assuming,' said Clive.

The next day when I came home from school, Eric Clapton was playing on the living-room speakers, and I heard Clive saying, 'And now, folks, catch this.' He was sitting with our father on the couch, and Mr and Mrs Cubano were on the two stuffed chairs. Clive's eyes were closed and he was leaning back into the corner of the cushions nodding his head, while our father sat forward at the edge of the pillows, nodding too. The song ended, and Clive got up to pause the tape machine. 'I'm turning the old folks on to Clapton,' he said.

181

'It's not bad,' said Mr Cubano. 'It's innovative.'

Clive smiled at him. 'You crack me up, Mr Cubano.'

'It's not bad,' said our father. 'The harmonies are standard, but the melody's innovative.'

'It's just me teaching you what *I* know, Dad.'

'I guess that's right, young man. I guess that's right.' Our father winked at Clive. 'I have to admit,' he said, 'you do seem to know a thing or two.' The Cubanos nodded. 'Now,' our father said, turning to me, 'why don't we all try the next number. William, come sit next to me. Rose!' he called into the kitchen, 'Rose, come hear this.' He closed his eyes, and I sat down next to him.

I moved as close as I could. 'Dad,' I whispered then, 'my report card is coming tomorrow.'

Without opening his eyes, he whispered back, 'It came *today*, sailor.'

Our mother appeared, and Clive started the tape. We sat through 'Bell Bottom Blues' and 'Layla', our father nodding every now and then without opening his eyes, Mr Cubano tapping his feet, Mrs Cubano shifting hers and our mother sitting at the cloth chair looking out the window into the yard. The tape clicked off at the end of the side.

'Well?' said Clive.

'I liked the second number,' said our father.

'Hip,' said Mr Cubano, quietly.

'All *right*, folks,' said Clive. He gave the peace sign. 'What about you, Mom?'

She looked up from the window. ' I have values and taste,' she said.

'*Birkahoosh*,' said Clive.

'Pardon?'

'Honey,' our father said to our mother, 'this stuff is all around us. It's the future.' He got up and slid his arm around her waist. 'We might as well learn about it.'

She looked right at him. 'You may listen to what you wish, Simon,' she said. Then she turned to Clive. 'And what did you say, young man?'

'*Nadj a hoshaig ma*,' said Clive.

'Pardon, honey?'

'*Nadjon melegem van.*'

Nobody spoke. Finally Mrs Cubano said, 'Tell us how you solved that problem with the antes, Clive. It sounds complicated.'

'He doesn't have to talk if he doesn't want to, dear,' said Mr Cubano.

'Yes, he does,' said our father.

'*Djerunk.*'

'Honey,' said our mother, 'the Cubanos don't understand you.'

Clive looked up. 'Sorry, Mr and Mrs Cubano,' he said. Then he looked over at me. '*Djerunk,*' he said again, as though I understood.

I lowered my eyes. Abruptly, next to me, our mother started to cry, and when I looked up I saw that our father, at the head of the couch, had braced back his shoulders the way, in the old days, he used to brace them back before he hit us. But then he lowered them again. He closed his eyes. He kept them closed for a few moments, and when he opened them he patted our mother's elbow, turned to the Cubanos and said, 'Isn't it great what kids do nowadays. They reinvent everything. Clive's invented a language.'

'Teach us a few words,' said Mrs Cubano, coming around the chair to lay her hands on our mother's shoulders.

That night after dinner I went back to our father's study, where he was listening to W-104 instead of the Cleveland Symphony. 'Afternoon Delight' came on, and I moved into the room and sat across from him on the corner of the desk. I could see my report card lying open among his stack of bills. 'What do you think of this music, William?' he said.

'It's all right.'

'Clive seems to be quite enamored of it.'

I nodded. 'Dad,' I said, 'I just had a bad semester.'

'Don't sweat it, sailor,' he said. 'At ease.' He tugged at his belt. Then he said, 'All this business with your brother, you know—the things he does, the music and the language—I want you to know that he's just trying to understand his life, that's all.' He looked out the window at the Cubano's house across the way, where the downstairs light went off and the staircase one came on. 'Do you understand what I'm saying?'

183

'Yes.'

'I knew you would.' He fingered his sideburns. 'Now, I'm not saying the things he does are bad. And if you want to do them yourself someday, why, that's just fine.'

'It is?'

'Yes. You know, my generation has a lot to learn from yours.' He unfastened his belt, loosened it a notch and refastened it. He walked to one corner of the room, thrust his hands into his pockets, pulled them out and walked across to the other. He returned to my side and we looked at ourselves in the glass. 'A fifty-year-old man in a purple tie,' he said at last. 'Look at me, William—your father.'

I was wearing one of my yellow and white tie-dyes, and in the window it looked like an egg with a broken yolk. I was trying to grow my hair past my shoulders. 'Look at me, Dad,' I said. 'Your son.'

He laughed through his nose. 'What a noble creature is man,' he said and punched me on the shoulder. He laughed again. 'Your old man sells insurance, will you ever forgive him?'

'I forgive you, captain.'

He smiled. 'I forgive you, too, sailor,' he said.

Across the way, the lights in the Cubano's upstairs bedroom came on. Then Mrs Cubano appeared in the window in a maroon evening dress. She looked down at us in the study, waved and pulled the shade closed. The faint dot of a satellite labored across the heavens, and when I looked away from it I could see that our father was watching me again in the glass.

'I just want you to know, William,' he said at last, 'that grades don't mean anything. I want you to know that. Why, I'm proud you don't care about them.'

'You are?'

'They're just an external source of approval for something you ought to be doing for yourself anyway.' He laid his hand on my shoulder. 'Affirmative, sailor?'

'Affirmative, captain.'

The satellite had cleared the zenith now and was edging down the far dome of the sky. 'In a hundred years we will never know,' he said. He pulled his hand from my shoulder and leaned closer to the window, this time looking at himself. 'Sweet Mercy!' he

whispered. 'How my very heart has bled, to see thee, poor old man. And thy grey hairs hoar with the snowy blasts.'
'It's not that bad.'
He ruffled my hair again. 'Samuel Taylor Coleridge,' he said. '*That's* what's important, William. Not your report card!'

The Cuyahoga County finals were held in April, in an auditorium at Oberlin College, where the three regional champions sat on stage and puzzled through their problems. Both of the other contestants wore ties and jackets, and one had a yarmulke clipped into his hair; Clive's eyes were red, his hair was tied in a leather headband and, as always, he pulled his sandals on and off as he worked. The other two boys bent over their desks and scribbled calculations while Clive gazed about, adjusted his sandals, occasionally noted something on paper, then looked up and thought some more. Mr Woodless, Clive's math teacher, was in the audience, along with Mr Sherwood and the Cubanos, Elliot and Sandra, who sat next to me. After each problem, the contestants were given a break in which the previous problem was handed out to the onlookers.

Mr Cubano whistled when the first problem was passed down the row and reached him. He handed the mimeographed stack to our mother, who looked down but did not take one, and then passed it on to Mr Woodless, who did. I took one too:

Of twelve coins, one is counterfeit and weighs either more or less than all the others. The others weigh the same. With a balance scale, on which one side may be weighed against the other, you are to use only three weighings to determine the counterfeit.

Next to me, Sandra's hands were clasped together. I looked at them and considered my brother onstage, his thoughts whirling with possibilities, moving deeper and deeper into the secret area of his being where none of us could ever go. His eyes fluttered and closed, and I knew that he had answered the question. They opened, and as he wrote something on his sheet, Sandra's hands opened too.

At the end of the afternoon, the judges graded the problems

while the audience milled in the hall, drinking lemonade; I tried to talk to Sandra about a Doobie Brothers concert that Billy DeSalz had gone to, pretending I had gone myself, but she was distracted; finally, a bell rang, and we went back in to hear the superintendent of schools tell us that with mathematics, the real winner was the mind and the country and the love of knowledge, but that in this particular case, today's winner, with a perfect score, was Clive Messerman.

The next afternoon, I filled my pockets with tangerines and knocked on the Philco refrigerator box, but when it opened, Elliot, not Sandra, was standing there. Behind him, on Sandra's bed, Clive sat holding the plexiglass smoke-bottle he had made in shop class. It was designed to conceal the smell of a joint. 'Well, well,' he said. 'Since when do you know about this place?'

'Don't worry, I haven't told anybody.'

'*Servoos*,' said Elliot.

'Who was worried?' said Clive.

'Dad says his generation has a lot to learn from ours anyway,' I said, ducking inside to sit down with them. 'He told me that.'

Clive nodded. His shirt was unbuttoned, and he reached inside it, retrieved a joint and slid it into the housing of the bottle. He touched it with a lighter, then examined it; the smoke filled the chamber but did not escape into the room. He held it up to the light for us to inspect. 'Like a drum,' he said.

'Like a clam's ass,' said Elliot.

'I just came down here to bring Sandra some food, you guys.'

Elliot laughed. 'Feeding the monster,' he said.

Clive nodded, then leaned forward and sucked hard on the bottle, clearing the dense smoke like a vacuum. 'What else did Dad say?' he rasped.

I thought for a moment. 'He said he thinks you're just trying to understand life.' Clive laughed, spraying a jet of smoke from his nostrils that he tried to direct out the window.

'I hear you,' I said.

Elliot took the bottle, waited for the smoke to gather again, then toked from it, turned to Clive and said, 'It's true, you know. William's right. We have to lead our parents through this stuff. If they don't see something, we have to show them. It's up to us.'

Clive shook his head. 'It ain't up to us,' he said.

Elliot handed the bottle to me, and I pretended to take a drag through the top. I held the smoke in my mouth without inhaling.

'We have to educate them,' Elliot said.

'Hold it in, William,' said Clive.

Upstairs, the back door opened, and when the two of them looked out the window under the deck I quickly exhaled. 'Supposedly you guys have your own dictionary,' I said.

'Who told you that?' said Elliot.

'I heard at school.'

'*Kipihenni magayat,*' Clive said.

'Well, not yet, William,' said Elliot. He hummed a quick Jefferson Airplane lick. 'But we're getting there. We're writing one.' He handed me the bottle again, and I took a small toke into my mouth.

'A whole dictionary?'

'Yeah.'

'Who's we?' I said.

'Don't talk,' said Clive. 'Hold it in.'

Elliot looked at him again. 'It's up to us to educate them,' he said.

'Nothing's up to us,' said Clive.

That night, early in the bluest hour of morning, I woke and found Sandra sitting at the end of my bed. 'Easy, tiger,' she whispered.

'How long have you been here?'

She put her hand on the blankets over my ankle. 'Not long. I was watching you.'

'Was I snoring?'

'You sleep like an angel.'

'Clive says I snore.'

'Well, you don't.'

I lay back down. She hummed a few notes. 'William,' she whispered, 'have you told your parents about me?'

'No way.'

'Are you sure?'

'Positive.'

'Well, I think your mother knows. She looks at me like she does.'

'Sandra,' I said. 'There is no way in the world that my mother knows about you.'

She smiled in the moonlight. Then I heard her shoes drop on to my area rug, one then the other. 'I *told* you I was clairvoyant,' she said.

'About what?'

'About this. I knew this would happen.' I smiled, and suddenly she was lying next to me, on top of the blankets. She draped her arm over my chest. 'You're sweet,' she said, 'for not telling them.'

'Thanks.'

'You smell like your brother.'

'I do not.'

'Yes, you do.'

'Well, he learned it from me.'

She giggled, then we both went silent, and it took her a long time, lying there looking at the moonswept walls with me, listening, I think, to my breathing, before she turned her head abruptly and kissed me on the lips. Then she turned away again. 'Really—' she said. 'That was sweet.'

I thought for a while, then turned and kissed her back, harder, and in another few moments let my hand move to her shoulder. At certain moments I could not help thinking about how I would describe this to Billy DeSalz: *She smelled like oranges*, and *her lips were as soft as margarine*. Finally, she pulled away. 'Oh, don't,' she whispered, closing her eyes, 'Not yet, William. Don't ruin it.'

When she had gone, I rose and went into the bathroom. Sleep had deserted me. I brushed my teeth with Clive's Ultra Brite and smoothed a palmful of his LectricShave on to my cheeks. I turned on the hot water and ran his razor underneath it, then stroked through the cream on my face in smooth, decisive zags. The mirror steamed and I cleared a blotch in its center, where I tried to see myself in the way I must have looked to Sandra. 'Hello, sweetheart,' I said in a low voice, leaning forward into the regathering mist. 'My name is Ariel Sheshevsky.'

That day, I began looking for Clive's dictionary. I looked in his room, the basement and the back yard; I considered his character, then checked in unlikely places, like the middle of the bookshelves in the living-room and underneath the silverware rack in the kitchen drawer. Then I decided that perhaps it would be in an unlikely form and not in a unlikely place—inside a book of matches, say, or recorded on one of his tapes. I combed through his wallet. I poured out all the bottles of vitamins in our medicine cabinet. In his desk, I sifted through his roach clips, his lighters and cigarette cases, his guitar picks, his articles on home cultivation and Grow-Lites, and his smoke bottles and water-pipes made in shop class. From behind his bookshelf I retrieved his envelope of love poems from Sandra, which were all from Shakespeare, written out in her cramped hand. But there were no new ones, and I had read the old ones many times before. All I could find of his new language was a torn scrap of paper among the poems that said, in pencil, '*bar, baratsag, barki,*' and, on the other side, in calligraphy, '*We must teach them what they do not know.*'

On a Sunday morning in April, in Columbus, Clive won the Western Ohio finals and moved on to the State's. We ate leg of lamb that afternoon for lunch, his favorite, and afterwards our father went upstairs to practice brain-teasers with him. I washed and then dried the pans and finally went to the living-room to study geometry. When I could resist no longer, I went upstairs to join them.

They were sitting on his windowsill, the *Moscow Puzzles* open between them, and our father was gazing at something in the corner of the pane. I came in and cleared my throat.

'I was just looking at the moldings around the window here, William,' he said. He looked up. 'Have you ever noticed them? They are made of a number of intricate pieces.'

I looked. 'Congratulations, Clive,' I said. 'I dried the dishes for you.'

'Thanks, William.'

'Clive's taught me a few words,' our father said suddenly. '*Agglegeny,*' he said, and looked at him.

Clive nodded. '*Servoos,*' he said.

'*Allat*,' said our father. He looked out the window again. '*Bayosh, Birkahoosh, Diznaw*,' he recited, staring out the glass.

Clive winked at me. 'Little brother,' he whispered, 'the old man has just tried a doob.'

'I don't see what this marijuana's supposed to do, William,' said our father.

'You tried it, Dad?'

'Yes, I did, sailor.' He winked at Clive. 'Look out, Sheshevsky!' he said. Then he looked up from the window and shrugged his shoulders. I sometimes wish he had been a different man. 'Bombs away,' he said.

'Bongs,' said Clive.

Clive reached behind his leg, pulled out his water-pipe and handed it to me. He tamped down the bowl with the end of the lighter and pressed the flame to it as I sucked; I held the smoke in my cheeks, then pretended to draw it into my lungs. I held it in my mouth until I couldn't any more, then blew it out slowly and took another hit. Finally I walked over and stood next to the windowsill, where our father put his arm over my shoulder and stretched his foot across to Clive's shin. We looked at the moldings for a time, and then out the window, and our father tapped his fingers to Clive's riffs. 'Interesting,' our father finally said, 'you didn't inhale, William.'

'Sure I did.'

'He never has,' said Clive.

At dinner that night, our father opened another bottle of wine that Colonel Byzantian had sent us. In the letter that our father read aloud as he poured glassfuls for our mother and himself, the Colonel included the history of his grape vines, which needed the exact climate and soil found in only two regions of the world. 'That is why I have come here,' he wrote, 'for soil this color. Too many years on ships and you forget the taste of women and wine.' Instead of 'sincerely,' or 'love,' the letter ended with, 'In the earth we shall find the hidden source.' Our father repeated this phrase, draining his wine, then went to the cabinet and took down a glass for Clive.

'Well,' he said, after he had filled it and another for himself.

'Here's to the champion. And here's to the hidden sauce.'

'Source,' said our mother.

Our father winked at me, drained his glass again, repoured it and pretended to look back at the letter. 'I see that you're right, dear,' he said. 'Well,' he yawned, leaning back in his chair, 'my wife is right, and I only have one son left.'

Nobody said anything for a moment. Then our mother said, 'What is that supposed to mean, Simon?'

'Why, I don't know,' he answered, swishing the wine in his cheeks. 'It surprised *me*, too. It just came right out.' He swallowed the wine, smiled at Clive and me, then drank again. 'Too many years on ships, I guess.'

'You're drunk, Simon,' said our mother.

'Yes, I suppose I am,' he said.

But that evening after dinner his words returned to me. I was in the living-room puzzling through my geometry when I suddenly realized that Clive was the one he was talking about, not me. Clive was the one he considered his only son. I heard guitar scratchings from upstairs, the churn of the dishwasher in the kitchen and the broadcast of the Cleveland Symphony in our father's office. I had always assumed that something was wrong with my brother, something dangerous and perhaps shameful, and that my parents and I were allied to repair it, but now, for the first time, I thought of it another way: that I was the one they loved less; that Clive was aloof in order to escape their love, and that I was zealous in order to win it.

I was in the middle of a difficult problem about river current which I had read over and over. I turned to the hint section at the end of the book and glanced quickly at the schematic diagram of a raft in a river, then turned back again and did more figuring. Outside, the Ceref boy from down the street was kissing a girl under the streetlight; his hands moved down to her hips. Clive had shown me how to do this exact sort of problem a couple of weeks before; the knowledge of mathematics resided inside him like an instinct, the way it resided in our father, and I felt a quick sadness again in my chest. But I made it disappear. From upstairs I heard Clive's steps on the floor joists, then his window sliding open and the tap of his feet as he sat on the sill-seat and bumped them against the house. Down the block, the girl had walked away from the Ceref boy, who was now pretending to kiss the lightpole.

I went back and knocked on our father's office. 'It's me, captain,' I said.

He was leaning back at his desk, and when I walked in he lost his balance in the chair and nearly toppled. I steadied him with my hand and went to the corner of the room, where I looked out the window on to our deck. The radio was playing W-104 again.

'Yes, sailor?' he said.

'I thought that was cool, what you said the other day about grades.'

'I thought you might.'

In the dark window I watched his reflection as he puckered and unpuckered his lips behind me, then shook his head ponderously. I had the sense he was going to say something I wouldn't like. 'Dad,' I said quickly, 'what would you say if I got into trouble?'

'What kind of trouble?'

I paused. 'Big trouble.'

He narrowed his eyes and thought for a moment. 'You won't, sailor.'

'How do you know?'

He raised his eyebrows. 'How do I know? I just do.' He stood and came up next to me at the window. 'Character is fate,' he said, looking out into the yard. 'Heraclitus said that, two thousand years ago.'

'What if I changed my character?'

He laughed. 'You won't,' he said. 'That's the point.'

The DJ announced the hour and put on 'Freebird', and our father and I stood looking out the window into the garden. The night was moonless. In the light from the Cubano's house, we watched a racoon from their yard appear atop our back fence, scrape for its balance, then scamper down on to our grass. It ambled across to the bin that held our garbage cans. 'Hmmm,' said our father, 'expensive taste—it likes anchovies.'

'Thank you, Ohio Mutual.'

He tousled my hair, and I felt better. The racoon reached its paws up to the latch, knocked it back and forth, then gave up and climbed back over into the Cubano's yard. The song ended and our father switched off the radio. 'All these creatures,' he said, 'going about their business.'

'What a noble creature is man.'

He smiled. Garbage cans suddenly clattered on to the Cubano's patio, floodlights came on and the racoon bolted down their driveway. In a moment Mrs Cubano came outside in her bathrobe, and our father swiftly turned off the light. 'Shhh,' he whispered.

We stood there. Across the way, she was picking up the trash and dropping it back into the can. Her breath clouded the air, and she pulled her robe tighter around her shoulders. Then she sat down on the deck rail and lit a cigarette. She smoked it gazing up into the sky, and after a few moments looked around, shook her hair out so that it fell down her back, then put her hand on the belt of her robe.

'Pull,' I whispered.

Our father smiled at me. 'Don't move, sailor,' he said. 'We could lose all reconnaissance.'

She looked across at our house.

'Stealth is utmost, captain.'

We watched, still as trees. After a time, she stood, tightened her robe, threw her cigarette butt into our yard and walked back into the house.

'Oh, well,' said our father.

'She forgot to latch the bin, Dad.'

'Elementary, my dear Watson.'

He turned on the radio again. 'Freebird' was still playing. 'You know, captain,' I said, 'Clive wouldn't have been interested in that.'

'In what?'

'In what we just saw.'

He rubbed my head. 'He's not a sailor,' he said.

'That's it,' I said. Across the way, the light in the Cubano's kitchen came on. 'Dad,' I said, 'What were *you* like in high school?'

'What was *I* like?'

'Were you a screw-off? Did you care about your grades?'

'We were at war in those days, William.' He went to his desk, took out his key ring, tossed it in the air and caught it. 'In geometry,' he said, 'we learned bomb trajectories. Yes, I cared about my grades, William. Then I went to war.'

'You can be smart without being smart,' I said.

He nodded at me.

'Clive, William,' called our mother. 'Dessert! We're having pie.'

I turned to the door, but he didn't move. He dialled the classical music station again, then looked back out the window. The racoon had appeared again at the end of the Cubano's driveway. 'You're a sailor,' he said. 'With you, we've got nothing to worry about.'

The music welled and the racoon climbed back up on to their porch. 'Do you recognize the composer?' he asked.

'Beethoven?' I said. 'No, wait a minute. Haydn?'

'No, Albinoni. Listen to this. Listen to the passion of the cellos.' He turned it up, and when the strings came to a crescendo his eyes closed.

'Dad,' I said, 'I've been stealing things.'

He opened his eyes again. 'Oh,' he said. 'I think I understand.' He gestured out the window. 'See that deck, William?'

'Yes.'

'That deck cost me sixteen-hundred dollars.'

'I know that, commander.'

'Well, how do you think I earned that money?'

I pointed at his insurance file. 'That,' I said.

He looked serious. 'Well, then, you must also know that what I said to you about grades was incorrect. Your grades are about as important as anything gets.' He shook his head again. 'Grades are all an employer has to judge you by. You know that, William, don't you? That what's right is right? That it's the squeaky wheel that gets the grease? You know, don't you, that these crazy times are going to pass?'

That week, spring arrived, and on Sunday Clive invited me to swim with him at the stone quarry. He, Sandra, Elliot and I snuck underneath the chain-link fence and followed the steep path down to the water, which was filled with rock powder that the wind had churned into an unearthly, opal green. Boulders lay along the shallows and the shore. Clive, Elliot and I stripped to the waist and lay down on them, and Sandra pulled off her T-shirt and stretched out in her white bikini on the one between Clive and me. Elliot unpacked four squares of carrot cake and passed them around. I ate mine and lay back down.

Clive held his up and examined it in the sun. 'Elliot baked them,' he said.

I nodded at Elliot with my eyebrows raised to show respect. 'It was good,' I said.

'*Kituno gomba*,' said Clive.

'*Saipen*,' said Elliot.

I nodded again and smiled. I scanned the surface for fish ripples, though it seemed certain nothing could live in these waters. I tossed in a stone. 'Thanks for inviting me, you guys.'

'No problem, little brother.'

I lay back down. After a few minutes Clive came over to me and looked at my face. '*Servoos*,' he said. He smiled. 'It's a greeting.' He laid his hand on my shoulder. '*Servoos*,' he said again.

'*Servoos*.'

'How do you feel, little brother?'

'Great.'

'You found our dictionary, didn't you?'

'Nope. I didn't even look for it.'

'I told you,' Elliot said.

Clive studied me. '*Djerunk*,' he said. He studied me again.

Elliot glanced at him. 'Hey,' he said. 'We're going swimming.'

'Skinny-dipping,' said Clive. Then he pointed at Sandra, who was sleeping. He leaned up close to me. 'You must have tired her out,' he whispered.

Elliot grinned. 'The monster eats a lot,' he said.

Then they stripped off their clothes, and by the time I had stood up they were both up to their chests in milky green water, splashing on the rock shelf a few feet from shore and jumping off the submerged boulders into the deep. I sat there watching them, when suddenly a haze dropped over me like a blanket. For a while I carried on watching, then I lay back on the rock again. I glanced out over the water: they were paying no attention. Next to me, Sandra was snoring. 'Sleeping beauty,' I whispered in a high voice; then, in a deeper one, I said, '*Servoos*.' But she didn't stir. I looked up at the sky, and thoughts of her began to drift over me. I could not shake them—the way she had blown smoke rings in her hideout, the way, in my bed, her hand had rested right above my heart. I turned to watch Clive and Elliot. Out in the deep, they had begun wrestling, pulling each other down into the water and twisting to regain the surface. They separated and then both submerged, while I watched from the shore for their forms in the choppy green. They did not reappear. I sat up, and finally, near the ledge, Elliot surfaced. In a moment, Clive did too, shaking his head like a dog and spitting out a rainbow. I saw the colors of it clearly, the indigo and violet fanning out from his whirling head, hanging in the air. They splashed at each other, and again I saw little jewels of color in their wake. Then these disappeared. They went under once more. I stared out as the surface grew stiller, and then calm, and then glassy, and then they erupted in the center again.

They emerged and stood on the shore. I pretended to be asleep, and when I felt shade on my face, I opened my eyes and found Clive standing over me. '*Servoos*,' he said.

'*Servoos*.'

'How do you feel, little brother?'

'Great.'

He looked down at me, his cheeks streaked with quarry sediment. 'I told you, *bayosh*,' he said, turning to Elliot. 'You baked them too long.'

They dried themselves with their shirts, whispering a few words in their language while I listened with my eyes closed. Sandra slept, waking now and then to turn herself over. I heard Clive and Elliot wringing out their hair and lying down on the rocks, and then the small, steady splash of pebbles being tossed into the water and Clive humming a Clapton lick between throws. Lethargy welled over me. Just before I slept, I was aware of all the smallest sounds of the quarry—the tiny chime of lapping waves, my brother's humming, the occasional groan of rock shifting in the heat and the plink of pebbles in the water. Sandra snored, just slightly. When I woke, the sun was gone.

Clive and Elliot and Sandra were gone also. I stood and rubbed my eyes and looked out over the water, which had turned dark and was ruffled by wind. Gusts darted across like flocks of birds. I sauntered to the edge and looked around. They had taken their clothes with them, too; disappointment chilled me. I tossed rocks into the water, one by one, gazing at the choppy, grey shallows as they began to go black

'The genius in thought,' Sandra said behind me. I turned around and she was standing in her T-shirt and bikini bottom, smiling. 'I was walking,' she said, 'but they're gone.'

'Where to?'

'Good question.' She stepped closer and I saw that her T-shirt was wet through. 'I waited for you,' she said.

'I guess you did.'

She climbed on to a flat slab of rock and patted the spot next to her. I sat. 'Tell me something,' she said. 'What are you going to think of me in ten years?'

'In ten years?' I said. 'In 1983?'

'Shhh,' she said.

This time her hands moved to my hips, then one of them was on my belt, then my zipper, and I became aware of a line I had never crossed, then crossed it. I tried to remember everything so I could tell Billy DeSalz. I was also trying to work her bikini bottom down over her legs without drawing attention to it, when she stopped, kissed me, and, just like that, pulled off her T-shirt and top. Her breasts bounced in the pale light and I leaned up and kissed them. *They were like cool melons.* She shook the bikini bottom the rest of the way down her legs, kicking it off finally so that it flew into the air and landed on the gravel shore next to us. I moved my hands to her belly. *Her skin was like cream.* I pulled off my own shirt, stood and removed my trunks, and when she lay down again I shrugged, looked quickly at her so that I would be able to describe the sight and then lay down alongside.

That weekend, in Columbus, Clive faced Ariel Sheshevsky for the state championship. Ariel was a slight, long-haired boy, with a leather headband in his hair and a derisive look on his features, and as soon as I saw him I knew he would be trouble. He looked like Clive. Both of them answered every question correctly, and although the Lieutenant Governor of Ohio laughed about this as he stood on stage at the end, holding the bronze plaque that my brother and Ariel would have to somehow split, our mother wept openly. In a moment, Mrs Cubano did too, and then, next to me, Sandra started as well, her tears cutting trails through the tiny flecks of glitter on her cheeks.

'It's only a math prize,' I said.

It was those tears I recalled that same night as I stood in the kitchen with our mother. She was mixing batter for victory cookies. 'Sandra's living in the basement,' I said.

She stopped mixing. 'Boys will be boys,' she said.

I moved in front of her. 'I mean, she's been living there all year. She doesn't go home. Her parents don't know where she is. They don't care. She lives behind the furnace.'

'Poor girl.'

'She lives behind *our* furnace.'

She dipped the spoon in the bowl, twirled it and handed it to me coated with batter. 'Sweetheart,' she said, 'don't you think I know about Sandra?'

'You know about her?'

'Of course. I'm no dummy, despite what your father thinks. Besides, I think it's kind of romantic.'

'Dad knows too?'

'No, he doesn't. And I don't think you should tell him, either.'

I sat down, and she went back to mixing. 'I want to ask you something,' she said finally. She didn't look up from the bowl. 'She's his girlfriend, right?'

'Clive's?'

'Yes.'

'You mean, are they *exclusive* or something?'

'Yes, that's what I mean. Are they boyfriend and girlfriend?'

'Well, I don't know. I guess so.' Then I said, 'Yes.'

'That's what I thought. It's fine with me if she wants to live in our house.'

That evening, in our basement, as I stood with the ping-pong paddle in my hand across from our father, it suddenly occurred to me that Sandra's attentions had been meant for nothing more than to insure her secrecy. I don't think so now—I know it's more complicated—but that night, standing alongside the cheerful green table, I did. 'Service,' I said.

Our father mis-hit the return and it sailed in high towards my forehand, where I leaned forward and hit the slam. I hit it too long and it missed the table, bounced once on the concrete floor and skipped through the crack by the Philco refrigerator box into her hideout. Our father put down his paddle and went after it.

If the spring of 1973 had taken place ten years later, I sometimes think, we might still have been at peace today, as we were then. Over the years, my brother became a college physics professor and a dean of students, and I became a reporter and now, recently, an editor, at the *Boston Globe*. A year ago, vacationing at the shore in New Jersey, I came upon two middle-aged women on the boardwalk, dark-eyed and thick-featured, and as I passed by I heard one say to the other, '*Servoos!*' When I stopped, they asked me if I, too, was Hungarian, and the shock was so great that they must have assumed, from the tears in my eyes, that I was.

But by then it was too late. I would never be able to laugh with Clive about his secret. As adults, we had become tender and comradely with each other, like soldiers wounded in the same battle, and we finally grew to talk to each other in almost the way I had hoped we would. We lived in different cities, but whenever we saw each other there was an ease between us that I felt with no one else in the world; and at Thanksgiving and Passover when we embraced at my door, I would hold him close and breathe in his particular smell—a smell I have since, as Sandra said, noticed on the collars of my own shirts—and while my wife moved to the door to greet his lover (a word I have learned to use) he would whisper '*Servoos!*' into my ear. Although even then it was still, amazingly, the only word of his I knew, I always whispered it back.

Things were changing so fast in 1973 that I admire my parents for trying to keep up. They were well-meaning people who were accepting what they could, one arena at a time, and I think it was a difficult period for them, especially for our father. What he found when he pulled back the Philco box in search of the ping-pong ball was my brother and Elliot, lying on the folded blankets that were Sandra's bed, their pants around their ankles, their penises standing up amid their jumbled legs. For a moment nobody moved. Then they began struggling with their pants. but suddenly Clive calmed, and presently Elliot did too, both of them straightening their backs and composing their expressions until they sat upright before us, placed and still, the way monks sat as they froze to death.

'*Batorsag*,' my brother said.

'*Szerelem*,' said Elliot.

Our father's arm flashed, and Clive flew back from the impact of the blow, hitting the wall with the loose wings of his shoulders and then crumpling. Elliot hugged his knees. Clive shook his head and let his mouth fall open, and then he turned to me standing behind our father with the ping-pong paddle in my hands. Flecks of blood streaked his tongue. Our father held his right hand in his left. Upstairs, our mother said, 'Clive, William, dinner! We're having macaroni!'

Then our father moved quickly to his knees, and though nobody in our family had ever prayed before, so far as I knew, that was what he did, he prayed, leaning forward and clasping his hands together in the hollow of his neck, his eyes closed, on his knees on the rolled blankets; and then my brother, the genius, the dope-smoker, the disguiser of languages, my brother the faggot leaned forward too, but he did not put his hands together. He merely lowered his head, and then Elliot did the same, and I knew from their nodding that they were weeping. I recognized with something like the profundity of religion that this was a sea change in our family and the great unturning of my brother's life, and though I moved to my knees as well and put down the paddle I felt no tears. All I could think was that now was the beginning of my own ascendance. For so long, I had known something was going to happen to my brother, and finally it had. The inevitability of it had always been a half-hidden secret to me, a fact that persisted just beyond where I could give it voice. Now at last, as I bowed my head, I recognized it, deep in my own character, as the fleeting ghostly shape of a wish; and for this, fifteen years later, in a stifling room at Columbia-Presbyterian Hospital in Manhattan, where the doctors told me I had better come on a late-night flight to say goodbye to my brother, I wept and wept and wept.

GRANTA

NICK HORNBY
FOURTEEN AND AFTER

Alison Ashworth (Aged Fourteen)

My friends and I used to mess about in a park just round the corner from where I lived. We were fourteen and had recently discovered irony—or at least, we had what I later understood to be an ironic attitude to the swings and roundabouts and other stuff rusting away there. We used them, but self-consciously, in the full knowledge that they were amusements for kids, not teenagers: we would jump off the swings when they could go no higher, leap on to the roundabout when it would spin no faster, hang on to the end of the swingboat as it reached an almost vertical position. If we could expose the potential to injure in these apparently innocuous machines, then playing on them became legitimate.

We had no irony when it came to girls, however. There had been no time to develop it. One moment they weren't there—not in any form that interested us, at any rate—and the next they were. One minute we wanted to clunk them round the ear for being so stupid, the next . . . well, we didn't know what we wanted.

What did *we* have that we didn't have before? Squeaky, two-pitched voices. But they served only to make us preposterous, not desirable. Our testicles had dropped, apparently, and some pubic hairs had sprouted (not that we were in the position to show these off).

Girls, on the other hand, quite clearly had breasts.

None of us had seen them, not without their protective layers of bra and school blouse, but they were obviously there, and to accompany them, there was a new way of walking: arms folded over the chest, a posture apparently intended both to disguise and accentuate what had recently happened. There was also make-up, inexpertly, sometimes even comically, applied, but nonetheless a terrifying sign that things had progressed without us, behind our backs.

Then one night, David Ashworth's sister Alison peeled off from the female pack that gathered by the park bench, smoking and laughing in the autumn dusk, tucked me under her arm and walked off with me.

I can't remember now how this kidnap was effected. I don't

Photo: Ian Berry (Magnum)

203

think I knew at the time, because I was aware, halfway through our first kiss, my first kiss, of an utter bewilderment, a total inability to explain how Alison Ashworth and I had become so intimate. I am not sure how I ended up on her side of the park, away from her brother and Mark Godfrey and the rest, or how we separated from her crowd, or why she tipped her face towards me in such a way that I knew I was supposed to put my mouth on hers. But all of these things happened, and the following evening, they happened again.

When I want to kiss people in that way now, it is because I want other things too: bed, company and conversation, Friday nights at the cinema, Lemsips brought to me in bed when I am ill, a little boy called Tom or Jack and a little girl called Holly, maybe— or Maisie; I haven't decided yet. But I didn't want any of those things from Alison Ashworth, not even sex, especially not sex. What was I doing? What was the significance of the snog in 1972?

The truth is, no significance. Two nights later I turned up, and Alison was sitting on the bench with her arm around Kevin Bannister. Nobody—not Alison, or Kevin, or me, or the sexually uninitiated retards hanging off the end of the swingboat—said a thing. I was stung. I blushed and I prickled. I suddenly forgot how to walk without being aware of every single part of my body.

Our relationship had lasted only four hours (the two-hour gap between school and *Nationwide*, times two); I could hardly claim that I had got used to having her around. But the humiliation was almost intolerable.

It was brought on, in part, by my teenage vanity. The year before, I had been told that I needed glasses but refused to wear them and so noticed Alison and Kevin being intimate and exclusive only when I was nearly on top of them. I stopped, looked at my watch, turned around and headed back towards the bachelors, my prominent and still exposed ears (a year later one would have had to delve around inside a poor imitation of a Rod Stewart haircut to find them) burning like a beacon. It was a symbolic, interminable and unbearably lonely walk, watched with great interest by those in both camps. I concentrated on the empty packets of Number Six that marked out the path between the boys and the girls.

Even now, I wish that I hadn't looked at my watch. I worry

that I will meet somebody who was in the park that night, somebody who, two decades later, will point out that the glance at the wrist fooled nobody. What sort of time could make a fourteen-year-old boy spin away from a girl and towards a roundabout, palms sweating, heart racing, trying desperately not to cry? Certainly not five forty-five on a late September Wednesday night.

I would like to think that as I have got older times have changed, relationships have become more sophisticated, females less cruel, skins thicker, reactions sharper, instincts more developed. But there is an element of that evening in everything that has happened to me romantically since. I have never had to take that long walk again, and my ears have not burnt with quite the same fury, and I have never had to count the Number Six packets in order to avoid mocking eyes, not as such, not literally.

Penny Hardwick (Aged Fifteen)

Penny Hardwick was a nice girl. She had a nice mum and dad, and a nice house, and a nice younger sister, and she wouldn't let me put my hand underneath or even on top of her bra, and I finished with her without telling her why. She cried, and I hated her for it.

I can't tell you what sort of person Penny was. (I can, however, tell you what sort of person Penny Hardwick became: a good person. She went to college, did well and became a radio producer for the BBC; she is bright, and naturally funny in a way that is often beyond many people of her education and class and, frankly speaking, sex; she is, or was, when I used to see her for a while in the early eighties, prone to an engaging and attractive self-doubt. I guess she was a version of all those things when we went out, but the signs were beyond me.) Penny was pretty. She went to the High School. She read a lot. Lots of people liked her. Her top five recording artistes were Carly Simon, Carole King, James Taylor, Cat Stevens and Elton John. But that was all I knew, because I don't think we ever talked. We went to the pictures, parties and discos. And we wrestled.

When I was fifteen, these were the questions boys asked other

205

boys: 'Are you getting any?' 'Does she let you have any?' 'How much does she let you have?'

Sometimes the questions were derisive: 'You're not getting anything, are you?' 'You haven't even had a bit of tit, have you?'

Girls, meanwhile, had to be content with the passive voice. Penny used the expression 'broken into': 'I don't want to be broken into yet,' she would explain patiently and maybe a little sadly (she seemed to understand that one day—but not yet—she would have to give in), when she removed my hand from her chest for the one hundred thousandth time. Attack and defence, invasion and repulsion . . . It was as if breasts were little pieces of property that had been unlawfully annexed by the opposite sex; they were rightfully ours, and we wanted them back.

In any woman's magazine, you'll see the same complaint: men, those little boys (ten or twenty or thirty years on), are hopeless in bed. They are not interested in 'foreplay'; they have no desire to stimulate the erogenous zones of the opposite sex; they are selfish, greedy, clumsy, unsophisticated. The complaints, you can't help feeling, are ironic. Back then, all we wanted was foreplay, and girls weren't interested. They didn't want to be touched, caressed, stimulated, aroused; in fact, they used to thump us if we tried. Is it surprising, then, that we're not much good? We spent two or three long and extremely formative years being told not to bother. Between the ages of fourteen and twenty-four, foreplay changes from being something that boys want to do and girls don't, to something that women want and men can't be bothered with. The perfect match, it would appear, is between the *Cosmo* woman and the fourteen-year-old boy.

If somebody had asked me *why* I was so hell-bent on grabbing a piece of Penny Hardwick's chest, I wouldn't have known what to say. What was in it for me? I wasn't asking for any sort of reciprocation. Why didn't she want her erogenous zones stimulated?

In any case, after a couple of months of fighting on the sofa with Penny, I'd had enough: I had admitted, unwisely, to a friend that I wasn't getting anywhere, and my friend had told some other friends and I was the butt of a number of unpleasant jokes (I was told I wasn't doing my duty). The word was out. I had to give Penny one last try, in my bedroom while my mum and dad were at

the Town Hall watching a local dramatic society interpretation of
Toad of Toad Hall. I used a degree of force that would have
outraged and terrified an adult female, but got nowhere, and when
I walked her home we hardly spoke.

I was offhand the next time we went out, and when Penny
went to kiss me at the end of the evening I shrugged her off.
'What's the point?' I asked her. 'It never goes anywhere.' The time
after that, she asked whether I still wanted to see her, and I looked
the other way. We had been going out for three months, which was
as near to a permanent relationship as you could get in the fourth
year (her mum and dad had even met my mum and dad). She cried,
then, and I loathed her for making me feel guilty.

I went out with a girl called Kim, who I knew for a fact had
already been invaded, and who (I was correct in assuming)
wouldn't object to being invaded again. Penny went out with Chris
Thomson from my class, a boy who had had more girlfriends than
all the rest of us put together. I was out of my depth, and so was
she. One morning, maybe three weeks after my last grapple with
Penny, Thomson came roaring into our form room. 'Oi, you
spastic. Guess who I knobbed last night?'

I felt the room spin.

'You never got so much as a bit of tit in three months, and I
shagged her first week!'

I felt stupid, and small, and much, much younger than this
unpleasant, oversized, big-mouthed moron. I couldn't understand
what had happened. How had Penny gone from being a girl who
wouldn't do anything to a girl who would do everything there was
to do? It was best not to think about it too hard; I didn't want to
feel sorry for anybody else except me.

Penny became a good person (it's easier for girls to become
good, of course); I suspect that even Chris Thomson turned out all
right. It is hard to imagine him skidding into his place of work, his
bank or his insurance office or car showroom, chucking his
briefcase down and informing a colleague with raucous glee that he
has 'knobbed' said colleague's wife.

Jackie O'Neill (Aged Seventeen)

Jackie O'Neill was my friend Phil's girlfriend, and I pinched her: slowly, patiently, over a period of months. Jackie and Phil had started going out around the same time as Penny and I, except they went on and on: through the giggly, hormonal fourth form, and the end-of-the-world 'O'-level and school-leaving fifth, and on into the mock-adult sobriety of the lower sixth. They were our golden couple, our Paul and Linda McCartney, our Paul Newman and Joanne Woodward, living proof that in a faithless, fickle world it was possible to grow old, or at least older, without chopping and changing every few weeks.

I'm not sure why I wanted to mess it all up. I suspect I had hoped that Jackie would confer some of her air of romantic permanence on me, but of course she needed Phil for that. (Perhaps I should have looked for a way to go out with both of them, but that sort of thing is hard enough to pull off when you're an adult; at seventeen, it could be enough to get you stoned to death.)

I liked her, of course; but what I liked most of all was the doom that attached itself to our relationship. For the first time I became aware that this business could be more than just fun. It could be thrillingly miserable, a way of tapping into grown-up angst that otherwise might take years to access. Going out with Jackie felt good because it felt bad.

At age seventeen, you can, I reckon, fuck up just about anyone's relationship, if you give yourself enough time. In the first month or so you've got no chance, but once things have settled down, all you have to do is ask questions and be very sympathetic. Jackie, I found out, was frightened by the way the Jackie-and-Phil train seemed to be heading unstoppably for a silver wedding party on a disco boat on the Thames; she was depressed by the way people of her own age seemed to regard her as some sort of matriarch (she didn't put it like that, but she mentioned the Queen Mother) just because she had only had one serious boyfriend; she was worried that Phil didn't want to go to college, and that he was already beginning to wonder aloud whether Jackie really wanted to study away from home.

I nurtured each doubt and complaint as if it were an ailing kitten; eventually they turned into sturdy, healthy grievances, with their own cat-flaps which allowed them to wander in and out of our conversations at will. And then we started to talk about what it would be like if we went out together.

You think this is childish? I have been the pointy bit of a triangle several times since then, but that first time was the sharpest—much more distressing than the affair with the married woman I had in the mid-eighties (which damaged nothing and nobody, apart from our eternal souls and her pig of a husband). Phil never really spoke to me again; our Saturday shopping crowd wouldn't have much to do with us either. My mum had a phone call from Phil's mum. School was, for a few weeks, uncomfortable.

Compare and contrast with what happens if I make that sort of mess now: I can frequent different pubs and clubs, change my phone number, go out more, stay in more, fiddle around with my social compasses and draw a new circle of friends (and anyway, my friends would never be her friends, whoever the 'she' might be), avoid all contact with disapproving parents. That sort of anonymity was unavailable then, though. You had to stand there and take it, whatever it was.

What perplexed me most of all was the feeling of flat disappointment that overtook me when Jackie called me . . . I had been plotting this capture for months, but when capitulation finally came, I felt nothing—less than nothing, even. I couldn't tell Jackie this, obviously, but on the other hand I was quite unable to show the enthusiasm I felt she needed. So I decided to have her name tattooed down my right arm.

Scarring myself for life seemed much easier than having to tell Jackie that it had all been a grotesque mistake, that I had just been messing about; if I could show her the tattoo, my peculiar logic ran, I wouldn't have to bother straining after words that were beyond me. I should explain that I'm not a tattoo kind of guy: I am, and was, neither rock'n'roll go-to-hell decadent or lager-squaddy muscular. But there was a disastrous fashion for tattoos at our school, and I know several men in their mid-thirties—accountants and schoolteachers, personnel managers and computer programmers—with shaming messages from that era burned into their flesh. I am sure that Guy Smith regrets the 'Lindsay' just below his right shoulder, and that Steve Reed occasionally fingers his 'MUFC' thoughtfully in the mornings, redeemed only by the fact that MUFC are still around while Lindsay is almost certainly not.

I was just going to have a discreet 'J heart R' done on my upper arm, but Victor the tattooist wasn't convinced.

'Which one is she? *J* or *R*?'

'*J.*'

'And how long have you been seeing this *J* bird, then?'

I was frightened by the aggressive masculinity of the parlour— the other customers (who were all firmly in the lager-squaddy muscular team and seemed inexplicably amused to see me), the nude women on the walls, the lurid examples of services offered, most of which were conveniently located on Victor's forearms.

'Long enough.'

'I'll fucking be the judge of that, not you.'

This struck me as an odd way to do business, but I answered anyway: 'A couple of weeks.'

'And you're going to marry her, are you? Or have you knocked her up?'

'No.'

'So you're just going out? You're not lumbered with her?'

'Yeah.'

'How did you meet her?'

'She used to go out with a friend of mine.'

'Did she now? And when did they break up?'

'Saturday.'

'Saturday.' He laughed like a drain. 'I don't want your mum in here moaning at me. Fuck off.'

I fucked off.

Jackie and I only lasted a few weeks, and then she and Phil got back together. Victor was spot on. But things didn't go back to the way they were. Some of the boys at our school, and some of the girls at hers, thought Jackie was a cow for using me to renegotiate her agreement with Phil. And then, for some reason, we no longer admired people who had gone out together for a long time: we were sarky about them, and they were even sarky about themselves. In a few short weeks, mock-marital status had ceased to be something to aspire to, and had become a cause for scorn. At seventeen, we had become as embittered and unromantic as our parents.

Sally Doyle (Aged Twenty-one)

When I first saw Sally, I suddenly realized that she was the sort of girl I had wanted to meet ever since I had been old enough to want to meet girls. She was tall, with short, cropped hair (she said she knew some people who were at St Martin's with friends of Johnny Rotten), and looked different and dramatic and exotic; she talked a lot, so that you didn't have those terrible strained silences which seemed to characterize most of my sixth-form dates; and when she talked, she said remarkably interesting things—about her course, about music, about films (I was doing a Media Studies course, but she knew far more about all that sort of thing than I did).

And she liked me. She liked *me*. *She* liked *me*. *She liked me.* I wasn't entirely sure what there was to like, but I wasn't about to go into that too deeply; what I did know was that by moving towns (I was now in London) I had made it easier to be liked by girls. At home, girls already knew me, or my mum and dad, or my sister—or knew somebody who knew me, or my mum and dad, or my sister. I always felt that my boyhood was about to be exposed. How could you take a girl out for an underage drink in a pub when you knew you had a scout uniform still hanging in your closet? Why would a girl want to kiss you if she knew (or knew somebody who knew) that just a few years before you had insisted on sewing souvenir patches from the Norfolk Broads and Exmoor on your anorak? There were pictures all over the house of me with big ears and uncool clothes, sitting on tractors, clapping with glee as miniature choo-choo trains drew into stations; and though later on, distressingly, girlfriends found these pictures cute, it all seemed too close for comfort then. When I was sixteen, that anorak with the patches on was only a couple of sizes too small.

Sally had only ever known me as a young adult, however. I was old enough to vote; I was old enough to spend the night with her, the whole night, in her hall of residence (I was in digs with an old lady), and have opinions, and buy her a drink in a pub secure in the knowledge that my driving licence with its proof of age was in my pocket . . . and I was old enough to have a *history.*

I still felt a fraud. I was like all those people who suddenly shaved their heads and said they'd *always* been punks, they'd been punks before punk was even thought of: I felt as though I was going to be found out at any moment, that somebody was going to burst into the college bar brandishing one of the anorak photos and yelling, 'You used to be a *boy!* A *little lad!*' and Sally would see it and pack me in. It never occurred to me that she probably had a pile of old pony books and some ridiculous party dresses at her mum's house in St Albans. As far as I was concerned, she had been born with enormous ear-rings, drainpipe jeans and an inexplicable enthusiasm for the works of Mark Rothko.

We went out for two years, and for every single minute I felt as though I was standing on a dangerously narrow ledge. I couldn't ever get comfortable. I was depressed by the lack of flamboyance in my wardrobe; was fretful about my abilities as a lover; I worried that I would never ever say anything interesting or amusing to her about any subject; I was intimidated by the other men on her design course, and became convinced that she was going to go off with one of them. She went off with one of them.

I lost the plot for a while. And I lost the sub-plot, the script, the soundtrack, the intermission, my popcorn, the credits and the Exit sign. I hung around Sally's flat until some friends of hers caught me and threatened to give me a good kicking. I decided to kill Marco (Marco, fucking hell), the guy she went off with, and spent long hours in the middle of the night working out how to do it. I did a spot of shoplifting. I took an overdose of Valium, and then stuck a finger down my throat. I wrote endless letters to her, some of which I posted, and constructed endless conversations, none of which we had. And when I came round, after a couple of months of darkness, I had jacked in my course and was working at the Record and Tape Exchange.

I had always hoped that my adulthood would be long and meaty and instructive, but it all happened in two years. Some people never get over the sixties, or a war, or the night their band supported Dr Feelgood at the Hope and Anchor (*'And* we blew them off the stage'), and spend the rest of their days walking backwards. I never really got over Sally. That was my time. That was when the important stuff, the stuff that defines me, went on.

What came first, the music or the misery? Did I listen to music because I was miserable? Or was I miserable because I listened to music? Do all those records turn you into a melancholy person? Some of my favourite songs: 'Only Love Can Break Your Heart' by Neil Young: 'Last Night I Dreamed Somebody Loved Me' by the Smiths; 'Call Me' by Aretha Franklin; 'I Don't Want To Talk About It' by anybody. And then there's 'Love Hurts' and 'When Love Breaks Down' and 'How Can You Mend A Broken Heart' and 'The Speed of the Sound of Loneliness' and 'She's Gone' and . . . some of these songs I have listened to about once a week, on average (three hundred times in the first month or so, every now and again thereafter), since I was sixteen or nineteen or twenty-one. How can that not leave you bruised somewhere, how can that not turn you into the sort of person liable to break into little bits when your first love goes all wrong?

People worry about kids playing with guns, and teenagers watching violent videos; we are scared that some sort of culture of violence will take them over. Nobody worries about kids listening to thousands of songs about broken hearts and rejection and pain and misery and loss. The unhappiest people I know are the ones who like pop music the most; and I don't know whether pop music has caused this unhappiness, but I do know that they have been listening to the sad songs longer than they've been living the unhappy lives. Conclude what you will.

Everyone has a Sally lurking around in their psyche, whatever they say now. It is not right to say that they do you no harm. Of *course* they do you harm. That is the whole point of them. At twenty-one, I could not see how it was possible to recover; I'd found the person I wanted to spend my life with, lost her through no fault of my own and now had to spend the rest of my life, fifty or sixty or seventy years, without her. How could you not hate someone for doing that to you?

Eventually, I stopped posting the letters; a few months after that, I stopped writing them, too. I still fantasized about killing Marco, although the imagined deaths became swifter (I allow him

213

a brief moment to register, and then BLAM!). I started sleeping with people again, although every one of these affairs I regarded as a fluke, a one-off, nothing likely to alter my dismal self-perception (and, like James Stewart in *Vertigo*, I had developed a 'type': cropped blonde hair, arty, dizzy, garrulous, which led to some disastrous mistakes). I stopped drinking so much; I stopped listening to song lyrics with quite the same morbid fascination (for a while, I regarded just about any song in which somebody had lost somebody else as spookily relevant, which meant I felt pretty spooked more or less the whole time). I stopped constructing the killer one-liners that left Sally writhing on the floor with regret and self-loathing.

I made sure, however, that I was never in anything, work or relationships, too deep: I convinced myself that I might get the call from Sally at any moment and have to leap into action. Marriage, mortgages and fatherhood were out of the question, just in case I got the call from Sally and then wasn't able to move quickly enough. And each devastating piece of information relayed to me by people who still knew her (She's living with Marco! They've bought a place together! She's married him! She's pregnant! She's had a little girl!) required a whole series of readjustments and conversions to keep this pathetic fallacy alive. (She'll have nowhere to go when they split! She'll really have nowhere to go when they split, and I'll have to support her financially! Marriage'll wake her up! Taking on another man's kid will show her what a great guy I am!) There was no news I couldn't handle; there was nothing she and Marco could do that would convince me that it wasn't all just a stage we were going through.

They are together still, as far as I know.

Sarah Quinn (Aged Twenty-six)

Sally was out of my class: too pretty, too smart, too witty, too much. What am I? Average. A middleweight. Not the brightest bloke in the world, but certainly not the dimmest: I have read books like *The Unbearable Lightness of Being* and *Love in the Time of Cholera* and understood them, I think—they were about girls, right? (The five greatest books ever written: *Catch-22* by Joseph Heller, *Breakfast of Champions* by Kurt Vonnegut, *Sweet Soul Music* by Peter Guralnick, *Red Dragon* by Thomas Harris, and, I suppose, *Catcher in the Rye*); I take the *Guardian* and the *Observer*, as well as the *NME* and the music glossies. I am not averse to going down to Camden to watch subtitled films (top five subtitled films: *Betty Blue, Subway, Tie Me Up! Tie Me Down!, The Vanishing, Diva*), although on the whole I am happier with an intelligent mainstream Hollywood effort (top five intelligent mainstream Hollywood efforts, and therefore the five greatest films ever made: *The Godfather, The Godfather 2, Taxi Driver, Annie Hall, Raging Bull*).

I'm not the best-looking bloke in the world, but not the ugliest, not compared with, say, Berky Edmonds, a kid from school, who had one eye about seven times the size of the other and terrifying acne scars. I'm average height, not slim, not fat, no unsightly facial hair. I keep myself clean, wear jeans and T-shirts and a leather jacket more or less all the time apart from in the summer, when I leave the leather jacket at home. I vote Labour. I can see what feminists are on about, most of the time, but not the radical ones.

My genius, if I can call it that, is to combine a whole load of averageness into one compact frame. I'd say that there were millions like me, but there aren't: lots of blokes have impeccable music taste but don't read; lots of blokes read but are really fat; lots of blokes are sympathetic to feminism but have stupid beards; lots of blokes have the Woody Allen sense of humour but look like Woody Allen. Lots of blokes drink too much, lots of blokes behave stupidly when they drive, get into fights, show off about money or take drugs. I don't do any of these things. I do OK with women not because of the virtues I have, but because of the shadows I don't have.

Even so, you've got to know when you're out of your depth. I was out of my depth with Sally; after her, I was determined never to get out of my depth again. People have got to *match* if they're going to stay together, I decided. They don't have to have the same interests, or the same background, or the same education, although I guess all of these things help; but if you look like Lyle Lovett, and she looks like Julia Roberts, you haven't got a chance. Your expectations are going to be different.

Sarah and I matched.

Sarah was average-attractive (smallish, slim, nice big brown eyes, crooked teeth, shoulder-length dark hair that always seemed to need a cut no matter how often she went to the hairdressers), and she wore clothes that were the same as mine, more or less. Favourite recording artistes: REM, Eurythmics, Bob Dylan, Joni Mitchell, Bob Marley. Favourite films: *Gone with the Wind*, *Diva* (hey!), *Gandhi*, *Missing* (she's probably changed her mind about those two by now), *Wuthering Heights*.

And she was sad. She had been dumped a couple of years before by a sort of male equivalent of Sally, a guy called Tom who wanted to be something at the BBC. (He never made it, the wanker, and each day we never saw him on television or heard him on the radio, something inside us rejoiced.) He was her moment, just as Sally was mine, and when they split, Sarah had sworn off men for a while, just as I had sworn off women. It made sense to pool our loathing of the opposite sex and share a bed at the same time. Our friends were all paired off; we were frightened of being left alone for the rest of our lives. Only people of a certain disposition are frightened of being alone for the rest of their lives at twenty-six; we were of that disposition. Everything seemed much later than it was, and after a few months she moved in with me.

We couldn't fill a room. I don't mean that we didn't have enough stuff: she had loads of books (she was an English teacher), and I have over two thousand records (1,844 albums, 307 twelve-inch singles, although it was less than that back then), and the flat is pretty poky anyway. I mean that neither of us were loud or powerful enough to fill a room: when we were together, I was conscious of how the only space we occupied was that taken up by our bodies. We couldn't *project* like some couples can. Sometimes we tried, when we were out with people even quieter than us; we never talked about why we suddenly became shriller and louder, but I'm sure we both knew that it happened. We did it to compensate for the fact that life was going on elsewhere, that somewhere her Tom and my Sally were together, having a better time than we were and with more glamorous people. The shrill noise we made was a sort of defiant gesture, a futile but necessary last stand. (You can see this phenomenon everywhere you go: young middle-class people whose lives are beginning to disappoint them making too much noise in restaurants and clubs and wine bars. 'Look at me! I'm not as boring as you think I am! I know how to have fun!' Tragic. I'm glad I learned to stay home and sulk.) Ours was a marriage of convenience as cynical and as mutually advantageous as any, and I really thought that I might spend my life with her. I wouldn't have minded. She was OK. I didn't really love her, though. Not until she left, anyway.

There's a joke I saw in a sitcom once—*Man About the House*, maybe?—a terribly unsound joke, wherein a guy takes a really fat, speccy girl out for the evening, gets her drunk, and makes a move on her when he takes her home. 'I'm not that kind of girl!' she shrieks. He looks at her aghast. 'But . . . but you *must* be,' the bloke says. It made me laugh when I was sixteen, but I didn't think about it again until Sarah told me she had met someone else. 'But . . . but you *can't* have,' I wanted to splutter. I don't mean that Sarah was unfanciable—she wasn't, by any means, and patently this other guy fancied her. I just mean that her meeting someone else was contrary to the whole spirit of our arrangement. All we really had in common (our shared admiration of *Diva* did not, if truth be told, last us much beyond the first few months) was that we had been dumped by people. This was where we matched. We were fervent anti-dumpers. So how come I got dumped?

I was being unrealistic, of course. You run the risk of losing anyone who is worth spending time with, unless you are so paranoid about loss that you choose someone unlosable, somebody who could not possible appeal to anybody else at all. (Joey Soul: 'If you want to be happy for the rest of your life/Never make a pretty woman your wife/So from my personal point of view/Get an ugly girl to marry you.') If you're going to go in for this lark at all, you have to live with the possibility that it won't work out, that somebody called Marco, say, or Mark (Sarah's obscure object of desire) is going to come along and upset you.

But I didn't see it like that at the time. All I saw at the time was that I'd moved down a division and that it still hadn't worked out, and this seemed a cause for a great deal of misery and self-pity.

And then I met Laura.

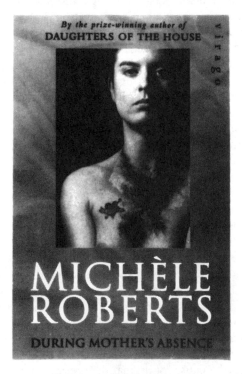

GRANTA

TIMOTHY GARTON ASH
THE VISIT

' **A** re you bringing any laundry?' asks the porter at the fortified entrance to Moabit prison.

When I laugh he says defensively, 'I was only asking,' and grimly stamps my permit to visit remand prisoner Honecker, Erich.

Into a waiting-room full of chain-smoking wives and spivs in black leather jackets. Wait for your number to be called from a loudspeaker. Through an automatic barrier. Empty your pockets and put everything in a locker. Body search. Another automatic barrier. Unsmiling guards, barked orders. *Moment! Kommen Sie mit!* Then you've come to the wrong place. Collect all your belongings again. Pack up. Walk around the red-brick fortress to another gate. Unpack. Sign this, take that. Another huge metal door. The clash of bolts. A courtyard, then the corridor to the prison hospital, bare but clean.

Somehow all this seems increasingly familiar. I have been here before. But where and when? Then I remember. It's like crossing through the Friedrichstrasse underground frontier station into East Berlin, in the bad old days. West Germany has given Honecker back his Berlin Wall.

Inside it is warm and safe. There is food to eat; plain fare, to be sure, but regular and ample. There is basic, free medical care for all. Good books are to be had from the library, and there is guaranteed employment for men and women alike. And life is, of course, very secure. Just like East Germany.

T he first time I saw, at close quarters, the Chairman of the Council of State of the German Democratic Republic and General Secretary of the Socialist Unity Party of Germany, Erich Honecker, was at the Leipzig trade fair in 1980. A horde of plain-clothes Stasi men heralded the arrival of the leader. Eastern functionaries, West German businessmen, British diplomats—all flapped and fluttered, bowed and scraped, as if at the Sublime Porte of Suleiman the Great. His every move, every tiny gesture, was studied and minutely interpreted, with all the arcane science of Sovietology. Significantly, graciously, the Chairman and General Secretary stopped at the Afghan stand, which displayed rugs and nuts. 'And these are peanuts and those are salted peanuts . . . ' came the breathless commentary of the rattled Afghan salesman.

Graciously, significantly, the Chairman and General Secretary clapped him on the shoulder and said: 'We regard your revolution as a decisive contribution to détente. All the best for your struggle!' Ah, happy days, the old style.

Now the the door opens and there he stands in a tiny corner room, sandwiched between the doctor's washbasin and a table. He is very small, his face pallid and sweaty, but he still stands bolt upright. 'Bodily contacts are not permitted,' says my permit. But he extends his hand—graciously, significantly—and I shake it. He is clad in khaki prison pyjamas, which remind me of a Mao suit. But on his feet he still wears, incongruously, those fine, black leather slip-on shoes in which he used to tread all the red carpets, not just in Moscow and Prague but in Madrid, in Paris and in Bonn. 'Fraternal greetings, Comrade Leonid Ilyitch,' and a smacking kiss on each cheek. 'How do you do, Mr President.' 'Guten Tag, Herr Bundeskanzler.'

We sit down, our knees almost touching in the cramped room, and the accompanying warder wedges himself into a corner. All my notes and papers have been impounded at the gate, but fortunately the doctor has left some spare sheets of lined paper and a pencil. Fixing me with his tiny, intense eyes—always his most striking feature—Honecker concentrates on answering my questions. He talks at length about his relations with Moscow, his friendship with Brezhnev, his arguments with Chernenko and then Gorbachev. Even under Gorbachev, he says, the Soviet Union never ceased to intervene in East Germany. The Soviet embassy's consular officials behaved, he says, like provincial governors. So much for the sovereignty of the GDR that he himself had so long trumpeted! At one point he shows staggering (and I think genuine) economic naïveté, arguing that East Germany's hard currency debt, in Deutschmarks, has to be set against its surplus in transferable roubles.

His language is a little stiff, polit-bureaucratic, but very far from being just ideological gobbledygook. Through it come glimpses of a real political intelligence, a man who knows about power. Was it his conscious decision to allow many more ordinary East Germans to travel to the West in the second half of the

221

1980s? Yes, definitely, a conscious decision. He thought it would make people more satisfied. But did it? *Nee*, he says, *offensichtlich nicht*. Nope, obviously not.

With the tiny pupils of his eyes boring into mine, he speaks with what seems like real, almost fanatical conviction—or at least with a real will to convince. This is somehow more, not less, impressive because of the humiliating prison surroundings, and because of the obvious physical effort it costs him. (He has cancer of the liver. The doctors give him only months to live.) Once he has to excuse himself to go to the lavatory, accompanied by the warder. 'You noticed I was getting a little restless,' he says apologetically on his return.

Then he resumed his defiant refrain. East Germany, he insists, was 'to the end the only socialist country in which you could always go into a shop and buy bread, butter, sausage etc.' Yet people wanted more? Yes, but now they regret it. Look at the unemployment in the former GDR! Look how few apartments are being built! He gets hundreds of letters from people in the east. They say they lived more *quietly* in the old days: *sie haben ruhiger gelebt*.

And look what's happening on the streets now, the racist attacks, the fascists. It reminds him of 1933. Really? 1933? Well, he concedes, perhaps 1923. Hitler's first attempt was also a flop. But look what happened then. He's warning us. We've been here before. At least: he's been here before. Which, indeed, he has: held as a remand prisoner in this very prison in the years 1935–37, after being caught working for the communist resistance.

And now he is here again. West Germany's leaders denounce him as a criminal. Yet only yesterday those same politicians were competing for the privilege of being received in audience by him. Oh, the tales he could tell! His talks with West German Social Democrats were, he says, 'comradely'. Some other West German politicians were more reserved. He had great respect for Franz Josef Strauss. Helmut Schmidt was the most reliable and punctilious partner. But he also got on well with Helmut Kohl. He had often talked on the telephone to Chancellor Schmidt, and to Chancellor Kohl. Why, he had even dialled the number himself.

Then the former Chairman of the Council of State of the

former German Democratic Republic and former General Secretary of the former Socialist Unity Party of Germany pulls out of the pocket of his prison pyjamas a slightly dog-eared card on which his former secretary had typed the direct telephone number to the Chancellor in Bonn. He places it before me, urges me to copy the number down. 0649 (West Germany) 228 (Bonn) 562001.

A quarter-century of divided Germany's tragic, complex history is, it seems to me, concentrated in this one pathetic moment: the defiant, mortally sick old man in his prison pyjamas, the dog-eared card with the direct number to Chancellor Kohl.

What would happen, I wonder, if he rang that number now? Would it, perhaps, give the standard German recorded message for a defunct number: 'no *Anschluss* on this number'? (The word *Anschluss* means simply connnection, as well as territorial incorporation.) But no, I try it later, and it still takes you straight through to the Chancellor's office in Bonn.

The warder clears his throat and looks at his watch. Our time is up. Honecker rises, again standing almost to attention. A formal farewell. Then the bare corridors, the clashing gates, the unsmiling guards, the belongings from the locker, the fortified entrance. But now I *am* carrying laundry. Scribbled in pencil on a doctor's notepad: the dirty linen of history.

ROYAL COURT THEATRE

Sloane Square SW1

everything
and the
kitchen
sink

Booking now open for:

- **HYSTERIA**
  by Terry Johnson

- **MSM**
  devised by DV8 Physical
  Theatre Company

- **NIGHT AFTER NIGHT**
  by Neil Bartlett

- **LAND OF THE LIVING**
  by David Spencer

- **LIVE LIKE PIGS**
  by John Arden

- **HAMMETT'S APPRENTICE**
  by Kevin Hood

Call the Box Office
(071-730 1745)
for further information
or a leaflet

GRANTA

MICHAEL IGNATIEFF
THE HIGHWAY OF BROTHERHOOD
AND UNITY

Wild strawberries were served in a silver cup at breakfast, I remember, followed by hot rolls with apricot jam. The dining-room overlooked the lake, and when the window was open, you could feel the mountain air sweeping across the water and the white linen tablecloth and then on to your face.

The hotel was called the Toplice, on the shores of Lake Bled in Slovenia. The diplomatic corps spent the summer there, in attendance upon the dictator who took up residence across the lake. My father, like the other diplomats, came to gossip and take the waters. Every morning, he visited the hot mineral water baths beneath the hotel. I played tennis, rowed on the lake and conceived a passion for an unapproachable Swedish girl of twelve.

We travelled everywhere in the Yugoslavia of the late 1950s—through Bosnian hill villages, where barefoot children swarmed up to the car; to the great mosque of Sarajevo, where I removed my shoes and knelt and watched old men pressing their foreheads on the carpets and whispering their prayers; to the Dalmatian islands and beaches, then unvisited by Western tourists; to Lake Bled in Slovenia.

Parts of southern Serbia, central Bosnia and western Hercegovina were so poor that it was not clear how ordinary people survived. Llubliana and Zagreb, by contrast, were neat, prosperous Austro-Hungarian towns that seemed to have nothing in common with the bony, bare hinterlands of central Yugoslavia.

At the time all expressions of economic resentment, as well as of nationalist consciousness, were banned by Tito. The society marched forward, willingly or unwillingly, under the banner of 'brotherhood and unity'. To call yourself a Croat or Serb first, and a Yugoslav second, was to risk arrest.

I had no idea how complicated and ambiguous the division between national and Yugoslav identity actually was. I knew that Metod, my tennis coach in Bled, always called himself, first and foremost, a Slovenian. I dimly remember him saying bitterly that he hated serving in the Yugoslav National Army, because both he and his brother were ragged by the Serbs for being Slovenian.

Was that the only time I saw the cracks that were to become fissures? Everywhere else, I remember people who told me, happily, that they were Yugoslavs. In retrospect, I was there at the most hopeful moment. Tito was still lionized for having kept the country out of Stalin's empire; there were the first signs of the economic boom of the sixties; soon to come was the liberalization of travel which allowed millions of Yugoslavs to work abroad and which for a time made Yugoslavia the most free of all the eastern European communist countries.

I hold on to my *ancien régime* memories. Everyone now says the descent into hell was inevitable. Nothing seemed less likely at the time. My childhood tells me that nothing is inevitable.

The Highway of Brotherhood and Unity

Between Belgrade and Zagreb is the Highway of Brotherhood and Unity, built by Tito to link the two central republics of Croatia and Serbia. For three hundred kilometres, it runs parallel to the Sava river, through the Slavonian plain, some of the flattest and richest farmland in Europe.

Driving along the highway this summer, I soon become aware what an odd road it is. For a start, all the green destination signs have been painted over. I stop at one and take a closer look. The sign says I am headed towards Lipovac. I peel back the Lipovac decal, and the word Belgrade appears beneath. As far as Croatia is concerned, the Serbian capital has disappeared. Officially, therefore, I am on a highway to nowhere.

About forty kilometres past Zagreb, the Croatian traffic begins taking the exits, leaving the highway to me. Apart from the UN Jeeps and lorries heading out from Zagreb, mine is the only civilian car on the road. I have a superb four-lane motorway all to myself. I stop. I get out, cross both carriageways and back again. No one. Then I get into the car, take it up to 115 miles an hour, feeling an adolescent zeal. I roar up to a toll-booth, only to discover that its windows are smashed and the booth is empty, though the hazard lights continue to blink on and off. I back up and take the toll-booth at full speed.

I have no company except the hawks circling above the deserted highway, looking for field mice, and the feral cats prowling along the grassy, uncut verges. But from time to time, I can just make out the flash of reflected sunlight on the binoculars of Croatian spotter teams dug into the motorway exit ramps. They must be puzzled by the civilian car using this deserted stretch of motorway as a drag-strip.

I have Austrian plates on the car. With Croatian or Serbian plates, I couldn't proceed beyond any of the checkpoints ahead. I am also equipped with a UNPROFOR pass, the essential passport for the UN protection zones I am about to enter. In the boot are canisters of extra petrol to get me through the Serbian zones, which are under petrol embargo. There is also a flak jacket. I put it on once and took it off immediately. It is ludicrously cumbersome and in practice useless. All you think about when you are wearing it are the parts of your body that remain exposed. In any case, the canisters of petrol have already leaked on to the flak jacket, ensuring that, if I do get hit while wearing it, I will burst into flames.

About an hour out of Zagreb, I see the first signs of war: the guard-rails on the central median strip have been chewed up and are scattered about one of the carriageways. I begin to feel the track marks left behind in the road surface by the passage of tanks and armoured personnel carriers. Further on, the road is pocked and pitted by mortar blasts. On one of the motorway bridges, I spot my first cross, the four cyrillic *S*s in each quadrant, standing for the Serbian motto: Only Unity Can Save the Serbs. On the next motorway bridge, I see the *U* for Ustashe and the chequered flag of the Sahovnica. On my left, near an exit ramp, a rusted and burnt-out bus is on its side, its roof sheared away by some form of incoming fire. I have reached the edge of the war zone.

Jasenovac

At Novska, seventy kilometres east of Zagreb, a UN Jeep meets me and leads my car down a shell-damaged slip-road, over a pontoon bridge, past the Serb and Croat checkpoints and drops me off at a wrecked building which used to house the Jasenovac museum and memorial centre.

Between 1941 and 1945, trains drew up at the rail-head ramp

on the other side of a vast, marshy field that slopes down to the Sava river. Jews and Serbs, gypsies and Croatian communists were herded out of the wagons and down the ramp to the barracks behind the barbed wire. They were put to work in the brick factory, and when they could work no longer, they were burned in the brick ovens or shot in the back of the head and dumped in the Sava river.

No one knows how many people died here on the bare field behind the museum where the barracks and barbed wire once stood. Serbs maintain the figure is 700,000. There isn't a Serb village in central Croatia which didn't lose someone in this place. Croats insist that the number is no more than 40,000. Independent researchers have put the number in the region of 250,000.

It is just as difficult to come to terms with what happened only two years ago, when the war of 1991 reached Jasenovac. For I am walking into a museum that has been systematically destroyed. Every book in the library has been ripped up and tossed on to the floor. Every glass exhibit case has been smashed. Every photograph has been defaced. Every file has been pulled out of every drawer; every table and chair has been up-ended; all the curtains have been shredded; all the windows have been smashed; all the walls have been daubed with excrement and slogans. An intense hatred, an overwhelming hatred from the past, has taken hold of the people who did this. As if by destroying the museum, they hoped to destroy the memory of what was done here.

I try to piece together what the exhibits might have been like. On the floor, a picture of a crowd of prisoners waiting at the barbed wire lies beside a photograph of a young woman, her hair in plaits, leaning on a fence. There is a photo of a prelate shaking hands with an SS officer; it is on top of a pile of prisoners' files and beside shredded portraits of Tito. The history of Yugoslavia seems to lie among the shattered glass and filth at my feet.

Museum guides would have tried to teach schoolchildren what happened here, and I can see how they struggled to understand it; their drawings lie scattered all over: barbed wire, bright barracks, water-colour guards, the walking skeletons at the brick works, as seen through the eyes of a nine-year-old.

I find scraps of film, ripped from the projectors in the museum cinema. I bend down and hold the frames up to the light from a shattered window. In one strip, there is an old man weeping; in another, a starved woman tottering down the road; in a third, eighteen frames of a headless corpse.

Light streams through a shell hole in the roof of the lecture theatre. A lectern is still standing; the seats, cinema screen and wall panelling have all been burnt out. On the front of the lectern there are the words, in Serbo-Croatian: Lest We Forget.

After 1945, Tito had the camp bulldozed in the hope that Serbs and Croats might forget. Then in the 1960s, when Tito had assumed that the wounds had now healed, the memorial centre was opened. But after all the school visits and lectures and film showings, Yugoslavia never came to terms with what happened here. The past remained unmastered and unforgiven.

When Croatia declared its independence in 1990, it made one central mistake, one that may have put the new state on the road to war: it failed to disavow publicly its fascist past, to disassociate itself from the Ustashe state and what it did at Jasenovac. The President of Free Croatia, Franjo Tudjman, fought the Ustashe as a young partisan, but in the euphoria of independence, he tried to unite all of Croatia's tortured past into what was called a national synthesis. He never visited Jasenovac. He never got down on his knees, as Willy Brandt did at the Warsaw Ghetto. Had he done so, the local Serb leaders would have had difficulty persuading their Serb followers that the new Croatia was the fascist Ustashe come again.

Serbs scoff when you say Tudjman should have atoned for Jasenovac.

Are you crazy? they say. His party was financed by Croatians abroad, in Toronto and Melbourne. And who were they? Old Ustashe.

But the problem runs deeper. The wartime Ustashe state was Croatia's first experience of being an independent nation. It has proved impossible for Croatian nationalists to disavow that nationhood, even if it was also a fascist one. Instead, they evade the issue. They dismiss tales of Ustashe atrocity as Serbian propaganda; they airbrush atrocity into crime by playing statistical sleight of hand with the numbers who died. Finally, it appears, some Croats have dealt with Jasenovac by vandalizing its remains.

It is said that aggression begins in denial and that violence originates in guilt. A nation that cannot repudiate a fascist past may condemn itself to a fascist future. True enough. But there is another equally imprisoning mechanism at work. If your enemies call you a fascist enough times, you begin to call yourself one too. Take your enemies' insult and turn it into a badge of pride. How many times in the weeks ahead do I meet Croats at checkpoints who say: 'They call us Ustashe. Well then, that is what we are.' And likewise, the Serbs. 'You call us chetniks. Well that is what we are.' The two sides conspire in a spiral of mutually interacting self-degradation. And where does that spiral begin? In the most ordinary form of cowardice, in telling lies about the past.

But that is not all.

Tito's Yugoslavia remembered the Croatians of Jasenovac only as murderers, never as victims. Tito never built a memorial for the thousands of Croatians who were massacred on the roads of north-eastern Croatia and Slovenia in May 1945, fleeing Tito's own communist partisans. The guilt of Jasenovac has become unbearable, not merely because it was great, but also because it was unjust. At Jasenovac you discern the lie that eventually destroyed Tito's Yugoslavia: that the Second World War was a national uprising against German occupation led by Tito's partisans. In reality it was a civil war fought among Yugoslavs.

Jasenovac makes you ponder liberal pieties. Somewhere in my childhood, I must have been taught that telling lies eventually makes you ill. When Vaclav Havel said that people need to live in truth, he also meant that nations cannot hope to hold together if they do not come to some common—and truthful—version of their past. But there are nations with pasts so hard to share that they need centuries before forgetting does its work. To ask for truth might be too much. Yugoslavia might be such a case. Fifty years was not enough time to forget.

Cry, girl, cry

Thomas Hobbes would have understood Yugoslavia. What Hobbes would have said, having lived through religious civil war himself, is that when people are sufficiently afraid they will do anything. There is one type of fear more devastating in its impact than any other: the systemic fear which arises when a state begins to collapse. Ethnic hatred is the result of the terror which arises when legitimate authority disintegrates.

On all the roads which lead north from the Highway of Brotherhood and Unity, there is a continuous swathe of devastation. I am in central Croatia now, in the heart of what was once one of the most complex, multi-ethnic communities in Europe: a Croatian majority, a Serbian minority along with several other groups—Germans, Italians and Hungarians. The 1991 war tore these villages apart, and now they are divided between Croatian and Serbian sectors, with UN checkpoints in between.

Roofless houses, their tiles and beams lying in deserted, weed-filled rooms; fire-edged window and door frames; brick walls pierced by artillery blasts. Some houses have been raked by so much automatic-weapon fire that the plaster has been torn away, leaving only the pitted brick. The tree trunks outside wear a glittering jacket of metal slugs. In the ditches lie small Yugoslav Zastovo cars, riddled with bullets or twisted into rusted sculpture by a tank's treads.

At first the destruction appears to have no rhyme or reason. In some villages, not a wall has been left unsprayed with bullets, while in others, scarcely a house has been touched. I work like an archaeologist, sifting through the clues to discern the pattern. There appear to be three forms of destruction.

The most surgical is dynamiting: the houses then collapse in neat piles, with minimal damage to the ones next door. Families are driven out by their neighbours or by paramilitaries, and their homes are simply blown up. Many of these dynamited piles are large, recently constructed houses. How many years as a *gastarbeiter* in a German car-plant were invested in them?

The second type of destruction is accomplished by artillery fire, from the Yugoslav National Army guns which punch round, tyre-sized holes in Croatian village walls.

The third type of destruction is fire-bombing, which leaves scorch-marks on all the windows. This would have been the work of marauding paramilitaries—from both sides.

Some houses are daubed by the Serbs with the letter *U*, for

Ustashe, marking them for ethnic cleansing. Others have the crudely painted names of those who lived in them. I spend hours in these ruins, the dust in my throat, the sound of broken glass under my feet, deciphering the clues to the shape of catastrophe.

Never say ethnic cleansing is just racial hatred run wild, just Balkan madness. For there is a deep logic to it. By 1990, this part of Yugoslavia was a Hobbesian world. No one in these villages could be sure of being protected. If you're a Serb, and are attacked, do you go to the Croatian police? If you're a Croat, in a Serbian village, being attacked at night by Serbian paramilitaries, usually led by a former policeman, where do you go? If you can't trust your neighbours, drive them out. If you can't live among them, live only among your own. Ethnic cleansing appears to offer people their only security. It alone gave respite from the fear which leaped like a brush-fire from house to house.

As you travel through the zones of devastation in central Croatia, you have the impression that you have fallen through some hole and are spinning backwards into the past. You are not in 1993, but 1943. In Serb villages, old ladies in black scarves and black wool dresses watch you suspiciously as you pass; ribbed haycarts go by, driven by old men in their World War Two khaki forage caps. In their back gardens, women are bending over their hoes. On the roads, militiamen, wearing the red, white and blue shoulder badge of the Serbian Krajina, emerge from dugouts to stop the car and search you. Everyone is wary. Few talk.

In one ruined farm, formerly inhabited by Croatians, I come upon an old Serbian couple camping in the remains of an outbuilding. They are in their eighties and have been driven by the Croatians from their home in Daruvar, forty kilometres to the north. The old man is sawing up a piece of charred wood for the stove. The old woman is tidying up their tiny room, with its bed, its cracked window, table, two cups and two chairs, and spotlessly swept floor. They have rebuilt the roof themselves, and have survived on what they get from neighbours and the Red Cross. We sit on a stump, in the middle of the ruins. I ask them if this war has been worse than the last one.

The old woman replies, with bitter scorn. 'In the last one, we all fought the Germans. This time, there is just betrayal.' Neighbour against neighbour, friend against friend.

Can you ever live together again? I ask, knowing the answer. They both shake their heads and look away.

I ask how they manage to survive, and they suddenly revive.

'God will arrange everything,' they both say in unison, exchanging a cheerful glance across what must be fifty years of marriage. When I get up to leave, the old man takes my hand and holds it in a long, intense grip. His bright, blue eyes stare deep into mine. 'Truth and national rights. That is all we want. Truth and national rights.'

A kilometre away, across another checkpoint, this time in the Croatian village of Lipic, I come across a man helping a team of six women in blue overalls stacking up the usable bricks from the rubble of a flattened house. It turns out that he is its owner, and the women are from a municipal detachment sent out to repair damaged houses.

Tomaslav Marekovic is his name, Yup to his friends. Yup is the caretaker in the local hospital and coach of the local football team in his spare time. I suspect, without knowing for sure, that he is also a prominent local supporter of the HDZ, the ruling Croatian party. Why else, I reason, is his the only house I can find in Lipic where the rubble is being cleared by a municipal work detail?

He shows me where his kitchen was, where the television set used to be, where his couch stood. Now there is nothing left but the foundations and a mound of bricks which the women are stacking in piles after chipping away the mortar. Next door's house was untouched. Why? I ask.

Serbs, he says. We always got on. Now, he says, they are in West Germany.

And the house next door to that?

My parents, he says laconically. He points to the street. 'That is where they left my father. There, in the street, for three weeks, before someone buried the body. And my mother, they took her to a barn and set her on fire.'

Yugoslav Army tanks, dug into the hills above Lipic, were pounding the town and, under directions from local Serbian paramilitaries, were targeting Croat houses. When Yup's house came under bombardment, he and his wife jumped in their car and fled to Zagreb, but his parents refused to come, thinking they would be safe. Days later, they were dragged out of their house by Serbian paramilitaries, possibly from the same village. They were shot. As Yup tells me all this, he sighs, pauses to light a cigarette, and stares glumly into the distance. The women work silently around us, stacking bricks.

Yup calls for a break, and I sit down with the women at a trestle table in his tiny back garden. I want to know why the work detail is all female, and they reply, with much laughter and winking: 'Because women are better workers.' Left unsaid is the fact that so many Croatian males are away serving in the army. I tell them that the Serbs nearby aren't rebuilding. They're living in the ruins, with their guns trained towards Croatia.

'They're not rebuilding,' says one woman, 'because they know they're done for.' Some women nod; the others look down silently at the table.

Yup says, 'Three of you are Serbs, isn't that right?' And the three women beside me nod and look back down at the table. In the silence, they leave it to me to figure out how it comes about that three Serbian women are helping to rebuild a Croat's house. It is because they were married to Croats, have lived here all their lives and find themselves now, torn in two, as their village is. The Serbian woman beside me begins to cry, and a stillness descends over everyone. The Croatian women across the table look at her dispassionately, while she crumples into herself. 'Cry, girl, cry,' says one and reaches over and takes her hand.

Warlords

Back in 1989, we thought the new world opened up by the breaching of the Berlin Wall would be ruled by philosopher kings, dissident heroes and shipyard electricians. We looked forward to a new order of nation states, released from the senile grip of the Soviets. We assumed that national self-determination had to mean freedom, and that nationalism had to mean nation building. We were wrong. We hoped for order. We got pandemonium. In the name of nationalism, dozens of viable nation states have been shattered beyond repair. In the name of state building, we have returned large portions of Europe to the pre-political chaos prior to the emergence of the modern state.

Large portions of the former Yugoslavia are now ruled by figures that have not been seen in Europe since medieval times: warlords. They appear wherever nation states disintegrate: in the Lebanon, Somalia, northern India, Armenia, Georgia, Ossetia, Cambodia, Liberia, the former Yugoslavia. With their car-phones, faxes and exquisite personal weaponry, they look post-modern, but the reality is pure medieval.

The warlord's vehicle of choice is a four-wheel-drive Cherokee Chief, with a policeman's blue light on the roof to flash when speeding through a checkpoint. They carry a gun but don't wave it about. They leave vulgar intimidation to the bodyguards in the back, the ones with shades, jeans and Zastovo machine pistols. They themselves dress in the leather jackets, floral ties and pressed corduroy trousers favoured by German television producers. The ones I met at the checkpoints leading off from the Highway of Brotherhood and Unity were short, stubby men who in a former life had been small-time hoods, small-town cops or both. Spend a day with them, touring their world, and you'd hardly know that most are serial killers.

Warlords dominate the war zones; they have also worked their way in to the heart of power in the authoritarian single-party states of both Croatia and Serbia.

Warlords are celebrities in the Balkans. They have seats in the Serbian parliament. One, Vojislav Seselj, the self-styled Duke of the Serbian chetniks, runs his own party as well as a full-time paramilitary unit. Another, Zeljko Raznjatovic—also known as Arkan—controls an eight-hundred-strong paramilitary unit called the Tigers, who raped and tortured their way through eastern Slavonia in the Croatian war of 1991. This odious thug—there is an Interpol warrant for his arrest for an attempted murder in Sweden—is a parliamentary deputy who also operates a number of immensely profitable sanctions-busting businesses, including one that sells smuggled petrol for hard currency. Ever the post-modern Prince of Darkness, Arkan has launched himself into celebrity franchising. In Serbian farmhouses in eastern Slavonia, the icon you are most likely to see, beside an image of Saint Sava, is a large coloured calendar with a different picture of Arkan for every month of the year.

That Arkan is allowed to serve as a deputy in the Serbian parliament is proof, Croatians will tell you, that Serbia is a fascist regime. It is not. Belgrade is no less democratic than Zagreb, with functioning opposition parties and newspapers. Milovan Djilas characterization of Serbian politics—'democracy with a tinge of banditism'—also explains how the warlords have worked their way into the heart of the system.

Because there are warlords on the Croatian side too, if not in Zagreb, then in the front-line towns. Osijek is run by council president and local party boss Branimir Glavas.

I tour the town in Glavas's Jeep; it is like being with a spectacularly popular local politician in a small American town. He comes across a wedding and is serenaded by the band; the bridegroom asks him to kiss the bride; the revellers hand him bottles of wine to try. This man is, however, also leader of the Glavas Unit, a paramilitary group responsible for the defence of Osijek; it is also responsible for the cleansing of Serbian villages and for the murder of Croatian policemen who sought to maintain good relations with Serbs.

Glavas flashes a policeman's badge at the police checkpoints and a military pass at the front line. The limits of his power are as imprecise as they are pervasive. He has translated the nefarious glamour of the warlord into peacetime power, but assures me that he could re-mobilize his paramilitaries overnight.

Thirty kilometres away, across the front line in Serb-held Vukovar, there is Mr Kojic, the Serbian equivalent of Mr Glavas. Same Jeep, same courteous manner. Same guns.

The warlords are nationalists, but their convictions are uninteresting. They are technicians of violence, rather than ideologues. Before everyone else, they understood that ethnic nationalism has delivered the ordinary people of the Balkans straight back to the pre-political state of nature where, as Thomas Hobbes predicted, life is nasty, brutish and short. In the state of nature, the man with a Zastovo machine pistol and a Cherokee Chief is king.

And the warlord not only offers protection. He offers a solution. He tells his people: if we cannot trust our neighbours, we must rid ourselves of them. If we cannot live together in a single state, we must create clean states of our own. Ethnic cleansing is not just motivated by nationalist hatred. It is the warlord's coldly rational solution to the Hobbesian war of all against all. Rid yourself of your neighbours, the warlord says, and you no longer have to fear them. Live among your own, and you can live in peace. With me and my boys to protect you.

Belgrade

On the Highway of Brotherhood and Unity, you never tell anybody where you've really come from or where you're really going. At the Croatian checkpoints, you say that you're going to the next Croatian town. At the Serb checkpoints, you smile, let them search your boot, rummage through the dirty underwear in your luggage, offer them Marlboros and tell them over and over that you are heading towards the bosom of Mother Serbia.

At the first toll-booth on the Serbian side of the highway, you do not hand them the toll card you picked up at the Zagreb entrance. You say instead that you've come from the Serbian Krajina, and then negotiate your toll in German marks.

About twenty kilometres from Belgrade, I see the first sign of the impact of Western sanctions: enormous queues of small Zastovos, Fiats and Renault 5s stretching from service stations, and large crowds of men gathered around the empty pumps, waiting. The men play cards, talk politics, sing to a harmonica, but when I approach them, and they discover that I'm a Western writer, they surround me, an angry knot of men. A short man with a pork-pie hat, mud-encrusted boots and the hands of a farmer pokes me in the chest: 'What the hell were we supposed to do with those Croats? Wait for them to cut our throats? And what do you do? You give us these sanctions. You call that fair?' And so it goes, with themes and variations, that soon have them blaming Churchill and the British for supporting Tito rather than Draza Mihailovic. The British are to blame for fifty years of Communism in Yugoslavia.

239

Their anger would be more threatening if it were not so comic. The men in the queue approach, then say they don't want to have anything to do with a Westerner, then turn on their heels—their friends all admire the splendid gesture of defiance—and then return and start talking, pausing to let me take notes, peering over my shoulder to see how I spell their names. This, I learn, is part of the ritual style of Serbian nationalism itself. The dance has its opening quadrille: we won't talk; the West never understands; we despise you; you tell nothing but lies; then they start talking and never stop. Ask anybody a simple question and you get that tell-tale phrase: 'You have to understand our history . . . ' Twenty minutes later and you are still being told about King Lazar, the Turks and the Battle of Kosovo. Everywhere there is a deep conviction that no one understands them, coupled with the fervent, unstoppable desire to explain and justify themselves.

Next morning, I visit a bank; there is a queue; the ritual repeats itself. People violently and vehemently refuse to talk, only to launch into a stream of Serbian self-justification that begins with their immemorial struggle against the Turks and concludes with their defence of Bosnian Serbia against the Muslim fundamentalists. Along the way, the invective sweeps up the anti-Serbian crimes of Churchill, Roosevelt, Stalin and Tito into a rhetorical flow as muddy as a spring torrent.

Bank queues are as fundamental a part of Belgrade life as the petrol queue. The economy is in a state of advanced hyper-inflation—running at two hundred per cent per month. In the restaurants, the price stickers on the menus change overnight. The only reliable hedge against inflation is a hard currency account. Many private banks have opened for business and promise to pay ten per cent per month on such accounts. How they manage to do so is a mystery. The rumour is that the private banks are deeply engaged in the nether world of smuggling, illegal oil imports from the Ukraine, arms-trading with Russia together with the laundering of Western drug money. Some banks have gone bust, and the fear is that if more do, the Milosevic regime itself might be swept away in the ensuing economic chaos.

So anxious are the small depositors about the fate of their accounts that many queue all night in order to ensure they can make a withdrawal. The queues stretch hundreds of yards, a pushing, shoving mass of cold, deeply unhappy, old-age pensioners, many weak with tiredness.

Tito's Grave

He liked greenhouses. So he built himself a greenhouse. He used to rest here, among the poinsettias and the cacti, like an old lizard in the sun. Now they have buried him in the greenhouse, in front of his residence in Belgrade. There is a large white marble slab, with bronze lettering: JOSIP BROZ TITO, 1892–1980.

No one much visits any more. On the day I show up, it is raining, and water is dripping from a broken skylight onto the Marshal's grave.

In 1945, on Tito's birthday, some teenagers ran a relay race from Kragujevic to Belgrade and presented him with a baton. Every year of his reign, the 'youth' of Yugoslavia repeated that race and at the end of it they presented the old dictator with the relay batons. His birthday became 'Youth Day'. Twenty thousand batons are kept in the museum next to his grave.

How quickly the legitimacy of power drains away. The batons were not ridiculous twenty years ago. The relay race meant something to people. Now it seems to belong to the rites of some vanished tribe.

What does one conclude? Dictators have no successors. Charisma is the most unstable of legitimacies. That much is obvious. But what about democracy? Was there ever, really, a chance of democracy here? The old lizard himself would have said: Never, they will tear themselves apart if you let them. From the hell where dead tyrants are sent, he is surveying the inferno that followed his reign and saying: I told you so. There must be a rule of iron. I was right.

But nothing proves the dictator right. Time was needed; time for old men to die and their shame to die with them. In a culture which never had the time to experience the banality of bourgeois politics, nationalism became the vernacular of democracy in Yugoslavia. Not real democracy, of course, but the manipulated plebiscitary democracy which ratifies one-man rule. In that kind of democracy, nationalism offers the immense appeal of a politics of permanent fever, of eternal exaltation. Instead of the banal politics of the real—the poverty, backwardness, stubborn second-rateness of ordinary Balkan existence—nationalism directs the mind to higher things. It offers the glorious politics of identity and self-affirmation. Instead of the interminable politics of interest and conciliation, there are enemies to defeat; there is the immortal cause, the martyrs of the past and the present to keep faith with. And it does not escape the attention of cynics and criminals that in this state of organized and permanent exaltation, there is no cynicism, no crime, no large or small brutality, which cannot be justified if the words 'nation', 'people', 'rights' and 'freedom' are suavely sprinkled over it.

And what about us?

Standing back from the disaster, one sees that the Western failure to act in time was caused by something deeper than inattention, misinformation or misguided good intentions. The very principles behind our policies were in contradiction. In the light-headed euphoria of 1989, we supported the right of national self-determination and the continuing right of existing states to maintain their territorial integrity. How could we support both?

Most of all, we allowed guilt over our imperial pasts to keep us from defining the terms of a post-imperial peace. Post-imperial societies felt guilty condemning the nationalism of peoples who have been kept under imperial control. When the 'captive nations', from the Baltic to the Balkans, demanded their freedom, we did not stop to consider the consequences. After Versailles, after Yalta, the collapse of the last empire in Europe offered us a third opportunity to define a durable peace and create a new order of nations in Europe. We could have ended the Cold War with a comprehensive territorial settlement, defining borders, minority rights guarantees and adjudicating *between* rival claims to self-determination. But so concerned were we to avoid playing the imperial policeman that we allowed every local post-communist demagogue to exploit the rhetoric of self-determination and national rights to his own ends. The terrible new order of ethnically cleansed states in the former Yugoslavia is the monument to our folly, as much as it is to theirs.

An Old Man's Wallet

I am standing in the street directly in front of the Moscow Hotel in downtown Belgrade in the middle of a listless, slowly disintegrating demonstration against the Milosevic regime. A crowd of several hundred people is slowly discovering that it is too small to make anything happen. In the middle of the crowd is an old man wearing a chetnik hat. I go up and talk to him. He is in his seventies and he fought with Mihailovic against Tito during the Second World War. Does he have sons? I ask him.

He takes out his wallet and shows me three passport-sized colour pictures: each of his sons, all in their twenties. Two are dead, killed during the Croatian war. The third is in prison.

Why is he in prison?

Because, the old man says, he took his vengeance. He found the killer of one of his brothers, and killed him.

The old man then takes out a small folded news clipping from a Croatian newspaper. There is a passport-sized photo of another young man. 'The bastard who killed my son. But we got him. We got him,' he says, neatly folding the picture of his son's assassin back into the wallet with the pictures of his sons.

From father to son, from son to son, there is no end to it, this form of love, this keeping faith between generations which is vengeance. In this village war, where everyone knows each other, where an old man keeps the picture of his son's killer beside the picture of the son who avenged them both. There is no end, for when he dies, this old man knows, and it gives him grim satisfaction, there will be someone to do vengeance for him too.

JOHN BERGER

'Berger can describe a painting, can evoke the aura emanating from the objects it represents, with such eloquence that he can inspire us with universal longings'
— *London Review of Books*

ART AND REVOLUTION

Written in a time of despair, yet conveying great hope, *Art & Revolution* is about the explosive rebirth of Russian art from the beginning of this century. It comprises stories, history and photographs, illuminating the meaning of revolutionary art and the choices and dangers facing the pre-*glasnost* Russian artist. This Granta edition includes a new preface by John Berger. £7.99

ABOUT LOOKING

As in his seminal, bestselling *Ways of Seeing*, John Berger considers the way we look at the world, and the small feats we perform when we observe: editing, analyzing, judging, feeling. With a vision as arresting and original as that of the great artists he describes, Berger proves again that he is one of our most radical observers. Like Don McCullin's, his is 'an eye we cannot shut'. £7.99

'Berger reminds us of something that most contemporary writing tempts us to forget: that the greatest writers are distinguished, ultimately, by the quality of their humanity' – *Sunday Times*

GRANTA BOOKS

For further information on Granta Books, please write to:
Granta Book Information, FREEPOST, 2 – 3 Hanover Yard,
Noel Road, London N1 8BR

STEVE PYKE
WORLD WAR ONE VETERANS

Horace Hannan. Born 1899. 9th East Surrey Regiment.

Horace Ham. Born 1895. Middlesex Regiment.

Justin Watrin. Born 1899. 1er Bataillon de Chasseurs à Pieds à Troyes.

Emile Richard. Born 1896. 166ème R.I.

Humbert Monaco. Born 1896. Quarter Master US Army.

Joseph Bilicki. Born 1899. Chief Yeoman US Navy.

Bruno Lange. Born 1898. Kanonier 17th Foot Artillery.

Fritz Strübing. Born 1894. 34 Brigade 54th Infantry Division.

THE COLLECTED STORIES OF T. CORAGHESSAN BOYLE

The complete short stories of one of America's most outrageous writers, gathered together for the first time in one volume.

'Boyle is a consummate entertainer, a verbal showman, an explosively gifted satirist.'
New York Times Book Review

Trade Paperback Original £9.99

GRANTA BOOKS